MERCHANT FLEETS

MERCHANT FLEETS

First published in 1982

British Library Cataloguing Publication Data

Haws, Duncan
Merchant fleets 5.
Royal Mail & Nelson Lines
1. Merchant marine—History
1. Title

387.2'09 HE735
ISBN 0 946378 00 2

Text photoset in 9 on 10 pt English Times
and printed in Great Britain by Planet Press Limited,
50 Providence Place, Brighton, Sussex for the publishers,
TCL Publications, PO Box 16, Crowborough, Sussex.

Contents

Funnels

ROYAL MAIL

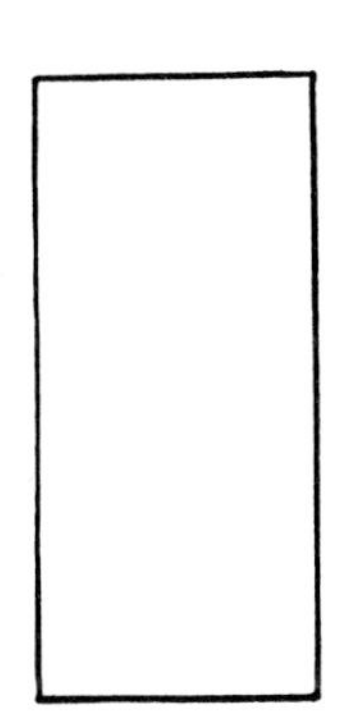

ROYAL MAIL

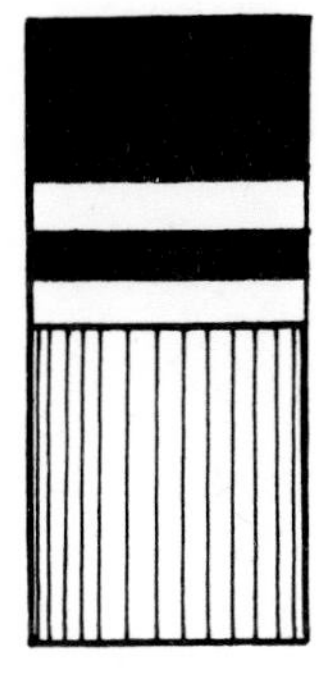

NELSON

1. Black.

2. Yellow-buff.

3. Red, white black white bands, black top.

Explanatory Notes

1 Company histories are arranged chronologically.

2 The ships owned are listed virtually chronologically except that sister ships are grouped together even when the period of their building covers more than one year.

3 Tonnage: the method of calculating tonnage has changed several times since 1830 and very few ships kept their initial tonnage. The gross and net tonnages shown are generally those recorded when the ship first entered service.

4 Dimensions: unless recorded as 'overall' the figures given are the registered dimensions between perpendiculars.

5 The speed given is service speed. This could vary according to route and ports of call.

6 Abbreviations: to assist all readers as few as possible have been used –

Apr	*April*
Aug	*August*
BHP	*Brake horse power*
Bt	*Built*
cabin	*Cabin class*
cm	*Centimetres*
cu m	*Cubic metres*
cu ft	*Cubic feet*
Cyl(s)	*Cylinder(s)*
dbl	*Double*
Dec	*December*
Dft	*Draught/draft*
diam	*Diameter*
Dim	*Dimensions*
disp	*Displacement*
dwt	*Dead weight*
E	*East*
Eng	*Engine*
exp	*Expansion*
fcsle	*Forecastle*
Feb	*February*
ft	*Feet*
fwd	*Forward*
g	*Gross*
GRT	*Gross registered tonnage*
H	*Hull*
HP	*Horse power/High pressure*
IHP	*Indicated horse power*
in	*Inch(es)*
Jan	*January*
kts	*Knots*
lb	*Pound(s)*
LP	*Low Pressure*
m	*Metre*
Mar	*march*
mm	*Millimetres*
MP	*Medium pressure*
mph	*Miles per hour*
n	*Net*
N	*North*
NHP	*Nominal horse power*
Nov	*November*
oa	*Overall*
Oct	*October*
Pad	*Paddle*
Pass	*Passengers*

quad	*Quadruple/four*	SHP	*Shaft horse power*
refrig	*Refrigerated*	Stm	*Steam*
reg	*Registered*	Stm P	*Steam pressure*
RHP	*Registered horse power*	SV	*Sailing vessel*
rmp	*Revolutions per minute*	T	*Tons*
S	*South*	tpl	*Triple/three*
scr	*Screw*	tst	*Tourist*
Sept	*September*	tw	*Twin/two*
sgl	*Single*	W	*West*

7 The technical data follows the same pattern throughout –

Bt (built); *T:* (tons), g (gross), n (net), dwt (dead weight). **Dim** (dimensions) oa (overall), length × breath × depth; *Dft:* (draught). **Eng** (engine) Pad (Paddle), sgl (single, dbl (double), scr (screw); Cyls: (cylinders); IHP, NHP, SHP, BHP, RHP, HP; Boilers; *Stm P:* (steam pressure) lb (pounds); kts (knots); By (engine builder). **H** (hull details); *Coal; Cargo; Pass:* (passengers), 1st (first class), 2nd (second class), 3rd (third class), tst (tourist class); *Crew.*

ROYAL MAIL LINE

Chronological History

1778 James MacQueen was born in Lanarkshire.

1797 He became manager of a Sugar Estate in the Island of Grenada and his main recreation was that of visiting as many of the Caribbean Islands as could be reached.

1820 MacQueen was immensely impressed with the potential of steamships for inter-island communication in the Caribbean but also he propounded his ideas of a worldwide system of communication by steamer.

1830 On his return to Glasgow he became the part owner of a newspaper and this he used to publicise his ideas. He paid particular attention to the delivery of the mails by sea and denounced the Admiralty sailing brigs which provided a very slow and unreliable service. There should be, announced MacQueen, a Royal Mail Line of Steamers.

1837 Sept: A plan for a mail steamship service to the West Indies was submitted to the Government entitled: "General Plan for a Mail Communication between Great Britain and the Eastern and Western Parts of the World; also to Canton and Sydney westward by the Pacific". He included an evaluation of "A Central American Canal at no distant date". The paper caused, amongst members of Parliament, an immediate upsurge of interest in the establishment of steamship routes for the carriage of the Mails.

1838 Jan: Mr MacQueen approached the Treasury with proposals for establishing a line of Royal Mail steamers to the West Indies. This was followed by the Directors of the Government sponsored West India Committee agreeing to find the necessary financial backing.

1839 July 24: The first meeting of the Directors of the Royal Mail Steam Packet Company was held in the counting house of the Merchant Bankers Reid, Irving & Co, in Tokenhouse Yard, London. Stemming from this James MacQueen was appointed General Superintendent of Affairs.

Sept 26: HM Queen Victoria granted a Royal charter incorporating the company. The Royal Coat of Arms thereafter formed a part of the livery of the company. The objects of the company were succinctly stated as:

"For the conveyance of the mails to and from Great Britain and the West India Islands and North and South America and other foreign parts and for this purpose to establish a regular supply of steam and other vessels".

The new company had an authorised share capital of £1,500,000. John Irving MP, a partner in Reid, Irving & Co, became the first Chairman.

1840 Mar 20: The Lords of Admiralty signed the contract for the carriage of the mails. This contract called for a main steamship service from Britain twice per month to Barbados, Grenada, Santa Cruz, St Thomas, Nicola Mole, Santiago de Cuba and Kingston (Port Royal).
The wording of the mail contract may be of interest:
"Between the Commissioners for executing the office of Lord High Admiral of the United Kingdom of Great Britain and Ireland on behalf of Her Majesty of the one part and the company of the other part . . . (agree) that one of such steam vessels so approved of and equipped and manned as aforesaid, with the said Mails on board, shall twice in every calendar month on such days (but at equal intervals of days), and at such hour, and from such port in the British Channel as the said Commissioners shall at any time or times, or from time to time signify in writing, under the hand of their Secretary, to the said Contractors, put to sea as soon as the said Mails are on board, and proceed to the Island of Barbados and after such an interval from her arrival there (not exceeding six hours) as the Governor or Senior Naval Officers present may require, such steam vessel as aforesaid shall forthwith proceed, with the said Mails on board, to the Island of Grenada, and there remain so long only (not exceeding twelve hours) as the Governor or Senior Naval Officer present may require and thence proceed, with the said Mails on board, to the Island of Santa Cruz, from Santa Cruz to St Thomas, from St Thomas to Nicola Mole, in the Island of Hayti, from Nicola Mole, to Santiago de Cuba, and from Santiago de Cuba to Port Royal in the Island of Jamaica".
Connecting services were rquired to serve all other principal West Indian islands with extensions to New York and Halifax, Nova Scotia.
The annual mileage involved in the contract was 684,816 miles. The contract called for the first mail sailing to be by 1st December 1841.
Mar 30: The Mail contract required 14 steamships and 3 sailing ships plus bunkering and repair facilities. All of which had to be completed in 20 months. An undertaking thought by the Press to be beyond the company's, or anyone's, capabilities. The prospectus inviting public participation was issued on this day. It called for £60 per £100 of stock and raised £900,000.
Apr: A 'building committee' was formed. They selected one design for the 14 steamers and spread the order widely as a hedge against delay. The orders were placed:
Caird & Co, Greenock and William Pitcher, Northfleet on Thames 4 each. Acramans, Morgan & Co, Bristol, 2 ships and one each at Robert Menzies Leith; Thomas & John White of Cowes, John Scott & Sons, Greenock, and James McMillan also of Greenock. The 3 schooners were to be Thames built. Half the fleet was to be built in Scotland. In several cases the hull was built away from the engine and was towed to the installation berth. In parallel the company set about establishing the necessary shore organisation and coaling services to meet the needs of the fleet. Southampton was to be the home port.

1841 Dec 3: The schooners *Lee* and *Liffey* (I) sailed together to take up local station in the West Indies.
Dec 16: *Forth* sailed for Nassau. Her station.
Dec 17: *Solway, Clyde* and *Tweed* (I) all left Southampton for stations.

1842 Jan 1: *Thames* (I) and *Tay* were at Falmouth waiting to sail with the mails. The contract specified Falmouth even though the Great Western Railway ran only to Bridgwater and horse drawn mail coaches were needed thereafter.
Jan 3: *Thames* departed with the first mails to Berbice–Havana–New York–Halifax. *Tay* left for Barbados.
Thereafter the mails left Falmouth on the 3rd and 17th of each month. The mail ships called at Corunna and Madeira for coal, outward bound, and at Bermuda inbound. The crossing averaged 19 days. As each of the new vessels entered service they sailed progressively to new ports prior to undertaking the homeward sailing; thus the round voyages averaged four to six months.

Identification at Sea
Each vessel was assigned its own flag. The fleet was placed in alphabetical order and assigned one of Marryats code flags. The flags were flown from the foremast. 55 different flags are known.

Night Signals
A Royal Mail vessel lit a yellow flare and a Roman Candle fired three white balls. If the other vessel, being Royal Mail, wanted to talk to its fellow member 3 yellow lights were displayed in a triangle (2 men stood on deck either side of the man on the bridge holding the apex light).
May 11: *Medina* became the the new company's first loss when she was wrecked on Turks Island.
July 31: James MacQueen retired at the age of 64. He lived to be 92.
During this year the routes were modified and, with Admiralty approval, shortened.
Oct 8: *Isis* was lost near Bermuda after damage at Puerto Rico. This loss together with the late delivery of the Acramans, Morgan pair (the builders were bankrupt) left Royal Mail without a mail ship.

1843 Jan 2: The hurriedly purchased *City of Glasgow* took one sailing and the *Trident*, chartered from the General Steam Navigation Co took the late January sailing. This is the only occasion in the history of the company when they have been without the necessary mail ships.
Apr 7: *Solway* was lost near Corunna; 17 passengers and 18 crew lost their lives. Because of the lack of navigational aids Corunna was omitted as a port of call.
June 1: *Severn* (I), the last of the initial order, sailed. In its first full year of trading Royal Mail lost £79,790 on trading as well as two ships valued at £53, 668.
Falmouth was discontinued as the mail port. Southampton being substituted bearing out the company's recommendations.

1844 Jan 15: Captain Philip Hart became Royal Mail's first Commodore. The Commodore flies a swallow tailed house flag instead of the usual rectangular version.
Princess Victoria became the embarkation tender at Southampton. The company's ships anchored off Netley at special buoys and the passengers had been embarked by rowing boat from Hythe.
July: The coaling hulk at Corunna, *North Britain,* returned to Southampton for use as a repair and depot ship. She also had engineering workshops installed.
Oct: William Pitcher of Northfleet, who had already built four of the original fourteen steamers, was given the contract for overhauling and re-caulking the ships, this was in spite of the need to journey the vessels round from Southampton. The reason being that the Royal Naval Dockyard at Portsmouth gave priority to naval vessels and thus hazarded Royal Mail's need to maintain its fleet in readiness to take the contractual mail sailings. William Pitcher built a new dry dock 500 ft (152.4 m) long × 78 ft (23.77 m) wide capable of accommodating 2 vessels at the same time.
Oct 9: *Actaeon* rounding Point Canoas near Cartagena, Colombia, in broad daylignt, ran onto a shore and was wrecked. The verdict being "inaccurate charts".

1845 Jan: *Reindeer* was purchased to augment the local WI services.

1846 Jan: *Eagle* was acquired to join *Reindeer.* These two vessels replaced the schooners, *Larne* (I) and *Liffey* (I). Sail was found to be too unreliable in areas of constant calm.
Nov 19: *Conway*, the first vessel designed solely for WI services, was launched.

1847 Feb 11: *Tweed* (I) was lost on Alecranes Rocks, near Yucatan. The survivors were rescued by the Mexican bridge *Emilio.* Having now lost 5 of the original fleet an immediate replacement for *Tweed* was needed. *Great Western* (Great Western Steamship Co) laid up at Bristol, was purchased and only slight modified before entering service.

A new service Southampton – Bermuda – New Orleans was inaugurated. *Teviot* (I) took the first sailing.
Conway (I), now completed, relieved *City of Glasgow* on the inter-island services which returned home and was laid at Blackwall for 2 years before being sold.

1848 *Lee* lost on the coast of Honduras. The last sailing ship in the fleet.

1849 Jan 14: *Forth* en route Havana – Vera Cruz, was wrecked on the Alecranes Rocks almost 2 years after *Tweed*.

1850 Jan 31: *Forth's* replacement *Derwent* launched.
July 5: An additional contract was entered into with the Admiralty. A monthly service was introduced to Rio de Janeiro with connecting steamer services to Monte Video (as then spelled) and Buenos Aires. This entailed an extra mileage of 152,000 and the contract added £30,000 raising the total to £270,000. In preparation for this the company had purchased *Esk* (I). She waited a year at Southampton for the day when the new contract would be signed. The new route was Southampton – Lisbon – Madeira – St Vincent (Cape Verde Islands) – Pernambuco – Bahia – Rio de Janeiro. In preparation the sailing ship *Southampton* took a full cargo of coal out to Rio for bunkering. An intermediate coaling station was established at St Vincent.
Nov 10: *Demerara* grounded badly in River Avon en route for engining; she did not enter Royal Mail service.

1851 Jan 9: *Teviot* took the first Rio de Janeiro mail service, arriving on Feb 7th. *Esk* then inaugurated the feeder service.
May: *Prince,* Royal Mail's first iron ship, was purchased to replace *Esk*. She sailed out to her station on July 2nd. *Esk* then returned north to St Thomas and became an inter-island steamer. The charter of 1839 was extended for 30 years. The new Rio contract demanded the addition of new vessels. Although the company preferred iron hulls the Admiralty still specified wooden hulls. Thus the 5 new vessels, the largest afloat, were of wood. They were *Orinoco* (I), *Magdalena* (I), *Amazon* (I), *Parana* (I) and *Demerara* (I).
Nov 10: *Demerara* grounded badly in River Avon en route for engining; she did not enter Royal Mail service.

1852 Jan 3: *Amazon* caught fire and burnt out on her maiden voyage. 115 lives were lost. The Admiralty thereafter decided that iron hulls were safer. Cunard's new *Arabia* was purchased as a replacement and was renamed *La Plata* (I). During this year fire precautions were incorporated, around the engine spaces, in the three remaining sisters.
Aug: in preparation for a projected Panama – Australia service Royal Mail opened a new route. Savannah (Georgia) – Nassau – Jamaica – Chagres (Colon).
Sept: In conjunction with the Pacific Steam Navigation Co, Royal Mail formed the Australian Pacific Mail Steam Packet Company. The new company ordered five ships. They were:
Kangeroo by Caird, Greenock.
Emeu and *Black Swan* by Robert Napier, Glasgow.
Dinornis by Reid & Co, Port Glasgow.
Menura by Miller and Ravenshill, London.
In preparation stocks of coal were built up at Panama, Tahiti, Wellington and Sydney. PSNC set up their Pacific West Coast offices in Panama City and they became managers of the company. Royal Mail were to operate the Atlantic connecting services and were to receive 30% of the through freights. The project was scheduled to commence in 1854.

1853 *Atrato* (I) became the first iron hulled mail ship built after the rescinding of the wooden hull ordenance.

Camilla was purchased from Samuel Cunard, to replace *Prince* which like *Esk*, proved too small for the growing Rio–River Plate traffic.

1854 Feb: *Emeu* was advertised to sail Southampton–Sydney–Panama but suddenly the whole project was abandoned. *Menura, Black Swan* and *Dinornis* were sold to Messageries Imperiales, France, and, after Crimean war service, *Emeu* went to Cunard and *Kangeroo* to Inman.
Tamar (I) became the last wooden hulled vessel built for the company. William Pitcher's era thus ended and as wood disappeared, so the company's connection with him ended.

1854/5 Crimean war. *Orinoco, Trent, Medway, Magdalena, Thames, Tamar* (I), *Severn* and *Great Western* were all used as transports.
Severn was converted into a hospital ship.
Medway carried out a cargo of Mr Page's seed so that vegetables could be grown in the Crimea instead of being freighted out, when most went rotten.

1855 Jan 27: The Panama Railway was completed. The Gulf of Mexico terminal was near Chagres in Navy Bay. The small township there was firstly called Aspinwall, after the railroad construction engineer, but it was soon renamed Colon.
The Pacific coast terminal was, of course, Panama City.

1856 Apr 23: After the ending of the Crimean war a Naval Review was held, on St George's Day, at Spithead. *Atrato* (I), *La Plata* and *Tay* represented Royal Mail. *Thames,* on charter to the British Government, was officially present.
The mail contract to Australia via Suez was secured from P&O by a new company, the European and Australian Company – but with onerous conditions. The company was so unprepared that it had no ships so Cunard's *Emeu* and P&O's *Etna* were chartered, meanwhile four steamers were built. They were the *European, Australian, Tasmanian* and *Colombian* with the purchased *Oneida* as relief vessel.

1857 The service Suez–Sydney commenced but, without repair facilities east of Suez, the new company soon ran into scheduling difficulties. It therefore sub-let to Royal Mail its UK–Egypt route Southampton–Marseilles–Malta–Alexandria.

1858 *Tamar* and *Teviot* were placed on the new service, but due to delays on the Australian side outbound passengers were stranded for long periods at Suez. Royal Mail were offered an amalgamation but refused the offer. However at the request of the British Government Royal Mail took over the whole contract, at £185,000 per annum, for an interim period. Because of the east of Suez problems Royal Mail were paid for delays and thus made a profit.

1859 *Tasmanian* and *Oneida* joined Royal Mail in repayment for unsecured monies. The other vessels were sold and the mail contract went back to P&O.
Mersey was specially built for the River Plate feeder service and *Camilla* was retired.

1861 Nov 7: The *San Jacinto* incident. *Trent* left Havana for England. Aboard were Messrs Slidell and Mason, the Commissioners to France for the Confederate States of America. On Nov 8, the Federal warship *San Jacinto* stopped *Trent* at the entrance of the Bahama Channel, 9 miles off Cuba. The commissioners were removed and imprisoned in Boston, Mass. Britain demanded their release on pain of war. In March 1862 the prisoners were finally released.

1862 Nov 21: *Avon* was lost at Colon.

1863 The company's first two screw driven steamers *Douro* (I) and *Rhone* built.
The mail contract was renewed for £215,300 annually.

1865 In a new attempt to operate a Panama–Australian service the Panama, New Zealand and Australian Royal Mail Company Ltd was formed. The company built *Kaikoura* (later *Tiber), Rakaia (Ebro* (I)), *Ruahine (Liffey* (II)) and *Mataura* and purchased *Prince Alfred* as reserve ship.

1866 June 2: *Atrato* took the Southampton–St Thomas sailing with *Danube* (I) connecting St Thomas–Colon. Thence 4 hours by rail to Panama where *Rakaia* took the onward Pacific service. The sailings from Panama were on the 23rd of each month. Although well run the service lost heavily.

1867 Oct 29: The great St Thomas hurricane. Of 60 vessels in the inner harbour only two were afloat next day. Over 1,000 lives were lost. Royal Mail lost *Rhone, Wye* and *Derwent. Conway* ground but survived without funnel and was demasted. *Solest* and *Tyne* were anchored in the outer roads. They weathered the hurricane but were both demasted. The sailing ship *British Empire* formerly the *Demerara* (1851) was also lost.

1868 The Panama, New Zealand and Australian RM Co ceased operations. Royal Mail was owed money and in settlement took over 3 of the vessels. They were refitted in UK and were compounded.

1868 Suez Canal opened.
Elbe was the first vessel fitted with compound engines for the company.
Arno and *Danube* were added to the Rio de Janeiro service.

1875 Jan 1: The mail contract was renewed but now for only £200,000 per year. Several ports were deleted from the mail contract and became non-contract ports so Royal Mail introduced their own 10 cent postage for local port to port conveyance. However the Postmaster General opposed the scheme and the omitted ports were re-contracted.
Aug 12: *Boyne* lost near Brest.
Sept 8: *Shannon* lost. PSNC's *Puno* and *Corcovado* were purchased to replace them. They became the largest vessels in the fleet, being renamed *Para* and *Don* respectively.

1876 Jan 21: *Severn* rammed and temporarily sank *Tagus* (I) at Colon.

1879 A West Indies revised contract came into force at £80,000 p.a.

1880 Royal Mail sailed out of London for the first time regularly since the 1841 *Thames* sailing.

1881 Feb: The Ashanti War. *Humber* was used to carry troops and mules from WI to Cape Coast Castle.

1882 Feb 10: *Tiber* (ex *Kaikoura)* lost at Porto Plata, San Domingo.
Apr: *Douro* was rammed and sunk by the Spanish vessel *Yrurac Bat,* which also sank.
The charter of 1839 was extended for a third time.

1883 *Eider,* the company's last paddler was sold out of service.

1884 A new route was introduced Santos to New York via Rio de Janeiro, Barbados and St Thomas.
Sept 11: *Dart* lost off Santos, en route New York.
The fortunes of the company reached a financial zenith when revenue reached £787,220 4s 3d, the highest total for the period 1880–1895.

1885 Feb 15: *Humber* left New York and disappeared at sea. 66 lost.
Apr: During a revolution in Colombia the company's offices at Colon were set on fire and destroyed.
June 20: *Guardiana,* on same route as *Dart* (I), was lost on coast of N. Brazil. The new service was withdrawn.

1886 Dec 2: *Orinoco* (II) entered service and was the company's first vessel to have electric light and triple expansion engines.

1887 July 23: Queen Victoria's Golden Jubilee was celebrated with a Naval Review at Spithead. *Tagus* (I) represented Royal Mail.

1888 The company introduced their first 'new look' ships *Atrato* (II), *Magdalena* (II), *Thames* (II) and *Clyde* (II). These vessels had the passenger accommodation in the superstructure and not below decks in the hull. They had pole masts and no sails.

1890 Sept 23: The company's offices at Colon again destroyed by fire.
Oct: Rotterdam was introduced as a port of call.

1891 Oct 29: *Moselle* was lost in a gale near Colon. Captain Rowsell went down with his ship.

1893 *Nile* (II) and *Danube* (II) straight stemmed enlarge *Atrato* class vessels entered service.

1894 Revenue from the carriage of mail reached £107,959.

1895 The capital of the company stood at £1,500,000 of which £900,000 had been issued, with debentures of £150,000. On the Stock markets the £100 share stood at a quoted £60 and the break up value at £50. This was a direct result of a period in ship owning of prolonged depression which in turn had been aggravated by excessive shipbuilding coupled with one of the cyclical trade recessions.
At that time Royal Mail owned 27 seagoing ships of 80,359 gross tons and an average age of 13 years. This was in fact an older fleet than P&O, Union Line or Castle Line at that time. The value of the fleet stood at £1,198,768 with a depreciation sum in the balance sheet of £50,000.

1897 June 26: Queen Victoria's Diamond Jubilee Naval Review was held at Spithead. *Danube* and *Orinoco* present. *Danube* conveyed the House of Lords and their guests. It was at this review that *Turbinia* dashed up and down the rows of anchored ships at 35 knots and effectively made known the Parsons Steam Turbine.

1899 *Tagus* (II) and *Trent* (III), smaller *Nile's* were commissioned.
The Boer war. *Nile, Tagus* (Transport 101), *Minho* (II), *Ebro* (II) and *Severn* (II) were all used as troop and supply transports.
Tagus took Boer prisoners to India.

1900 Yellow funnels were introduced when *Eden* and *Esk* were repainted at St Thomas.

1901 The Government subsidised Imperial Direct Line opened its sailings from Bristol to WI in direct competition with Royal Mail. Their *Port Morant* took the first sailing. Royal Mail encountered economic problems and profits fell.
Oct 16: *Para* suffered a violent explosion in her experimental frozen fruit hold. 3 killed.

1902 Mar: *Elbe* was chartered by Cunard to repatriate the passengers from *Etruria* who were stranded in the Azores following the loss in mid-Atlantic of *Etruria's* rudder.

Mar 31: The Boer (or South African) war ended at Pretoria. All the vessels in Government service were released by the year end.

Aug 16: King Edward VII's Coronation Naval Review took place at Spithead. It had originally been planned for June 28 but the King was ill with appendicitis. *Clyde* and *La Plata* (IV) attended.
For the first time in its history the company paid no dividend.

1903 Owen Philipps, later Lord Kylsant became Chairman of the company which was at a low ebb. He commenced a policy of revitalisation. The capital was increased by the simple expedient of calling up the 40% of unpaid stock which had, for 63 years, since the foundation of the company, remained unsubscribed. Six new cargo-only vessels were ordered and the new era of "A" class passenger liners for the South American service was planned and implemented.

1905 *Aragon* (I) the first "A" commissioned.
The West Indian Mail contract came up for renewal but Imperial Direct Line (an Elder Dempster subsidiary) obtained a £40,000 p.a. Avonmouth – Jamaica licence and Royal Mail carried on without a subsidy.

1906 Royal Mail restricted its mail service and an new inter-island contract was negotiated at £25,000 p.a. In order to maintain its frequencies two miniature "A"s *Berbice* (I) and *Balantia* (I) were ordered and delivered in 1909.

Feb: Royal Mail purchased PSNC's interest in the Orient – Pacific Line. *Oroya, Oruba, Orotava* and *Ortona* were transferred. The company was renamed Orient – Royal Mail Line. The ports of call were London – Plymouth – Gibraltar – Marseilles – Naples – Port Said – Suez – Colombo – Fremantle – Adelaide – Melbourne – Sydney.
The cargo service to Brazil was augmented by the purchase of two Bucknall vessels renamed *Marima* and *Manau.*
A new service was introduced Southampton – Cuba – Mexico. Union Castle's *Greek* and *Gaul* were purchased and renamed *Sabor* (I) and *Segura.*
3 "A"s *Amazon* (II), *Araguaya* and *Avon* (III) came into service.

1907 The Orient – Royal Mail Line's Australian mail contract came up for renewal. Orient Line bid for and obtained the contract and gave notice of their intention to dissolve the joint agreement.

Apr: An interest was acquired in Jenkin's Shire Line. *Monmouthshire, Denbighshire* and *Flintshire* were purchased and operated under the title Shire Line of Steamers Ltd. The shares of this company were held by Jenkins & Co, Thos & Jno Brocklebank and Royal Mail. Three months later Jenkins & Co dropped out.

1908 *La Plata* was sold to the Polytechnic Touring Association for cruising.
Asturias (I) took her maiden voyage in Orient – Royal Mail's Australian service.
The Forward Line was acquired and with them the London – Gibraltar – Moroccan ports – Madeira – Canary Isles routes. The *Agadir* and *Arzila* came under the Royal Mail flag.

1909 The dissolution of the Orient – Royal Mail joint service came into effect and Royal Mail withdrew from the Australian run.

1909 *Oroya* was sold. *Orotava* and *Oruba* went onto the WI route and *Ortona* was converted for cruising and renamed *Arcadian* (II). With these moves *Orinoco* went for breaking up.

1910 To augment the Southampton–South American service by the "A"s 5 "D" class ships were ordered for the Liverpool–South American meat run.

1911 *Deseado* (I) and *Demerara* (II) entered service, the remaining three *Desna, Darro* (I) and *Drina* (I) followed in 1912.
June 24: King George V's Coronation Review at Spithead. *Thames* and *Agadir* were present.
Nile was sold to Pacific Mail SS Co.
The last mail contract was entered into; 5 years at £63,000 p.a.
The Brocklebank shares in Shire Line of Steamers were purchased, together with five ships. Five more Brocklebank vessels necessary for operating the join service were withdrawn. To replace them *Radnorshire* (I) and *Merionethshire* were purchased and four more were built *Cardiganshire, Carnarvonshire, Pembrokeshire* and *Brecknockshire*. Glen Line bought the Brocklebank vessels.

1912 Apr 1: A supplementary Royal Charter was granted extending the company's powers and widening the field in which it could operate.
Shortly after the share capital of Elder Dempster Lines was acquired. Their *Jamaica* was transferred to Royal Mail.

1913 Four years earlier in 1909 Lord Balfour's Royal Commission had reported that communications between Canada and WI were poor. Eventually Royal Mail agreed, with the Government of Canada, to operate a fortnightly service with four ships. *Pembrokeshire* (ex *Sabor,* ex *Greek)* and *Carmarthenshire* (ex *Segura,* ex *Gaul)* were ideal in both size and passenger capacity. They were again renamed; this time after Canadian rivers. *Segura* became *Chignecto* and inaugurated the new service. *Sabor* became *Chaleur*. The second pair of ships were acquired from Union Castle. *Goth* became *Cobequid* and *Guelph, Caraquet*.

1914 Jan 13: On her first voyage *Cobequid* was lost in the Bay of Fundy. Elder Dempster's *Mandingo* was transferred to the route and renamed *Chaudiere*.
The Canadian contract was for 5 years at £70,000 p.a. with ports of call Halifax–St John–Bermuda–St Kitts–Antigua–Montserrat–Dominica–St Lucia–St Vincent–Grenada–Barbados–Trinidad–Georgetown (British Guiana) and vice versa.
Aug 4: First World War started. 38 Royal Mail vessels saw war service. Newport, Monmouthshire became the company's temporary home port. *Essequibo* (II) and *Ebro* (II) were launched for transatlantic service. The "A"s were now operating a weekly service to S. America.
Aug 15: The Panama Canal was opened.
A new company RMSP Meat Transports Ltd was formed to operate refrigerated meat cargo ships to River Plate ports.
War losses: *Tyne, Tamar, Potaro, Caroni, Aragon, Amazon, Oruba, Arcadian, Marima, Drina, Alcantara, Caribbean, Radnorshire, Merionethshire* and *Brecknockshire*.

1918 Nov 11: With the war over there were still standard ships on the stocks and no-one really wanted them. Royal Mail agreed to take over 14 of the A, B, C, G and N standard types.
The company also undertook the management of 11 vessels of the Russian Volunteer Fleet. Painted in Royal Mail colours they were operated by a special Royal Mail unit called "The Government Ship Management Department".
The vessels managed were:
Ekaterinoslavl, Kamenetz Podolsk, Koursk, Krasnoiarsk, Mogileff, Novorod, Omsk, Tambov, Vologda, Voronej and *Yaroslavl*.

1919 Due to war shortages PSNC's *Quilpue* and *Quillota* were chartered for Southampton–WI services, however the priority was for S. American ports.

1920 Aug 4: Royal Mail's passenger service to West Indies ended after almost 80 years.

1921 The company's first motor ship *Lochkatrine* entered service on the joint service, with Holland America Line to the N. Pacific ports of USA and Canada.
Because of the shortage of North Atlantic Tonnage Royal Mail were induced to operate a North Atlantic passenger service from Hamburg. PSNC, their subsidiary, had surplus tonnage, including *Orduña* which had been on the route under Cunard colours. She was joined by *Orbita* and *Oropesa*.
In April *Orbita* took the first sailing Hamburg–Southampton–Cherbourg–New York.

1922 Business on the route became so good that Royal Mail chartered *Vestris, Vauban* and *Vandyck* from Lamport & Holt.
In December *Orca* joined the Atlantic ships and *Oropesa* returned to PSNC.

1923 USSR petitioned for the return of the 11 Russian Volunteer fleet vessels. They won their claim but immediately writs for the payment of outstanding bills were served from many quarters and the majority of the vessels never returned to Russia.
Feb: Sir Owen Philipps became Lord Kylsant of Carmarthen and Amroth.
Ebro and *Essequibo* joined PSNC. *Ohio* (ex *Munchen)* was added to the Southampton–New York "Comfort Route".

1924 Quebec and Halifax were added as ports of call on New York run.

1925–1926 For the S. American run *Asturias* (II) and *Alcantara* (II) entered service as the largest motor vessels.

1925 Hamburg ceased to be a port of call.

1927 Royal Mail acquired the shares of White Star Line from the International Mercantile Marine Co *Ohio* and *Orca* went to White Star as *Albertic* and *Calgaric, Orbita* and *Orduna* were returned to PSNC and Royal Mail withdrew from the New York service. The Canada–WI service also ended.

1929–1931 The company encountered financial problems which eventually enforced a reconstruction of the group. PSNC was separated.

1932 Royal Mail Lines Ltd was formed to take over the assets of Royal Mail Steam Packet Co Ltd, RMSP Meat Transports Ltd, Nelson Steam Navigation Co Ltd and David MacIver & Co Ltd. Lord Essendon became the first Chairman.
The vessels transferred from Nelson were: *Meissonier, Murillo* and *Moliere* (former Lamport & Holt ships whose names had not been changed). The were renamed *Nasina, Nalon* and *Nela*. Together with the five 14,000 ton *Highland* Liners and *Highland Warrior* which became *Nagoya*.
From MacIver came *Thessaly* (I), *Sicily, Lombardy* (I), *Araby* (I), *Gascony* and *Brittany* (I).

1939–1945 Sept 2: The Second World War. All the company's vessels were engaged in some official capacity.
War losses were *Nalon, Nasina* (under Italian flag as *Asmara), Highland Patriot, Brittany, Lochkatrine, Lochgoil* (as *Empire Rowan), Culebra, Nebraska, Navasota, Natia, Nagara, Sabor, Sambre, Somme, Siris, Sarthe, Araby, Nagoya, Lochavon* and *Pampas*.

1945 The surviving passenger ships *Atlantis, Almanzora, Asturias, Alcantara* and *Andes* together with the four *Highland* sisters were all engaged in trooping, repatriation, hospital ship duties. *Almanzora* carried emigrants to Australia.

1947 *Highland Brigade* and her 3 sisters progressively re-entered the S. American service. New cargo tonnage was initiated, including *Loch Avon* and *Loch Garth*. The fleet included a few *"Empire"* type British standard ships and four ex SAM ships of the US *Liberty* class. *Almanzora* ended her 33 year career and was broken up.

1948 Jan *Andes* (II), built in 1939, made her first commercial voyage; next *Alcantara*, reconditioned at Belfast, joined her on the S. American run.

1949 *Magdalena*, a replacement for war losses and in particular *Highland Patriot* was lost on her maiden voyage.

1952–1958 Fleet building continued.

1959–1960 3 replacement ships for the *Highland* class came into service. They were *Amazon, Aragon* and *Arlanza* with white hulls.

1959 *Andes* rebuilt and converted to cruising being given a white hull.

1965 Furness Withy acquired the share capital of Royal Mail; they already controlled Shaw Savill & Albion. This brought together one of the largest British shipping groups. From this time onward an interchange of ships took place, frequently without change of name, all being operated by Furness Ship Management Ltd.

1968 The three new "A"s were unable to pay their way and were transferred the Shaw Savill & Albion for service to Australasia.
Abedesa and *Duquesa* were operated by Royal Mail without a change of name.

1968 The Royal Mail's N. Pacific route was merged with Furness Withy & Co Ltd.

1972 Royal Mail as a separate shipping line virtually disappeared into the combined Furness Withy fleets.
No new ships were built for Royal Mail as such; tonnage, as in the case of *Drina* (III), was transferred as appropriate.

1973 *Darro* (III) joined her sister in Royal Mail service.

1976 *Deseado* (III), formerly *Iberic*, was operated on Royal Mail routes.

1980 In the Furness Withy and Shaw Savill & Albion fleets only two Royal Mail names remain *Deseado* and the small service vessel *Tweed*. Once again the virtual elimination of one of the great names of the sea is regretfully recorded.

1981 *Orduna, Orbita* and *Orotega*, although operated by PSNC, were registered as being owned by Royal Mail.

Routes

1840–1920 Falmouth (1843: Southampton replaced Falmouth)–Barbados–Grenada–Santa Cruz–St Thomas–Nicola Mole (Haiti)–Santiago de Cuba–Kingston (Jamaica). Coaling calls were Corunna, Madeira outbound and Bermuda inbound plus local West Indies services.

1847–1850 Southampton–Bermuda–New Orleans.

1850–1980 Southampton–Lisbon–Madeira–St Vincent–Pernambuco (Recife)–Bahia–Rio de Janeiro–Montevideo–Buenos Aires. Over the years the ports of call changed, e.g. Madeira and St Vincent were dropped with the introduction of oil fuel.

1852–1868 Savannah (Georgia)–Nassau–Jamaica–Colon (Chagres).

1857–1859 Marseilles–Malta–Alexandria.

1884 Santos–Rio de Janeiro–Barbados–St Thomas–New York.

1906–1909 London–Plymouth–Gibraltar–Marseilles–Naples–Port Said–Suez–Colombo–Fremantle–Adelaide–Melbourne–Sydney.

1906 Southampton–Cuba–Mexico.

1913–1927 Halifax–St John (NB)–Bermuda–St Kitts–Antigua–Montserrat–Dominica–St Lucia–St Vincent–Grenada–Barbados–Trinidad–Georgetown (British Guiana).

1921–1927 Hamburg–Southampton–Cherbourg–New York.

1921–1980 London–Cherbourg–Vigo–Lisbon–Las Palmas–Rio de Janeiro–Santos–Montevideo–Buenos Aires.

1921–1968 Pacific cargo service. South Wales/Middlesbrough/London–Bermuda–Bahamas–Dominican Republic–Haiti–Jamaica–Puerto Rico–Venezuela–Curacao–Aruba–Colombia (Atlantic ports)–Panama (Cristobal)–Costa Rica–Nicaragua–Honduras–El Salvador–Guatemala–Mexico–Pacific USA ports–Vancouver. Not all ports were visited on every voyage.

Livery

Funnels 1841–1899: Black. Steam pipes were of polished copper with brass flange tops. Funnel stays were white; 1900–1972: Buff-yellow, including steam pipes; Jenkin's Shire Line: Red funnel black top.

Masts 1841–1899: Biscuit brown (straw coloured), white yard arms. Had a naval look about them; 1900–1972: Funnel buff. Mainmast top mast black.

Ports Early vessels: Red edged ports with green venetian shutters.

Hulls 1841–1899: Black. A thin white band appeared during 1880s on vessels which had not white painted fcsles or poops. Ended 1900; 1900–1903: Mail ships and cruising ships had white hulls. Mail ships reverted to black because of cost also coaling made them look dirty; 1903–1958: Cruising ships only had white hulls; 1959: Passenger and cruising ships had white hulls.

Boat Topping 1841–1860 (circa): None. But copper sheathing showed pink. Iron hulled ships none; 1860–1972: Salmon pink.

Boats 1841–1870s: Black; 1870s–1982: White.

Flags – House Flags The crown on the flag is only shared with 3 other companies. PSNC, Elder Dempster and Orient Line; The crown denoted a Royal Mail vessel with a naval agent aboard; The flag is seen first at the launch of *Forth* at Leith, May 22, 1841.

Fleet index

Illustrated fleet list

CLYDE, TWEED (I), THAMES (I), FORTH, TAY, MEDWAY (I) and MEDINA

1 **CLYDE**

Bt 1841 Robert Duncan, Greenock; *T:* 1,841 g, 1,285 n.
Dim 275 ft (83.82 m) oa, bowsprit to taffrail, 245 ft (74.68 m) × 60 ft (18.29 m) over paddle boxes and 30 ft (9.14 m) keel to spar deck.
Eng Pad, simple, side liver; 2 cyls; 400 NHP, 4 cast iron boilers with brick flues, 2 per cylinder. 4 furnaces per boiler. Stm P: 6 lb; 9 kts; By Caird & Co, Greenock. Paddles were of birchwood 8 ft 9 in (2.67 m) long, 3 ft (0.91 m) depth of blade and 2½ in (6.47 cm) thick.
H Wood. British and African oak with diagonal iron and wood fastenings; iron braces. Copper sheathed against Teredo worm, oakum caulked. The vessels had forecastles and poops but looked flush decked because of an oak spar deck which joined them. This provided an open promenade deck with large square ports. In appearance they were heavy and cumbersome and looked more like warships. they were referred to as being "Ocean Stage Coaches" not passenger liners. The Clyde class (1–10) carried an inverted lifeboat across the top of the paddle box.
Rig Initially built as 3-masted barquentines, square rigged on the foremast only. Later many had the mizzen mast removed to ease rolling. After about 10 years the surviving vessels were brigs (i.e. square rigged on fore and main masts) to increase speed by about 1 knot.
Pass 100. The best cabins were aft adjoining the saloon which occupied the square galleon like stern with its ornate scroll work.
Costs Engines £20,000, hull £28,500, sails 2 sets £650 each, spares £3,000 (mainly engine), furnishings £5,000, say £60,000 each. The Acramans Morgan pair *(Severn* and *Avon)* cost £6,000 more due to the collapse of the company.
General All were designed with funnels (Royal Mail called them chimneys) forward of the paddle boxes. However Scott Sinclair and Acramans Morgan had engine room layouts which placed the funnel abaft the paddels. Royal Mail reluctantly agreed to the variation.

1841 Feb 25: Launched. Dec 18: Maiden voyage Southampton – Corunna – Madeira – West Indies; Captain H. Woodruff, Lieutenant Royal Navy.
1865 Sold and broken up.

2 **TWEED** (I)

Details as *Clyde* (1) except:
Bt Ordered from Caird & Co but sub-contracted to Thompson and Spiers, Glasgow; *T:* 1,800 g, 1,172 n.

1841 Apr 24: Launched. Dec 18: Maiden voyage Southampton–West Indies; Captain E. Franklin.
1846 Dec 17: Sailed on what was to be her last voyage with 62 passengers and 89 crew; Captain Parsons.
1847 Feb 12: Wrecked en-route Havana–Vera Cruz on the infamous Alacranes Reef, Campeche Bank, Yucatan, 72 lives lost. The ship left Havana on the evening of February 9 and struck at 3 am on February 12 in fresh cross seas. These rolled *Tweed* from side to side on the rocks, until she lay on her starboard beam and before daybreak had broken into three parts. The survivors struggled onto a reef which was above water at low tide and submerged to about three feet at the flood. All the wood was assembled to form a raft upon which the survivors rested in turns whilst others prevented the raft from drifting off the reef. A small gig was salved and made seaworthy. Ten set off in this craft to seek help. They were found by the Spanish brig *Emilio* and were taken into the port of Sisal, on the northwest corner of the Yucatan, here canoes were obtained and towed by *Emilio* to the wreck. It took another twenty-four hours to ferry the 69 off the raft so that the survivors became 79 in all. The survivors paid immense tribute not only to the Captain and crew of *Emilio* but also to the Mexicans. For all the aid and clothing provided to the survivors no-one would accept a penny in payment.

3 **THAMES** (I)

Details as *Clyde* (1) except:
Bt 1841 William Pitcher, Northfleet, Thames; *T:* 1,889 g.
Eng By Maudsley, Sons & Field, London.

1841 May 20: Launched. Dec 29: Maiden voyage Gravesend–Falmouth. Captain P. Hast RN.
1842 Jan 3: Sailed with first mails, accompanied by *Tay*.
1850 The first to be fitted with feathering paddles. Increased speed by 2 knots.
1854 Crimean war transport. Aug 11: Took 400 passengers to Queen Victoria's Naval Review at Spithead. The first cruise of the company.
1859 Jan: Served on Southampton–Alexandria service for a brief period.
1865 Broken up at St Thomas, West Indies.

4 **FORTH**

Details as *Clyde* (1) except:
Bt 1841 Robert Menzies, Leith; *T:* 1,939 g, 1,147 n.

1841 May 22: Launched. Dec 17: Maiden voyage Southampton–St Thomas–Havana–Belize–Vera Cruz–Havana–Nassau (Mar 18)–Bermuda–Fayal–Falmouth–Southampton (Nassau outwards was missed due to engine trouble). Captain Favrer. The first mail vessel in service, she went to St Thomas to await the mails from *Thames* (3).

1848 Sept 2: Last voyage started. Southampton–West Indies.
1849 Jan 14: Lost on Nigrellos rock near Cartagena en-route Havana–Vera Cruz. Captain Sturdee. All saved.

SOLWAY, SEVERN, AVON and DEE

5 **SOLWAY**

Details as *Clyde* (1) except:
Bt 1841 James McMillan, Greenock; *T:* 1,700 g, 1,109 n.

1841 May 22: Launched. Dec 18: Maiden voyage Southampton–Nassau–Havana.
1843 Apr 8: Lost, outward bound, on Baldargo rocks, Sisargo, 20 miles west of Corunna. Captain R. C. Duncan. Carried 45 passengers and 88 crew; 35 lives lost.

6 **TAY**

Details as *Clyde* (1) except:
Bt 1841 Chas. Wood, Dumbarton, Clyde; *T:* 1,858 g.
Eng By Caird.

1841 July 6: Launched.
1842 Jan 3: Sailed with *Thames* (3). Voyage to West Indies took 19 days. Captain T. Hayden.
1851 On S. American run to Rio de Janeiro.
1853/4 Rebuilt and lengthened at Whites Yard, Cowes, Isle of Wight.
1856 Aug 30: Wrecked on Cape Roxo near Vera Cruz. No passengers aboard.

7 **MEDWAY** (I)

Details as *Clyde* (1) except:
Bt 1841 William Pitcher, Northfleet; *T:* 1,895 g.
Eng By Maudsley, Sons & Field, London. The Illustrated London News shows this vessel with white strake about 4 ft (1.22 m) thick at upper porthole level.

1841 July 7: Launched.
1842 Jan 31: Maiden voyage Blackwall–West Indies to take up station at St Thomas. Captain H. Smith.
1854 Crimean War transport.
1861 Sold for breaking up.

8 **SEVERN** (I)

Details as *Clyde* (1) except:
Bt 1841 William Patterson, Bristol (hull only); *T:* 1,886 g.
Eng By Acramans, Morgan & Co.

1843 June 1: Maiden voyage Southampton–West Indies. Captain W. Vincent. *Severn's* entry into service was delayed due to the financial collapse of Acramans, Morgan. She became the last of the 14 to be delivered. Built in dry dock. No launch.
1854 Crimean War transport.
1855 Hospital ship, one of the first, with 240 berths.
1856 Released to company. Not worth rebuilding, broken up at Vauxhall.

9 **MEDINA**

Details as *Clyde* (1) except:
Bt 1841 Thos. & John White, Cowes, Isle of Wight; *T:* 1,800 g.

Eng By Edward Bury, Liverpool.

1841 July 6: Launched.
1842 Jan 27: Maiden voyage Southampton – West Indies. Southampton – St Thomas 3,662 miles. May 12: Lost on a coral reef on Turks Island, 64 passengers and 104 crew; all saved. Captain C. F. Burnley.

10 **DEE** (I)

Details as *Clyde* (1) except:
Bt 1841 John Scott & Sons, Greenock; *T:* 1,849 g.
Eng By Scott, Sinclair & Co.

1841 July 10: Launched.
1842 Jan 14: Maiden voyage Southampton – West Indies. Captain C. Oman.
1849 Feb 1: When at Mobile *Dee* heard reports of a British steamer well aground on the Nigrellos Rocks, one of the Alacranes Reefs that had claimed *Tweed* (2) in 1847. She set sail at once and found that it was her sister ship *Forth* (4).
1860 Oct: After the Italian Civil War which founded the Kingdom of Italy *Dee* repatriated the Irish Brigade to Queenstown (Cobh).
1862 Dry rot; sold for demolition.

TRENT (I), TEVIOT (I) and ISIS

11 **TRENT** (I)

Details as *Clyde* (1) except:
Bt1841 William Pitcher, Northfleet; *T:* 1,856 g.
Eng By Miller, Ravenhill & Co, London.
Identification Thinner funnel not belled. Lifeboat ahead of paddle box which is black to deck level then white; also had an almost imperceptible rake.

1841 Oct 2: Launched.
1842 Mar 2: Maiden voyage from Southampton. Captain E. C. Miller.
1854 Apr: Crimean War transport. Carried the 23rd Regiment, Royal Welsh Fusiliers, 1,180 men to Eupatoria. Captain Woodward.
1861 Nov 8: Mr. Slidell and Mr. Mason, the Confederate States Commissioners to France were taken off *Trent* by the USS *San Jacinto*. This caused an international incident which almost caused Britain to declare war on the Northern States of America.
1865 Returned from West Indies. Laid up.
1867 Broken up at Woolwich.

12 **TEVIOT** (I)

Details as *Clyde* (1) except:
T: 1,744 g.
Eng By Caird.

1841 Oct 4: Launched.
1842 Feb 15: Maiden voyage Southampton – West Indies. Captain H. Crocker.
1847 Nov 2: Inaugurated Southampton – New Orleans service.

1851 Jan 9: Inaugurated S. American Southampton–West Indies–Rio de Janeiro direct service. Arrived Rio February 7.
1857 Placed on Southampton–Alexandria service of European & Australian R. M. Co. until operations ceased in 1858.
1864 Mar: Sold and broken up.

13 **ISIS**

Details as *Clyde* (1) except:
Bt 1841 Wm. Pitcher, Northfleet; *T:* 1,900 g.
Eng By Miller Ravenhill & Co, London.

1841 Nov 16: Launched.
1842 Apr 1: Maiden voyage Southampton– West Indies. Oct 8: Grounded on island off Puerto Rico. Refloated in damaged condition. Moved to Bermuda for repairs. Hit heavy weather and foundered off Bermuda. One lost.

14 **AVON** (I)

Details as *Clyde* except:
Bt 1842 Wm. Patterson, Bristol; *T:* 2,069.
Eng By Acramans, Morgan & Co.

1842 Floated out of dock. Completion held up due to the financial problems of Engine builders.
1843 Feb 1: Maiden voyage. Southampton–West Indies.
1852 Rebuilt and lengthened by Wm. Pitcher, at Northfleet.
1863 Nov 21: Whilst moored at Colon a gale blew up which tore *Avon* from her moorings and wrecked her on the nearby rocks.

LEE, LARNE and LIFFEY (I)

15 **LEE**

Bt 1841 Griffith Taylor, Barking, River Thames: *T:* 250 g.
Dim 150 ft (45.72 m) × 24 ft (7.31 m).
H Wood, 1 deck.
Pass 12.

1841 Dec 3: Maiden voyage Thames–West Indies. Captain Henderson. Sailed with her sister *Larne* (16). These two vessels were therefore the first in service with Royal Mail. They were to be used on inter-island services.
1848 Grounded and broke up near Belize, British Honduras. Captain Greaves. No lives lost.

16 **LARNE** (I)

Details as *Lee* (15) except:
T: 300 g.

1841 Dec: Sailed on maiden voyage with *Lee* (15). Thames–West Indies. Captain T. Restarrick. For local inter-island services.
1851 July: Sold and broken up. 10 years being about the life of a wooden sailer in Caribbean waters.

17 **LIFFEY** (I)

Details as *Lee* (15) except:
Bt 1841 Henry Wimshurst, Limehouse; *T:* 350 g.

1841 Dec (probably mid): Maiden voyage Thames–West Indies.
1847 Out of service. Little is known of this vessel.

18 **AURORA**

Details: Sailing ship stripped of top masts and used as a coal hulk at Falmouth during the period 1841-1843.

NORTH BRITAIN

19 **NORTH BRITAIN**

Details: Sailing ship; stripped of top masts and used as a coal hulk at Corunna from 1841-1843. After Corunna ceased to be a port of call *North Britain* returned to Southampton in June 1843. Here she became the Engineers depot ship carrying out maintenance and repairs to the mail ships. Boilers were constructed aboard her. In 1843 her foremast was removed and main and mizzen only remained with a large derrick on each.

1853 Sold and broken up.

The illustration depicts the donkey engine in use and four unknown signal flags on the main mast.

20 **CITY OF GLASGOW**

Bt 1840 Glasgow; *T:* 1,700 g.
Eng Pad, simple side lever; 2 cyl; 350 NHP; 8 kts.
H Wood, 1 deck.

1840 Entered service for Thomson & McConnell of Glasgow.
1841 Dec: Acquired to replace the non-delivery of *Severn* (8).
1842 Jan 2: Maiden voyage Glasgow-West Indies. Captain T. Boxer. Used as an inter-island ship based at St Thomas.
1846 When *Conway* (25) entered service withdrawn and laid up at Blackwall.
1848 June: Sold for further trading.

ACTAEON

21 **ACTAEON**

Bt 1841 Glasgow; *T:* 650 g.
Eng Pad, simple side lever; 2 cyls; 9 kts.
H Wood, 1 deck.

1841 Purchased from Martin & Burns, Glasgow, for use as a West Indies feeder service vessel. Jan 2: Maiden voyage to West Indies.
1844 Oct 9: Wrecked on Point Canoas near Cartagena, New Grenada (now Colombia).

22 **PRINCESS VICTORIA**

Details: 1844 Mar: Purchased for use as passenger tender at Southampton. Served from Southampton dock to Hythe anchorage. Replaced the rowing boats previously used. Remained in service until Southampton's 13 ft (3.196 m) depth was doubled about 1850.

EAGLE and RHEINDEER

23 **REINDEER**

Bt 1840 Liverpool; *T:* 600 g.
Dim 210 ft (64 m) × 35 ft (10.67 m).
Eng Pad.
H Wood.
Pass 24.

1840 Built for George Langtry & Co, Liverpool. Liverpool – Dublin service. Langtry started this steamer service as early as 1820.
1845 Acquired by Royal Mail to replace *Liffey* (17). Captain Revett. Disposal not known.

24 **EAGLE**

No details of this vessel seem to have been recorded. There were many ships with the name *Eagle* so that isolating this vessel is not conclusively possible.

1846 Jan: Purchased from Taylor & Scott, Dublin as consort to *Reindeer* (23). Refitted by Wm. Pitcher at Northfleet. May 13: First voyage for Royal Mail. Gravesend – West Indies.
1856 July: At Belize when town was burned by fire; acted as relief vessel to the inhabitants.
1861 Sold out of service at Jamaica.

CONWAY (I)

25 **CONWAY** (I)

Bt 1846 Wm. Pitcher, Northfleet; *T:* 895 g.
Dim 215 ft, (65.53 m) × 35 ft (10.67 m) × 16 ft (4.88 m)
Eng Pad, simple, oscillating; 2 cyls; 9 kts.
H Wood, 2 decks.
Pass 40.
As built this ship had 2 small funnels athwartship each serving one boiler. Drawing is 1862 profile.

1846 Nov 19: Launched. First vessel solely for West Indies service.
1847 Apr 11: Maiden voyage Southampton – West Indies.
1862 Re-engined. Re-entered service with one large funnel. When refitted *Conway* was

equipped with feather paddles. A rod and cam pivoted the paddle so that each blade entered and left the water in a vertical position. With fixed paddles the blades entered and left the water at an inefficient angle and were only vertical at the one instant when directly below the axle.
1867 Oct 29: Grounded but survived the great St Thomas hurricane. Both masts and funnel were blown out of the ship.
1870 June: Sold.

GREAT WESTERN

26 **GREAT WESTERN**

Bt 1838 William Patterson, Bristol; *T:* 1,340 g.
Dim 212 ft (64.62 ft) × 35 ft (10.67 m).
Eng Pad, simple, side lever; 2 cyls; 9 kts. By Maudsley, Sons & Field.
H Wood.
Pass 1st: After saloon 128, forward saloon 20.

1836 July 28: Laid down for Great Western Steam Ship Company.
1838 Apr 8: Maiden voyage Bristol–New York. Captain Lt James Hosken RN.
1840 1,700 g.
1843 Transferred to Liverpool–New York route.
1846 After 37 round transatlantic voyages withdrawn from service and laid up.
1847 Acquired by Royal Mail to replace the lost *Tweed* (2).
1854 Crimean war transport
1856 Returned to Royal Mail. Not worth refitting. Broken up at Vauxhall.

Life aboard ship in the 1840s
Lights were by candle affixed in lanterns. There was one lantern to two cabins and these were placed in a small head-height cubicle from outside the cabin. They could not be tampered with from inside the room.
Lights out for the whole ship's company was 9 pm. This included the cook's fires in the galley. Passengers lights were extinguished at 11 pm by the midshipman of the watch who, from the passageway, removed each lantern.
Scuttles and port holes were secured by 8 pm except for the majority of the passenger cabins which opened off the main saloon and had their windows facing inwards. The scuttles they had did not open. Ventilation was by means of opening cabin doors.
There was a saloon for the exclusive use of ladies. In some instances the lady's cabin was sold for passenger use and even when so occupied it was available to all ladies from 9 am to 9 pm.
In West Indian waters deck passengers were carried. They had to feed themselves, supply their own bedding and remain forward of the funnel.
Meal hours differed. Breakfast at 10 am was followed by Dinner (lunch) at 4 pm and tea or supper at 7 pm. The Captain was the ship's "Providore" and the stewards reported to him. The company gave a victualling allowance for each passenger and crew member aboard ship. There were safeguards against profiteering by Captains, for example the passengers knew their food entitlement for each type of meal.
Navigation was the Captain's responsibility, as well as ship's discipline, he and he alone plotted the course of his ship.
Mail bags were originally made of hide the same as on the mail coaches. However, aboard ship it was found that rats liked and ate them. Canvas oakum bags were substituted. Additionally every Royal Mail ship had to have at least one cat.

Wooden ships had to have their own timbers kept 'sweet' and water was frequently pumped into the ship to dampen the wood. The introduction of boilers and furnaces into the hulls of wooden ships led to the progressive drying out of the surrounding timbers and beams. This in time resulted in the vessels developing a fairly pronounced 'sag' amidships. To combat this, and as fire precautions, ships in the later forties had the areas around the machinery plaged with iron and the decks had iron grilles let into them.
Dry Rot was one of the major problems. It could develop after only two or three years and ships became 'sick'. Various remedies were used, such as felting and rock salting and using woods resistant to the fungus.
Sailing at night. No navigation lights were carried prior to 1847. Individual captains used their own arrangement of night lights. Many used none since their boast was that they could see or smell or hear another vessel. From 1848 the present system of navigation lights became mandatory.
Cargo. The early wooden paddlers carried almost none. Their holds were full of coal. It was 20 years before cargo pay-loads influenced steamship design. For cargo there were thousands of sailing vessels. Steam was for mail and passenger punctuality.
Sails were used extensively for another 40 years. Two sets were carried and in some ships a light set was used in West Indian waters to respond to the faintest breeze. Many captains used the fore and aft stay sails, when steaming, to keel the ship over at a slight angle; it was said to reduce rolling substantially to the benefit of the passengers.
The profile of the ship varied. At the beginning of a voyage the paddles were deeply covered and the vessel squatted like a duck. At the end of a voyage she rode high like a cork and her paddles thrashed and foamed with only 6 ins (15.24 cm) immersed.

ESK

27 **ESK** (I)

Bt 1849 Robert Menzies, Leith; *T:* 232 g, 142 n.
Dim 112 ft (34.14 m) × 21 ft 6 in (6.55 m) × 14 ft 4 in (4.37 m)
Eng Sgl scr, simple; 1 cyl; 70 HP; Stm P: 8 lb, 1 boiler, 8¼ kts. The propeller was detachable when not in use.
H Wood. 2 masts, rigged as a Brigantine with square sails on foremast. Dining saloon 12 ft (3.66 m) × 9ft 9 in (2.97 m) × 6 ft (1.83 m) with 4 twin berth cabins off. Separate ladies saloon.
Pass 29. Crew: 8 officers, 14 crewmen.

1849 Building as *Regulus*; purchased on stocks. Apr 10: Launched as *Esk*. Royal Mail's first screw steamer. Intended for the new mail contract which called for a connection from Rio de Janeiro to Montevideo and Buenos Aires. Lay at Southampton for a year.
1850 Nov 10: Maiden voyage. Southampton–Lisbon–Madeira–St Vincent (Cape Verde Is)–Pernambuco (Recife)–Bahia–Rio de Janeiro with 6 passengers. Captain Wm. Valler.
1851 After 10 months withdrawn as too small. Returned to St Thomas for local use.
1854 Returned to Britain. Sold to Thomas Hill of Southampton.
1855 Sold to Turkey.
1856 Apr 9: Lost in Black Sea after leaving Constantinople.

28 **DERWENT** (I)

Bt 1850 William Pitcher, Northfleet; *T: 794 g*.
Dim 175 ft (53.34 m) × 26 ft 1 in (7.95 m) × (7.95 m) × 14 ft 7 in (4.45 m).

Eng Pad, simple; 2 cyls: By *North Britain's* engineering shop.
H Wood, 1 deck.
Pass 40.

1850 Jan 31: Launched. Built to replace lost *Forth* (4). July 9: Maiden voyage. Southampton–St Thomas. Used as reserve steamer.
1867 Oct 29: Wrecked at St Thomas during the great hurricane together with *Rhone* (49) and *Wye* (41) although *Conway* (25) escaped. Over 1,000 lives lost in the area.

ORINOCO (I)

29 **ORINOCO** (I)

Bt 1852 William Pitcher, Northfleet; *T:* 2,245 g.
Dim 301 ft (91.74 m) oa, 269 ft (81.91 m) × 41 ft (12.5 m), 71 ft 10 in (21.89 m) over paddle boxes × 26 ft (7.92 m).
Eng Pad, simple; 2 × 2 cycls; 800 HP; 12 kts; 4 boilers, 16 furnaces.14 rpm. By Maudsley, Sons & Field. Paddle diam. 40 ft (12.19 m).
H Wood, 2 decks. Although the company wished to build iron hulled vessels the Government mail contract in 1851 still called for wooden hulls.
Pass 100 1st, 360 troops.

1852 May 17: Launched.
1853 Jan 23: Trials. 12 kts. easily maintained. Feb 2: Maiden voyage Southampton–West Indies. Captain Chapman.
1854 Feb 22: Crimean war transport. Conveyed 1st Battalion Coldstream Guards.
1858 Found to have extensive dry rot. Broken up at Castle's yard Vauxhall. Engines removed and installed in *Paramatta* (44).

AMAZON (I), MAGDALENA (I) and PARANA (I)

30 **AMAZON** (I)

Details as *Orinoco* (29) except;
Bt 1851 R & H Green, Blackwall; *T:* 2,256 g.
Dim 316 ft (96.32 m) oa, 282 ft (85.95 m) × 73 ft (22.25 m) over paddle boxes × 26 ft (7.92 m).
Eng By Seawall & Capel, Millwall; 800 HP.

1851 June 28: Launched by Lady Paget. The largest then English-built paddler; cost £100,000.
1852 Jan 2: Friday. *Amazon* left Southampton on her maiden voyage commanded by

Captain Symons and with Lieut. Grady as mail agent. She carried 50 passengers, a crew of 109, the mail agent and his servant plus the Captain, 162 in all. Her cargo included the mails, £20,000 of specie and coined money plus £5,000 worth of mercury for mining in Mexico. By 9 pm she was hove to off Portland Bill while water was hosed onto the paddle shafts which were overheating. extra grease was ladled into the bearings to assist them in running in and settling down. This manoeuvre was repeated twice more. Jan 4: At 12.45 am Second Officer Treweeke, on the bridge saw flames coming out of the forward stokehold. At the same instant Fourth Engineer Stone encountered flames coming through the forward boiler casings. He tried to reach the controls to shut off the engines by was driven back by flames. By 12.48 the amidship section of the ship was a wall of flame and the ship was driving at about 10 kts into a moderate gale. Firefighting made no impression and clearly the ship was doomed. The fifty passengers were safely assembled right aft. Captain Symons now turned the ship about so that the flames were blowing forward away from the passengers. This move trapped most of the crew in the forward part of the ship and in an area without lifeboats. A few came after over the paddle boxes but within minutes the heat was too great for this route to be used.

Amazon was still surging along at something like 9 kts – too fast for the boats to be launched. Another problem was now encountered. Each lifeboat nestled in a metal cradle. To launch a lifeboat it had first to be raised by pulley and then swung out over the side. Passengers had already climbed in to the boats and there were insufficient crew to hoist the weight. Chaos reigned as, amidst vast roaring sheets of flame, the struggle to free the boats continued. Worse still some of the lifeboats swung to and fro with the rolling ship and were stove in by the metal supports. In the end only three lifeboats and a dinghy (with four aboard) were safely launched; any others were capsized by the speed of the ship. A 4 am driving rain moderated the wind and the survivors, in one of the boats, in case more could be rescued, sailed towards the wallowing wreck whose red hot funnels glowed in the darkness. They then watched as *Amazon* slid beneath the sea amidst a hissing roar. At 8 am the British brig *Marsden*, en route form London to Carolina, rescued 21 and returned them to Plymouth. Two more boat loads were taken to Brest in the Dutch galliot *Gertruida;* 24 in all. Yet another boat, without oars or a mast but with 13 survivors was found by the Dutch ketch *Hellechene*. This boat was the last to leave the ship and was assisted by Captain Symons who pushed the lifeboat clear of its supports even though his clothes were then on fire. Thus 58 were saved. 36 passengers and 68 crew were lost including all the officers and the two midshipmen.

39 **MAGDALENA** (I)

Details as *Orinoco* (29) except:
T: 2,318 g.
Eng By Robert Napier, Glasgow.
H Had Morgan patent feathering paddles.

1852 The largest wooden ship built for Royal Mail by Pitcher. Towed to the Clyde for the installation of her engines. May 17: Maiden voyage Southampton–West Indies.
1854 Crimean war transport.
1860 Served mainly on Brazil run.
1866 Broken up at Vauxhall.

32 **PARANA** (I)

Details as *Orinoco* (29) except:
Bt 1851 Money Wigram, Southampton; *T:* 2,943 g.
Dim 316 ft (96.32 m) oa, 282 ft (85.95 m) × 73 ft (22.25 m) over paddle boxes × 26 ft (7.92 m).
Eng By Caird & Co.

1852 Apr 17: Maiden voyage Southampton–West Indies.
1855 Chartered by French Government as Crimean war transport.

1868 Engines removed. Stationed as a hulk at St Thomas.
1876 Sold and broken up at St Thomas. Last wooden vessel in fleet.

DEMERARA (I)

33 **DEMERARA** (I)

Details as *Orinoco* (29) except:
Bt 1852 William Patterson, Bristol; *T:* 2,318 g.
Eng Never installed.

1852 Grounded fore and aft on the voyage downriver from Bristol to the Clyde for engining. The bow rammed the Gloucestershire bank, her stern swung round and wedged across the Avon on a falling tide and broke her back. Never delivered to Royal Mail. £48,000 insurance claimed; rebuilt as world's larget sailing ship; renamed *British Empire.*
1867 Oct 29: Lost in the great hurricane at St Thomas.

34 **PRINCE**

Bt 1851 Sunderland; *T:* 398 g.
Dim 121 ft (36.88 m) × 26 ft 6 in (8.08 m) × 18 ft (5.49 m).
Eng Pad.
H Iron. The first in the fleet, 1 deck.

1851 May: Purchased to replace *Esk* (27) which was too small for her work. July 2: First voyage St Thomas–Rio de Janeiro.
1862 Sold out of service.

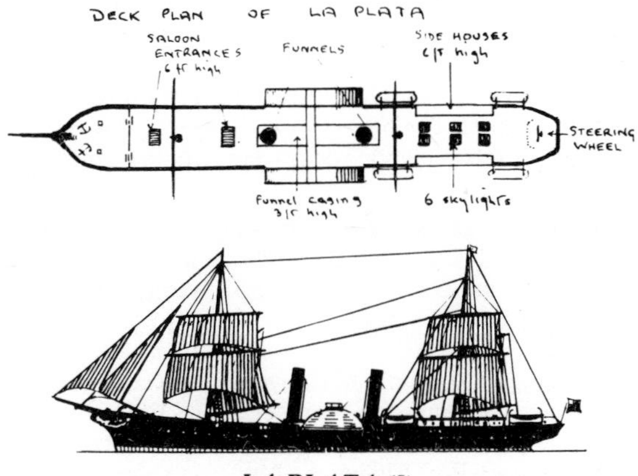

LA PLATA (I)

35 **LA PLATA** (I)

Bt 1852 Robert Steele, Greenock; *T:* 2,292 g.
Dim 314 ft (95.71 m) oa, 285 ft (86.87 m) × 40 ft (12 19 m) × 27 ft (8.23 m).

Eng Pad, simple, side lever; 2 cyls; 940 HP; 12 kts; By builder. Paddles 36 ft (10.97 m) diam.
H Wood, 2 decks.
Pass 116 1st, 20 2nd. Crew: 115.

1851 Laid down as *Arabia* (I) for Cunard. Purchased for £120,000 to replace loss of *Amazon* (30); renamed *La Plata*. Dec 24: Launched.
1852 Aug 17: Maiden voyage Southampton–West Indies. Captain W. Allan. Nov 18: Yellow fever aboard. 9 died including Captain Allan.
1860 Nov 24: Caught fire at Southampton. Burnt for 7 hours. Saved mainly by efforts of crew of *Tagus* (58).
1867 Nov 18: Escaped a 60 ft (18.29 m) tidal wave at St Thomas moving at 50 m.p.h. after an earthquake.
1871 Sold.

36 **CAMILLA**

Bt 1850 Canada; *T:* 539 g.
Eng Pad.
H Wood.

1853 Purchased from Samuel Cunard's Canadian organisation for the West Indies–Rio de Janeiro–Buenos Aires route.
1859 Replaced by *Mersey* (43) and sold to the Brazilian Government. Used on their Rio de Janeiro–Buenos Aires mail service.

ATRATO (I)

37 **ATRATO** (I)

Bt 1853 Caird & Co, Greenock; *T:* 3,466 g.
Dim 350 ft (106.68 m) oa, × 72 ft (21.95 m) over paddle boxes, 42 ft (12.8 m) beam × 34 ft (10.36 m).
Eng Pad, simple, side lever; 2 cyls: 12 kts; By builder. This was the engine intended for *Demerara* (33) but never fitted. The boilers were, however, new.
H Iron (the first build for the company), 4 decks. Headroom on main deck 7 ft 6 in (2.28 m).
Pass 224.

1853 Apr 27: Launched. Largest steamer in the world.
1857 Came upon fully rigged sailing ship *Rovers Pride* with no-one abroad but a nest on the mizzen mast indicated that at least one survivor had lived there for some period.
1864 Inaugurated on the Southampton–Colon service to commence the Panama City–Australian direct service.
1870 Sold to J. Morrison & Co, London. Converted to screw propulsion.
1872 Sept 7: Chartered to Thompson's Aberdeen Line for London–Plymouth–Cape–Port Phillip one voyage then no other steamer voyage for the company for ten years.
1874 Feb 2: London–Cape–Port Chalmers–Lyttleton service.
1875 Broken up.

Note: *Atrato was the first mail ship built after the Lords of Admiralty relented on its 'wooden hulls for mail ships' policy. This change arose from the burning of Amazon* (30) in Jan 1852.

SOLENT (I), TAMAR (I) and TYNE (I)

38 **SOLENT** (I)

Bt 1853 T & J White, Cowes; *T:* 2,230 g.
Dim 310 ft (94.49 m) oa, 296 ft 7 in (90.4 m) × 36 ft (10.97 m) × 28 ft (8.53 m).
Eng Pad, simple, side lever, oscillating; 2 cyls (twin casting); 400 HP; 12 kts (15 kts on trials). By Miller & Ravenhill and fitted in the West India Dock, London.
H Wood, composite with iron frames. The only such vessel owned.
Pass 100 1st, 350 deck (inter-island services in the West Indies).

1852 Jan 8: Launched by Doña Manuelita de Roxas y Tivierro. Oct 3: Maid voyage, Captain John H. Jellicoe (father of Admiral Jellicoe).
1853 Stationed in West Indies at St Thomas and used for local services.
1869 Sold, broken up.

39 **TAMAR** (I)

Details as *Solent* (38) except:
Bt 1854 William Pitcher, Northfleet; *T:* 1,850 g.
Eng By Maudsley, Sons & Field.
Tamar's funnels were taller and thinner giving the ship a spindly look.

1854 Jan 31: Launched. Last wooden vessel for Royal Mail.
1854 Crimean war transport.
1855 West Indies service.
1857 Sept: Placed on Southampton – Alexandria service in conjunction with European and Australian RM Co's services until they ceased in 1858.
1871 Sold.

40 **TYNE** (I)

Details as *Solent* (38) except:
Bt and **Eng** 1854 Miller & Ravenhill, Newcastle; *T:* 1,603 g.

1854 West Indies service inter-island.
1857 Jan: Ashore St Albans Head, Dorset. Salved.
1875 Sold for breaking up.

WYE

41 **WYE**

Bt 1853 Caird & Co, Greenock; *T:* 819 g.
Eng Sgl scr, 2 cyls; 9 kts.
H Wood.

1853 Local West Indies service.
1858 Operated Southampton–Alexandria service for a few months just before the Australian and European RM Co's service ceased. Then operated Marseilles–Malta route for winter 1858/59 before reverting to West Indies services.
1859 June 30: Stood by the wreck of *Paramatta* (44). Took off passengers.
1867 Oct 29: Wrecked, together with *Derwent* (28) and *Rhone* (49), in the great hurricane at St Thomas, 41 out of the 69 aboard died.

ONEIDA

42 ONEIDA

Bt 1855 John Scott & Sons, Greenock; *T:* 2,293 g.
Dim 306 ft 9 in (93.5 m) × 38 ft 10 in (11.84 m) × 19ft 2 in (5.84 m).
Eng Sgl scr, simple, direct acting; 3 cyls; 530 NHP; 10 kts. By Scott, Sinclair & Co, Greenock.
H Iron, 2 decks, fcsle 66 ft (20.12 m).
Pass 75 1st, 75 2nd, 100 steerage.

1855 Mar 20: Launched for Canada Ocean Steam Ship Co, Montreal. Became Crimean troop transport *No. 222.*
1856 Acquired by European & Australian RM Co.
1857 Jan: First voyage Sydney–Suez.
1858 Taken over with *Tasmanian* (47).
1865 Sept 3: Rescued the complement of SV *Duncan Dunbar,* 116 passengers and crew, wrecked on Roccas Reef, Brazil.
1872 Compounded.
1874 Sold to Ellis & Sons, London; converted into a sailing ship; same name. Further career not known.

MERSEY

43 MERSEY

Bt 1859 Thames Ironworks, Blackwall; *T:* 1,039 g, 767 n.
Dim 260 ft 5 in (79.37 m) × 30 ft 2 in (9.19 m) × 16 ft 6 in (5.03 m).
Eng Pad, simple, side lever; 2 cyls; 10 kts. 250 HP. By John Penn & Co., London.
H Iron, 2 decks.

1859 This vessel resembled *Solent* (38); for the service she was a great advance on all previous vessels. Built to replace *Camilla* (36) on Rio de Janeiro–Buenos Aires feeder service.
1876 Sold.

PARAMATTA (I), SHANNON and SEINE

44 **PARAMATTA** (I)

Bt 1858 Thames Iron Ship Building Co, Orchard Yard, Blackwall; *T:* 3,439 g.
Dim 330 ft (100.58 m) × 44 ft 2 in (13.46 m) × 19 ft 6 in (5.94 m). 66 ft (20.12 m) over paddles. paddles.
Eng Pad, simple, side lever; 2 cyls; 800 NHP; 12 kts. By Maudsley, Sons & Field, London. The engine was taken from *Orinoco* (29).
H Iron.
Pass 60 1st, 100 2nd. Crew: 120.
Ident Paddle box black, 3 parallel white bars, white disc and gold 5 point star on.

1858 Nov 8: Launched. Rolled violently and almost capsized.
1859 June 17: Maiden voyage Southampton – West Indies. Full complement of passengers. June 30: Wrecked on Horseshoe Reef, Anegada, West Indies. Grounded at 12½ kts. Attempts were made unsuccessfully for 12 months to get the vessel off the reef. At the enquiry Captain Baynton was dismissed.

45 **SHANNON**

Details as *Paramatta* (44) except:
Bt 1859 Robert Napier, Glasgow; *T:* 3,609 g.
Dim Length 338 ft (103.02 m).
Eng By builder.

1859 Mar 19: Launched by Mrs Napier for Southampton – West Indies service.
1860 Dec: Broke down at St Thomas; set off on tow to England by *Trent* (76). 12 days later the tow parted and she reached Plymouth under sail.
1875 Converted to sgl scr. The ship was remodelled by Walker Crouch & Lindwall by lengthening and the fitting of a clipper bow with finer lines forward. This increased the speed by 1 kt. In appearance *Shannon* was now a sister of *Elbe* (56) and *Moselle* (57).

Eng 2 cyls; Stm P: 56 lb. By Maudsley, Sons & Field, Deptford. The propeller was two bladed and 19 ft (5.79 m) diam.

1875 Sept 8: Re-entered service but wrecked during her second voyage inbound from Colon, on Pedro Bank.

46 **SEINE**

Details as *Paramatta* (44) except:
Bt 1860 Thames Ironworks, Blackwall; *T:* 3,440 g.

1860 Southampton – West Indies service.
1871 Broken up earlier than her condition warranted due to the phasing out of paddle steamers. Also her passenger accommodation was less than half of the new vessels being built.

TASMANIAN

47 **TASMANIAN**

Bt 1857 Laurence Hill & Co, Glasgow; *T:* 2,956 g.
Dim 360 ft (109.73 m) oa, 338 ft (103.02 m) × 42 ft 1 in (12.83 m) × 20 ft 11 in (6.38 m).
Eng Sgl scr, vertical, direct acting; 2 cyls, Stm P: 60 lb; 6 boilers, 30 furnaces, 11 kts.
H Iron, 2 decks and spar deck. Clifford patent lifeboat launchers fitted. Cargo: 1,100 tons with 400 tons edible oil in a deep tank. Fuel: 1,180 tons coal.
Pass 200 saloon, located in the poop, 60 2nd located forward.

1857 Laid down as *Melbourne.*
1857 Built for the Suez–Australia service of the European and Australian RM Co. Cost £110,000.
1859 Taken over with the *Oneida* (42) by Royal Mail in settlement of monies due. Her sister ships were *European* and *Australasian,* to Cunard, and *Columbian,* to P&O.
1860 Placed on Barbados route.
1871 Compounded; voyage coal consumption reduced from 1,088 tons to 466 tons.
1872 Made the then record passage Barbados–Plymouth in 11 days 18 hours 30 mins at a speed of 12½ kts.
1878 Sold.

DOURO (I) and RHONE

48 **DOURO** (I)

Bt 1864 Caird & Co, Greenock; *T:* 2,824 g.
Dim 326 ft (99.36 m) oa, 310 ft (94.49 m) × 40 ft (12.19 m) × 19 ft 10 in (6.05 m).
Eng Sgl scr, compound inverted; 2 cyls: 12 kts. By builer.
H Iron, 2 decks. First iron screw vessel in Royal Mail fleet.
Pass 253 1st, 30 2nd, 30 3rd. Crew: 129.

1864 Placed on the West Indies service.
1869 June: Introduced Southampton–Montevideo–Buenos Aires run.
1882 Apr 1: Off Cape Finisterre was run down and sunk by the Spanish steamer *Yruruc Bat.* Lost 5 passengers and 12 crew. The Spanish vessel also sank. Until 1914–18 war these were the last passenger fatalities.

49 **RHONE**

Details as *Douro* (48) except:
Bt 1865 Millwall Ironworks, Thames; *T:* 2,738 g.

1865 Oct 9: Maiden voyage Southampton–Brazil.
1867 Oct 29: Wrecked at St Thomas, together with *Wye* (41) and *Derwent* (28) in the great hurricane. Captain F. Woolley and 124 lives lost.

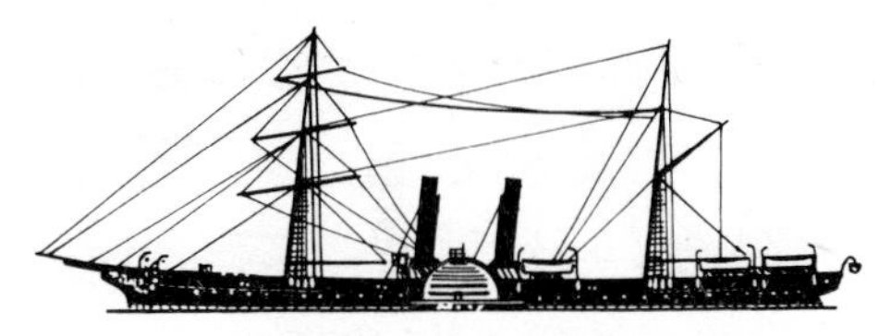

EIDER (I) and ARNO (I)

50 **EIDER** (I)

Bt 1864 Caird & Co, Greenock; *T:* 1,569 g.
Eng Pad, simple; 2 cyls; 9 kts.
H Iron.

1864 Completed.
1883 The last paddle steamer in the fleet. Sold to the Government of Haiti, converted into a gunboat and renamed *La Patrie*. Took part in the suppression of a local revolution. Grounded in Port-au-Prince harbour and remained there as a water logged hulk for over forty years.

51 **ARNO** (I)

Bt 1865 Caird & Co, Greenock; *T:* 1,038 g.
Dim 261 ft 7 in (79.73 m) × 30 ft 2 in (9.19 m) × 17 ft (5.18 m).
Eng Pad, simple, oscillating; 2 cyls; 250 HP; 10 kts. By builder.
H Iron, 2 decks.

1865 Stationed at St Thomas, West Indies. Remained on this berth all of her career.
1882 Sold.

DANUBE (I)

52 **DANUBE** (I)

Bt 1865 Millwall Ironworks, London; *T:* 2,039 g, 1,462 n.
Dim 332 ft (101.19 m) × 34 ft 5 in (10.49 m) × 24 ft 5 in (7.44 m).
Eng Pad, compound; 2 cyls; 275 HP. By Humphrys & Tennant.
H Iron.
Pass 140 1st, 68 2nd, 30 3rd. Crew: 180.

1865 Feb 27: Launched. Maiden voyage Southampton–West Indies.
1869 Used on Rio de Janeiro–Buenos Aires service. A large vessel to combat growing French competition.
1871 Sold to Union SS Co; same name. Rebuilt with one funnel and converted to screw. 2 cyls; 300 HP; Stm P: 60 lb; 12 kts. By Day, Summers & Co, Northam.

1879 Took Prince Imperial of France to South Africa where he died during the Zulu campaign.
1886 Sold and then re-sold for scrap.

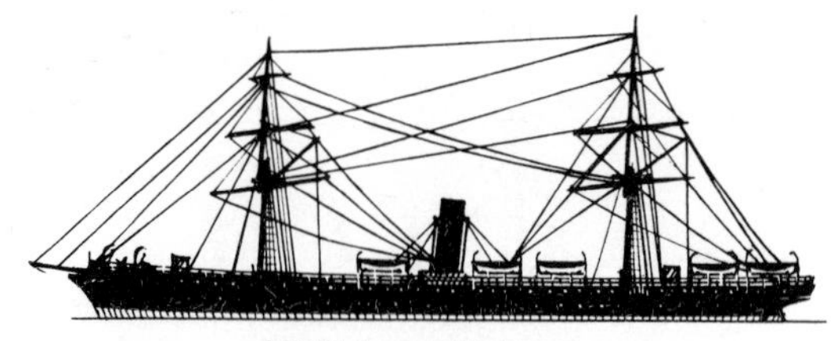
NEVA and NILE (I)

53 **NEVA**

Bt 1868 Caird & Co, Greenock; *T:* 3,025 g.
Dim 369 ft 6 in (112.62 m) oa, 348 ft (106.07 m) × 40 ft 4 in (12.29 m) × 33 ft 2 in (10.11 m).
Eng Sgl scr, simple, direct acting; 2 cyls; 450 HP; 13 kts; By builder.
H Iron, 3 decks, 10 watertight compartments.
H Introduced ventilating cowls into the fleet. Dining saloon sat 160.
Pass 272 1st, 58 2nd, 42 3rd.

1867 Laid down for Norddeutscher Lloyd as *Rhein*. Purchased on the stocks to replace *Rhone* (49).
1868 Feb 10: Launched. June 11: Trials, achieved 14½ kts. July 2: Maiden voyage Southampton – West Indies.
1880 Recorded as still using sails extensively on her voyages.
1890 Sold and broken up.

54 **NILE** (I)

Details as *Neva* (54) except:
Bt 1869 Day, Summers & Co, Northam, Southampton; *T:* 2,994 g, 1,642 n.
Eng By C A Day & Co, Southampton.

1869 Entered Southampton – West Indies service.
1890 Sold to Union SS Co; renamed *Roman* (II) for South African intermediate service.
1891 Sold for breaking up. The ship was too slow in service.

CORSICA

55 **CORSICA**

Bt 1863 J & G Thomson, Glasgow; *T:* 1,134 g, 681 n.
Dim 224 ft 3 in (68.35 m) × 32 ft 2 in (9.8 m) × 24 ft (7.31 m).
Eng Sgl scr, simple, oscillating geared; 2 cyls; 182 NHP; 2 boilers, 8 furnaces; 10 kts. By builder.
H Iron, 1 deck.

1863 Built for Cunard's Mediterranean service.
1868 Purchased to replace *Wye* (41); same name.
1877 Sold to R Foll Jr, same name.
1879 Re-engined by Wallsend Slipway, Wallsend.
1888 Out of register.

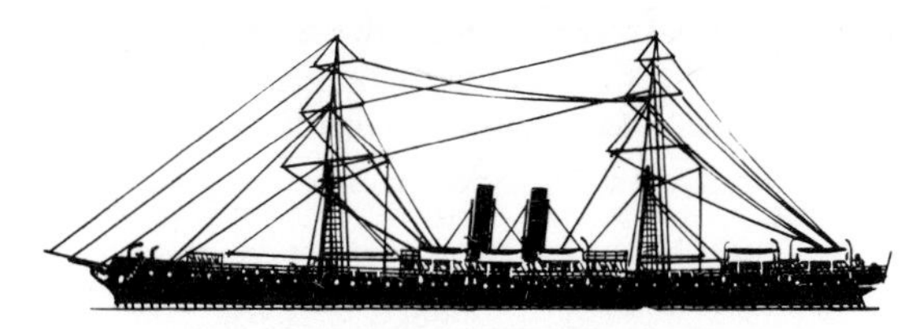

ELBE, MOSELLE and TAGUS (I)

56 **ELBE**

Bt1870 John Elder, Fairfield Yard, Govan; *T:* 3,108 g.
Dim 350 ft (106.68 m) × 40 ft 2 in (12.24 m) × 33 ft 4 in (10.16 m).
Eng Sgl scr, compound vertical direct acting; 2 cyls; 600 HP; 12 kts. By builder.
H Iron.
Pass 100 1st, 50 2nd, some 3rd.

1869 Nov 20: Launched. The first compound engined ship built for the company.
1870 Maiden voyage. Captain Gillies.
1902 Royal Mail's last square rigged ship. However fore and aft sails remained to give stability in a cross sea.
1902 When Cunard's *Etruria* lost her rudder the passengers were landed at Azores. *Elbe* was chartered to bring the stranded passengers to England.

57 **MOSELLE**

Details as *Elbe* (56) except:
Bt 1871; *T:* 3,298 g.
Pass 173 1st, 26 2nd, some steerage.

1871 May 20: Launched.
1872 Mar 18: Inaugurated Southampton–Barbados direct service.
1891 Oct 29: Wrecked near Colon. Only the Commander, Captain Roswell lost. He went down with his ship.

58 **TAGUS** (I)

Details as *Elbe* (56) except:
Bt 1871; *T:* 3,298 g.
Dim 358 ft (109.12 m) × 41 ft 1 in (12.52 m).

1871 Jan 21: Launched.
1871 Maiden voyage Southampton–West Indies.
1876 Jan 21: Rammed by *Severn* (66) and sank. Salvaged.
1880 When the S. American service was extended to Amsterdam as the turn-round port *Tagus* took the first sailing.
1897 Sold and broken up.

BELIZE

59 **BELIZE** (I)

Bt 1871 J & G Thomson, Glasgow; *T:* 1,038 g, 590 n.
Dim 231 ft 1 in (70.43 m) × 28 ft 2 in (8.58 m) × 22 ft (6.7 m).

Eng Sgl scr, compound, vertical direct acting; 2 cyls; 160 HP; 10 kts; By builder.
H Iron. This ship appears to have no deck houses.

1871 Built as *Bison*. Purchased and renamed. But there is no entry in Lloyds Register before 1874. The owners of *Bison* are thus not recorded.
1888 Sold out of service.

TIBER, EBRO (I) and LIFFEY (II)

60 **TIBER**

Bt 1865 Millwall Ship and Graving Co, Millwall; *T:* 1,591 g, 1,436 n.
Dim 265 ft (80.77 m) × 34 ft (10.36 m) × 25 ft 8 in (7.82 m).
Eng Sgl scr, simple, direct acting; 2 cyls; 300 HP; Stm P: 40 lb; 10 kts. By Humphrys & Tennant.
H Iron, 2 decks.
Pass 100 1st, 60 2nd, 65 3rd.

Note: Illustrated London News 1865 shows these ships with two funnels. Drawings with one funnel exist.

1865 Built as *Kaikoura* for the Panama, New Zealand and Australian Royal Mail Steam Packet Co. White funnels.
1866 Feb 28: Delivery voyage Southampton–Cape Town–Sydney. June 15: Maiden voyage Sydney–Wellington–Panama.
1868 Laid up.
1869 Apr: The owners went into liquidation.
1871 Taken over by Royal Mail; renamed *Tiber*. Placed on River Plate service.
1872 Compounded 2 cyls: 350 HP; Stm P: 40 lb; 12 kts; By Randolph Elder & Co, Glasgow.
1882 Feb 10: Wrecked at Porto Plata, San Domingo.

61 **EBRO** (I)

Details as *Tiber* (60) except:
T: 1,509 g, 1,080 n.

1865 Built as *Rakaia* for same owners as *Tiber*.
1866 Delivery voyage Milford Haven–Panama via Cape Horn. 11,315 miles in 46½ days at 10.37 kts average. June 24: Maiden voyage Panama–Wellington–Sydney.
1868 Laid up.
1871 Taken over and renamed *Ebro*.
1872 Aug: Inaugurated Antwerp–Southampton–Brazil service. Compounded as *Tiber* prior to taking this service.
1881 Sold; renamed *Baldomero Iglesias,* Compania Trasatlantica, Barcelona. Havana–New York route.
1898 Broken up in France.

62 **LIFFEY** (II)

Details as *Tiber* (60) except:
Bt 1866 J & W Dudgeon, Blackwall; *T:* 1,504 g, 1,020 n.
Dim 288 ft (87.48 m).

Eng Tw scr, simple, side lever; 2×2 cyls: as *Tiber*.

1865 Built as *Ruahine*. The first ocean-going twin screw ship. Her engines were in line fore and aft hence the extra length and lower net tonnage.
1866 Mar 31: Delivery voyage Southampton–Cape Town–Sydney. July: Maiden voyage Sydney–Wellington–Panama.
1868 Laid up Panama.
1871 Taken over and renamed *Liffey*. Placed on South American service.
1872 Reduced to sgl scr and compounded.
1874 Aug 27: Stranded at Point Jose Ignacio, Uruguay. Finally abandoned as a total loss.

63 **ESSEQUIBO** (I)

Bt 1871 Richardson Duck & Co, Stockton-on-Tees; *T:* 1,831 g, 1,317 n.
Dim 275 ft 5 in (83.95 m) × 34 ft 7 in (10.54 m) × 25 ft 6 in (7.77 m).
Eng Sgl scr, compound inverted, direct acting; 2 cyls; 170 NHP; 10 kts; By C D Holmes, Hull.
H Iron, 3 decks of iron ribs with wood planking.
Pass Deck passengers and cargo.

1871 Built as *Bladworth,* Brownlow & Co, Hull.
1873 Purchased and renamed *Essequibo*. Inter-island services supply ship.
1900 Sold and broken up.

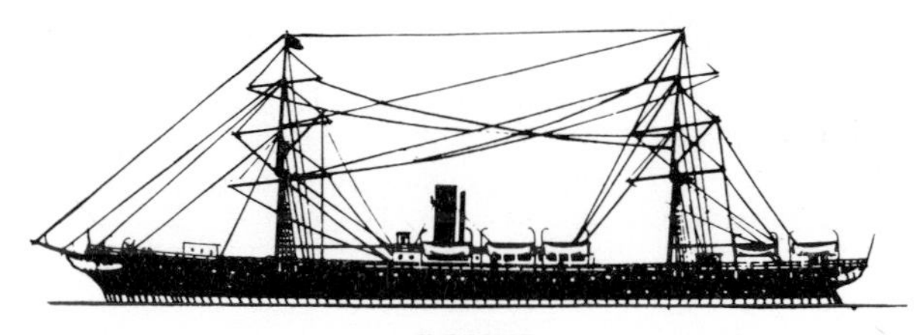

BOYNE

64 **BOYNE**

Bt 1871 Denny Bros, Dumbarton; *T:* 3,318 g, 2,483 n.
Dim 372 ft (113.39 m) × 40 ft 7 in (12.37 m) × 38 ft 5 in (11.71 m).
Eng Sgl scr, compound; 2 cyls; 500 HP.
H Iron, 3 decks.
Pass 108 1st. Crew: 113.

1871 Built for Southampton–West Indies service.
1875 Aug 13: Wrecked near Brest, France, at Molene. Grounded between 7 and 8 p.m. in thick fog. Captain MacAuley and all aboard saved. Gold specie of £20,682 was partially looted, presumably by the crew.

LARNE (II) and SEVERN (II)

65 **LARNE** (II)

Bt 1870 C. Mitchell & Co, Newcastle; *T:* 1,670 g, 1,068 n.
Dim 260 ft 2 in (79.3 m) × 34 ft 7 in (10.54 m) × 25 ft 11 in (7.9 m).

Eng Sgl scr, compound inverted, direct acting; 2 cyls; 180 HP; 10 kts; By T Clarke & Co, Newcastle.
H Iron, 1 deck.
Pass 200 1st.

1870 Built as *De Ruyter,* Engels & Co, Antwerp. Antwerp–India service then Antwerp–South America. Also served on Antwerp–Java route. The maiden voyage of this ship was, however, Liverpool–Bombay–Antwerp.
1873 May: Acquired by Royal Mail and renamed *Larne.*
1894 Feb 13: While homeward bound *Larne* was caught in a hurricane and lost her rudder. A sea rudder of sail was rigged and tried but this washed away. A jury rudder of wooden planking was constructed and fixed with the greatest difficulty. Eventually *Larne* reached port. At the time it was regarded as an incredible performance.
1900 Sold: renamed *Little Mary,* Italian.
1900 Sold again and renamed *Mario,* Italian.
1906 Broken up at Naples.

66 **SEVERN** (II)

Bt 1873 Oswald & Co, Sunderland; *T:* 1,736 g, 1,119 n.
Dim 281 ft 6 in (85.8 m) × 33 ft 9 in (10.29 m) × 24 ft (7.31 m).
Eng Sgl scr, compound direct acting; 2 cyls; 220 HP; 11 kts; By builder.
H Iron.

1873 Built for West Indies service.
1876 Jan 21: At Colon rammed and sank *Tagus.*
1881 Aug 4: Lost propeller. With sail only averaged 27 miles per day. Tug *Amy Dora* towed her to Punta Delgada, Azores.
1887 Sold to Government of Turkey (Ottoman Government).
1892 Out of sea going service.

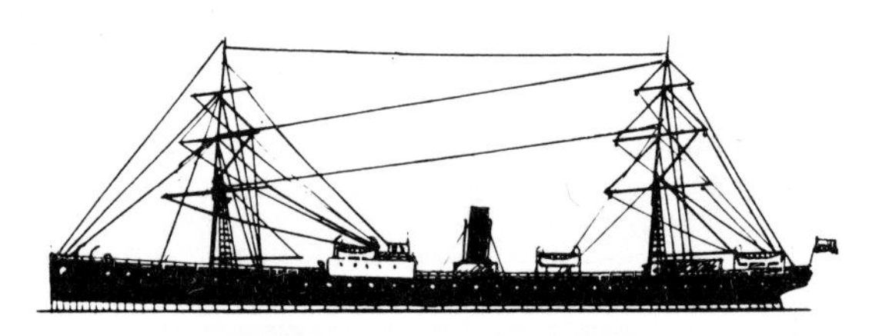

MINHO (I) and MONDEGO

67 **MINHO** (I)

Bt 1872 Barclay Curle & Co, Glasgow; *T:* 2,540 g, 1,491 n.
Dim 362 ft (110.34 m) oa, 350 ft 5 in (106.81 m) × 36 ft 9 in (11.2 m) × 27 ft 6 in (8.38 m).
Eng Sgl scr, compound inverted, direct acting; 2 cyls; 450 HP; 14 kts; By builder.
H Iron, 3 decks. Described as fitted with steam cranes but none are visible.
Pass 100 1st, 500 3rd (also called "Emigrant" and "Deck").

1872 Oct: Built for the Belgian Royal Mail, Ryde & Co as *Leopold II.*
1874 Purchased by Royal Mail and renamed *Minho;* Captain Jones.
1878 Sold to A. Ross, Glasgow.
18?? Sold to Turkey; renamed *Aslan* owned by Idarei Massousieh.

68 **MONDEGO**

Details as *Minho* (67) except:
Bt 1872 Tod & MacGregor, Glasgow; *T:* 2,564 g, 1,494 n.

1872 Dec: Delivered to Ryde & Co, as *Santiago*.
1874 Acquired with her sister by Royal Mail; renamed *Mondego*.
1885 Dec 21: In daylight and during a flat calm sea her Captain, Mr Green, disappeared. The officers of the watch saw and heared nothing nor did any of the passengers strolling the decks. The mystery of his disappearance has never been solved.
1888 Sold to A. Ross, Glasgow.

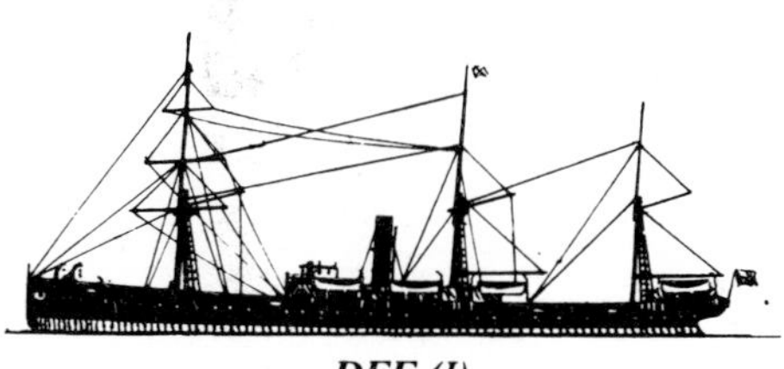

DEE (I)

69 **DEE** (II)

Bt 1872 Thomas Wingate & Co, Glasgow; *T:* 1,864 g.
Dim 300 ft 6 in (91.59 m) × 35 ft 4 in (10.77 m) × 24 ft 7 in (7.49 m).
Eng Sgl scr, compound; 2 cyls: 220 HP; 12 kts; By builder.
H Iron, 2 decks.

1872 Built as *Minnesota,* State Line, Glasgow for New Orleans service.
1873 Became *State of Minnesota,* same owner.
1875 Bought by Royal Mail and renamed *Dee;* placed on Southampton–West Indies service.
1901 Broken up.

70 **GUARDIANA**

Bt 1874 London & Glasgow Shipbuilding Co, Glasgow; *T:* 2,504 g, 1,597 n.
Dim 332 ft 1 in (101.22 m) × 36 ft 4 in (11.07 m) × 28 ft 7 in (8.71 m).
Eng Sgl scr, compound inverted; 2 cyls; 400 HP; Stm P: 70 lb; 12 kts; By builder.
H Iron, 3 decks, fcsle 38 ft (11.58 m); 3 masts.

1874 Purchased after launching as *Guardiana* and not renamed.
1875 Stationed at St Thomas and used on the North America to South America services.
1885 June 20: Lost of Paredes Rocks, Brazil en route New York–Santos. Her loss led to the ending of the New York–Buenos Aires run.

DON and PARA

71 **DON**

Bt 1872 Laird Bros, Birkenhead; *T:* 4,028 g.
Dim 387 ft 6 in (118.11m) × 43 ft 1 in (13.13 m) × 33 ft 7 in (10.24 m).
Eng Sgl scr, compound inverted; 2 cyls; 600 HP; Stm P: 65 lb; 11 kts; By builder.
H Iron.
Pass 60 1st, 70 2nd, 240 3rd.

1872 Built as *Corcovado* for the Pacific Steam Navigation Co's Valpararso service.

1875 Acquired to replace *Shannon* (45).
1876 Jan 15: First RMSP sailing Southampton–West Indies. Captain Woolward who remained with the ship for 81 voyages; 18 years.
1879 Tpl exp by Earle's Co, Hull.
1901 Broken up.

72 **PARA**

Details as *Don* (71) except:
Bt 1873; *T:* 3,805 g, 2,406 n.

1872 Built as *Puno* for the Pacific Steam Navigation Co.
1875 Acquired to replace *Boyne* (64).
1876 June: Southampton–West Indies service. Oct 16: The after hold exploded. 3 killed. The hold had been experimentally converted to carry bananas in CO_2 at low temperatures.
1890 Modernised. Tpl exp by Day Summers & Co, Northam.
1901 Broken up.

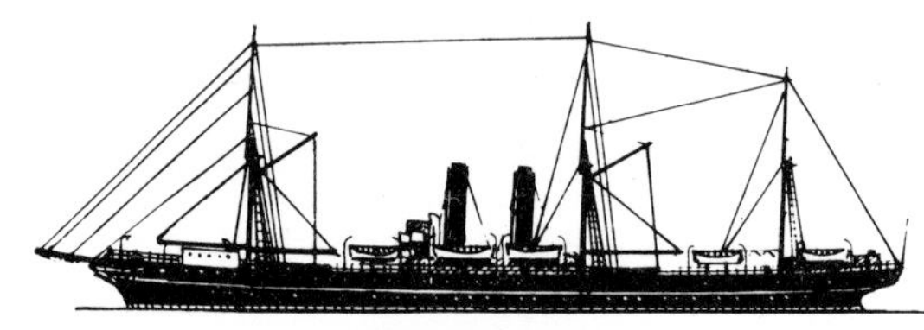

MEDWAY (II)

73 **MEDWAY** (II)

Bt 1877 John Elder & Co, Glasgow; *T:* 3,687 g, 2,353 n.
Dim 382 ft 2 in (116.48 m) × 42 ft (12.8 m) × 33 ft 2 in (10.11 m).
Eng Sgl scr, compound inverted; 2 cyls; 600 HP; 11 kts; By builder.
H Iron.
Pass 232 1st, 30 2nd.

1877 Built for the Southampton–West Indies service.
1886 Shown in Lloyds as Owned by J F Ure.
1886 Dec: Ashore on Isle of Wight for 2 weeks.
1888 Tpl exp installed; 3 cyls; 791 NHP; 12 kts; By Earle's Co, Hull.
1890 Square rigging on the foremast removed.
1899 Sold and broken up.

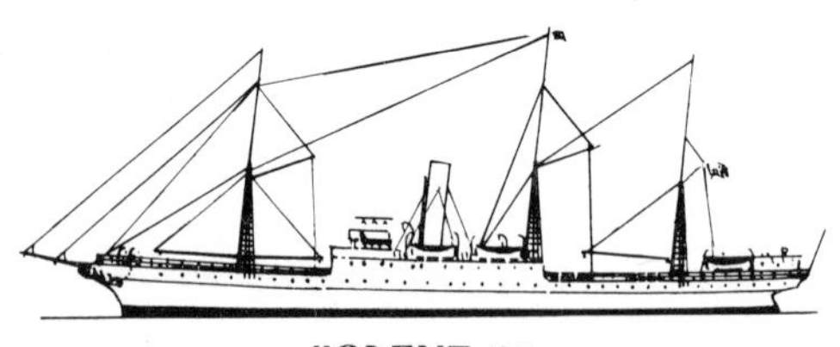

SOLENT (II)

74 **SOLENT** (II)

Bt 1878 Oswald Mordaunt & Co, Southampton; *T:* 1,908 g, 1,206 n.
Dim 321 ft 5 in (97.97 m) × 35 ft (10.67 m) × 16 ft 7 in (5.05 m).
Eng Sgl scr, compound inverted; 2 cyls; 280 HP; Stm P: 70 lb; 11 kts; By builder.
H Iron, 2 decks and spar deck. Her mainmast was removed about 1900.
1878 Sept: Inter-island serviced based at Barbados with *Esk* (82) and *Eden* (81). Black hull.

1902 May 12: Arrived as rescue ship at St Pierre after the Mount Pelée destruction. Over 35,000 died. *Solent* found one survivor in a cell in the town jail but he died 2 days later.
1905 Was Royal Mail's first full time cruising ship. White hulled.
1909 Broken up.

TAMAR (II) and TRENT (II)

75 **TAMAR** (II)

Bt 1873 Henderson & Co, Renfrew; *T:* 2,923 g, 1,988 n.
Dim 349 ft 7 in (106.55 m) × 37 ft (11.28 m) × 24 ft 6 in (7.47 m).
Eng Sgl scr, compound inverted; 2 cyls; 530 HP; 12 kts; By Henderson, Coulborn & Co.
H Iron, 3 decks and awning deck. Load line limited to 22 ft (6.70 m).
Pass 122 1st, 23 2nd.

1873 Nov: Built as *Vancouver* for China Transpacific SS Co Ltd (Fernie & Sons), Liverpool.
1875 Chartered to Pacific Mail Steamship Co, San Francisco – Sydney service.
1876 March 18: Sailed to Hong Kong in Macondray & Co service.
1878 Purchased and renamed *Tamar*. Southampton – West Indies service.
1897 Sold and broken up.

76 **TRENT** (II)

Details as *Tamar* (75) except:
T: 2,912 g.

1873 Built as *Vasco De Gama* (note wrong spelling: Da) for China Transpacific SS Co Ltd (Fernie & Sons), Liverpool.
1875 Chartered to Pacific Mail. San Francisco – Sydney route.
1876 March 30: Entered Macondray & Co service.
1878 Purchased and renamed *Trent*. Southampton – West Indies service.
1897 Sold for scrapping.

77 **DERWENT** (II)

Bt 1879 R. Thompson Jr, Sunderland; *T:* 2,471 g, 1,479 n.
Dim 329 ft 1 in (100.3 m) × 36 ft (10.97 m) × 25 ft 6 in (7.77 m).
Eng Sgl scr, compound inverted; 2 cyls; 350 HP; Stm P: 80 lb; 12 kts; By North East Marine.
H Iron, 2 decks; fcsle 34 ft (10.36 m), bridge 68 ft (20.73 m), poop 70 ft (21.33 m).

1879 Oct: Delivered.
1902 Broken up.

HUMBER

78 **HUMBER**

Bt 1880 London and Glasgow Co, Glasgow; *T:* 2,371 g, 1,528 n.
Dim 330 ft (100.58 m) × 35 ft 9 in (10.9 m) × 25 ft 7 in (7.8 m).
Eng Sgl scr, compound; 2 cyls; 340 HP; Stm P: 80 lb; 12 kts; By builder.
H Iron, 2 decks; fcsle 45 ft (13.72 m), bridge 32 ft (9.75 m), poop 38 ft (11.58 m), 3 masts.
Pass 80 1st.

1880 Sailed to station at St Thomas.
1881 Left Kingston, Jamaica with 2nd West India Regt for Ashanti War.
1885 Feb 15: Left New York homeward bound from West Indies. Never heard of again. No passengers aboard but 66 crew lost.

79 **AVON** (II)

Bt 1880 James Laing & Co, Sunderland; *T:* 2,225 g, 1,353 n.
Dim 283 ft 4 in (86.36 m) × 35 ft 2 in (10.72 m) × 29 ft 4 in (8.94 m).
Eng Sgl scr, compound inverted; 2 cyls; 200 HP; Stm P: 75 lb; 12 kts; By North East Marine.
H Iron, 2 decks.

1880 Entered service. Captain Spooner.
1903 Sold and broken up.

LA PLATA (II)

80 **LA PLATA** (II)

Bt 1879 R & H Green, London; *T:* 3,240 g, 2,069 n.
Dim 332 ft 5 in (101.32 m) × 40 ft 1 in (12.22 m) × 32 ft 11 in (10.03 m).
Eng Sgl scr, compound; 2 cyls; 500 HP; 12 kts; By Humphrys & Tennant, London.
H Iron, 2 decks and shade deck.
Pass 223 1st, 90 2nd.

1879 Built as *Norfolk* for Money Wigram. Their largest ship. Oct 18: Maiden voyage London–Suez–Melbourne, Sydney.
1882 Purchased by Royal Mail and renamed *La Plata.*
1893 Sold for cruising; renamed *Orienta,* Orienta Steam Yachting Association, London.
1895 Became *Norse King,* Norse King SS Co.
1896 Sold to Albion SS Co, same name.
1898 Renamed *Argonaut,* R. Galbraith & J. Moorhead, London.
1908 Sept: Collided with steamer *Kingswell* off Dungeness and sank.

EDEN (I) and ESK (II)

81 **EDEN** (I)

Bt 1882 Barrow Shipbuilding Co, Barrow; *T:* 2,145 g, 1,374 n.
Dim 309 ft 6 in (94.34 m) × 36 ft 2 in (11.02 m) × 16 ft 8 in (5.08 m).
Eng Sgl scr, compound inverted; 2 cyls; 350 HP; Stm P: 77 lb; 12 kts; By builder.
H Iron, 2 decks; bridge 77 ft (23.47 m).

1882 Based at Barbados for inter-island service.
1900 Painted white with buff funnels at St Thomas. This introduced the present yellow funnel.
1909 Aug 28: On last journey to St Thomas was wrecked on Cabrit Island.

82 **ESK** (II)

Details as *Eden* (81).

1882 Based at Barbados for inter-island service.
1900 Repainted after *Eden* (81) in the same livery.
1902 May 8: St Pierre was destroyed by the Mount Pelee eruption. *Esk* was the first Royal Mail vessel to arrive; as she approached ss *Roraima* exploded. Seeing no sign of life she left for St Lucia to summon help. *Solent* (38) went with relief supplies.
1910 Broken up at Firth of Forth.

83 **DART** (I)

Bt 1883 Raylton Dixon & Co, Middlesbrough; *T:* 2,641 g, 1,934 n.
Dim 320 ft (97.54 m) × 38 ft 4 in (11.68 m) × 26 ft (7.92 m).
Eng Sgl scr, compound inverted; 2 cyls; 350 HP; Stm P: 80 lb; 12 kts; By T Richardson & Son, Hartlepool.
H Iron; fcsle 40 ft (12.19 m), bridge 77 ft (23.47 m), poop 77 ft (23.47 m).

1883 Entered service St Thomas–S. American run.
1884 Sept 11: Wrecked on Zapato Rocks near Santos. Only the Captain, Edey, lost.

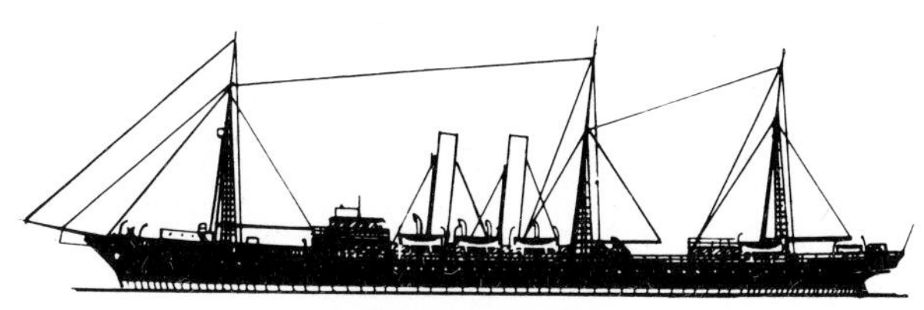

ORINOCCO (II)

84 **ORINOCO** (II)

Bt 1886 Caird & Co, Greenock; *T:* 4,434 g, 2,349 n.
Dim 409 ft 8 in (124.87 m) × 45 ft (13.72 m) × 25 ft 5 in (7.75 m).
Eng Sgl scr, tpl exp inverted; 3 cyls; Stroke: 66 in (167.64 cm); 5,800 IHP; Stm P: 150 lbs; 14½ kts; By builder.
H Steel, 3 decks and spar deck; 10 bulkheads, 4 hatches.
Pass 257 1st, 26 2nd.

1886 Sept 13: Launched. The company's first steel ship, the first with electric light and the first with triple expansion engines but also the last square rigged vessel built for Royal Mail, and the last ship to be flush decked with only wooden deck houses. Dec 2: Maiden voyage Southampton–West Indies; Captain Jellicoe.
1897 Took part in the Diamond Jubilee Naval Review at Spithead; she was accompanied by *Danube* (52).
1901 White hull.
1903 Black hull with white band.
1906 Nov 21: Collided in Cherbourg Roads with Norddeutscher Lloyd's *Kaiser Wilhelm der Grosse,* four of whose passengers were killed. *Orinoco* lost three of her crew when a lifeboat capsized. Her clipper stem saved the ship from greater damage.
1909 Broken up in the Firth of Forth during which she was badly damaged by fire.

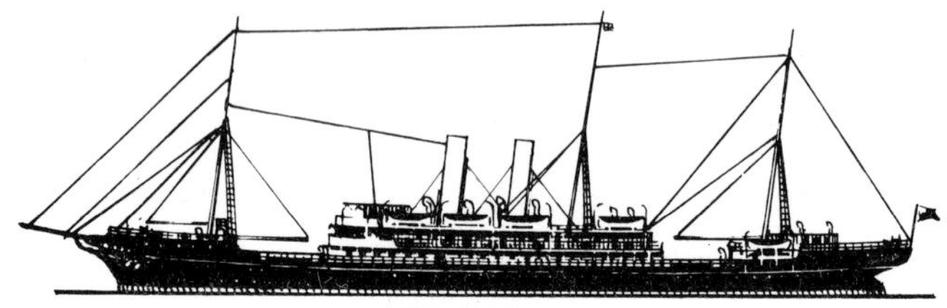

ATRATO (II)

85 **ATRATO** (II)

Bt 1888 Robert Napier & Sons, Glasgow; *T:* 5,366 g, 3,069 n.
Dim 421 ft 2 in (128.37 m) × 50 ft (15.24 m) × 25 ft (7.62 m).
Eng Sgl scr, tpl exp; 3 cyls; 1,000 HP; 8 sgl ended cylindrical boilers; Stm P: 150 lb; 15 kts; By builder.
H Steel, 3 decks; fcsle 61 ft (18.59 m), poop 41 ft (12.5 m), 2 hydraulic cranes at fore funnel worked the coaling hatches.
Pass 221 1st, 32 2nd, 26 3rd.

1888 Sept 22: Launched. Dec: Delivered. The first Royal Mail liner without yards.
1889 Jan 17: Maiden voyage Southampton–South America; Captain R. Dickenson. Then placed on the West Indies service for which she was designed.
1901 White hull.
1912 Oct: Sold for cruising to Viking Cruising Co as *Atrato.*
1913 When *Viking,* ex *La Plata* (105) was broken up *Atrato* was renamed *The Viking.*
1914 Taken over by the Admiralty; became HMS *Viknor,* Armed Merchant Cruiser. Attached to 10th Cruiser Squadron and employed on the Northern Patrol. The name change arose from the existence of a destroyer HMS *Viking.*
1915 Jan 13: Lost at sea by mine off Ulster. All aboard were lost in the gale that was blowing at the time. It was so rough that a submarine would not have been able to discharge torpedoes, hence the attribution of the loss to a floating breakaway mine.

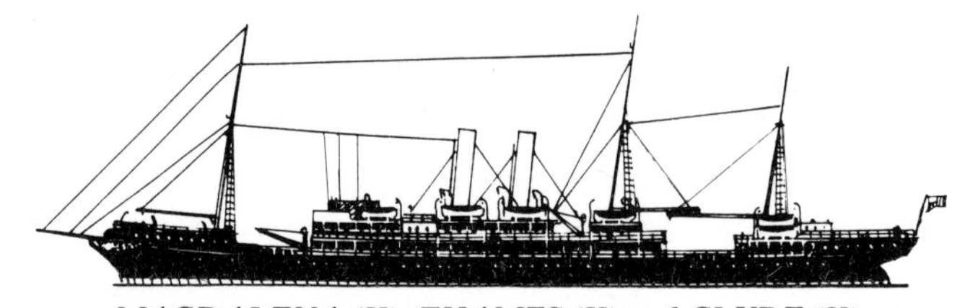

MAGDALENA (II), THAMES (II) and CLYDE (II)

86 **MAGDALENA** (II)

Details as *Atrato* (85) except:

Bt 1889; *T:* 5,362 g; 3,066 n.
Pass 170 1st, 40 2nd, 330 3rd.

The last Royal Mail liner built with square sails but no yards.

1889 Aug 2: Maiden voyage to Royal Naval Review at Spithead called by Queen Victoria in honour of her nephew Kaiser Wilhelm II. Due to bad weather the review itself was postponed until Aug 5. Chartered by Mayor and Corporation of London. The only merchant ship in the official procession. Captain W. Chapman. Then Southampton – West Indies route.
1910 Went ashore at Cartagena, Colombia and was fast for 4 days.
1915 Taken over by Admiralty. Served on West Indies Station as a troopship.
1921 Sold and scrapped.

87 **THAMES** (II)

Details as *Atrato* (85) except:
Bt 1890; *T:* 5,645 g, 3,369 n.
Dim 436 ft 4 in (132.99 m).
Eng HP cyl 43 in (109.22 cm).
H Fcsle 68 ft (20.73 m), poop 48 ft (14.63 m).

1889 Dec 10: Launched. Intended for South American service.
1890 Apr 24: Maiden voyage Southampton – S. America. Captain G. M. Hicks.
1914 Aug: Sold to Forth Shipbreaking Co but resold and used as a block ship in Holm Sound, Scapa Flow.

88 **CLYDE** (II)

Details as *Atrato* (85) except:
Bt 1890; *T:* 5,645 g, 3,377 n.
Other details as *Thames* (87).

1890 Apr 5: Launched. July 31: Maiden voyage Southampton – South America. Captain J. D. Spooner.
1913 June: Broken up Forth Shipbreaking Co.

TYNE (II), TAW, TEES and WEAR

89 **TYNE** (II)

Bt 1891 Ramage and Ferguson, Leith; *T:* 615 g, 374 n.
Dim 177 ft (53.95 m) × 28 ft 1 in (8.56 m) × 14ft 7 in (4.45 m).
Eng Sgl scr, compound; 2 cyls; 120 HP; Stm P: 160 lb; 12 kts; By builder.
H Steel, 1 deck; fcsle 25 ft (7.62 m).

1891 Built for West Indian inter-island services.
1897 Sold and renamed *P. de Sotolongo* Cia Gen. de Tabacos de Filipinas, Manila.
1909 Renamed *Union,* same owners.
1912 Reverted to *P. de Sotolongo,* same owners.
1916 Out of register.

90 **TAW**

Bt 1892 J. McArthur & Co, Paisley; *T:* 180 g, 71 n.
Dim 120 ft 1 in (36.6 m) × 21 ft 1 in (6.43 m) × 8 ft 8 in (2.64 m).
Eng Sgl scr, compound; 2 cyls; 114 HP; Stm P: 120 lb; 10 kts.
H Steel.

1892 Based at Grenada, West Indies with *Wear* (92).
1915 Sold to T. H. Scott, Trinidad, West Indies for coasting.
1921 Out of register.

91 **TEES**

Details as *Taw* (90).

1892 Based at St Lucia, West Indies.
1915 Sold to T. H. Scott, Trinidad, West Indies, for coasting, same name.
1922 Owned by Vestey Brothers, London; same name.

92 **WEAR**

Details as *Taw* (90).

1892 Based with *Taw* (90) at Grenada.
1915 Sold to T. H. Scott, Trinidad for coasting, same name.
1921 Bought by French Line (CGT), renamed *Balata,* based Fort de France.
1925 Sold then broken up.

SPEY

93 **SPEY**

Bt 1892 S. McKnight & Co, Ayr; *T:* 470 g, 224 n.
Dim 167 ft (50.9 m) × 26 ft (7.92 m) × 11 ft 8 in (3.56 m).
Eng Sgl scr, tpl exp; 3 cyls; 75 HP; Stm P: 160 lb; 10 kts; By Muir & Houston, Glasgow.
H Steel, 1 deck; fcsle 27 ft (8.23 m), bridge 14 ft (4.27 m), quarter deck 84 ft (25.6 m).

1892 Stationed at Jamaïca with *Arno* (104). Employed on Inter-island services.
1913 Sold to V. Kibrit, London; same name; no further trace.

NILE (II) and DANUBE (II)

94 **NILE** (II)

Bt 1893 J & G Thompson, Glasgow; *T:* 5,855 g, 3,425 n.
Dim 435 ft (132.59 m) oa, 420 ft (128.02 m) × 52 ft (15.85 m) × 33 ft 6 in (10.21 m).
Eng Sgl scr, tpl exp; 3 cyls; 3,500 IHP; Stm P: 160 lb; 4 dbl ended boilers, 32 furnaces; 15 kts; By builder.
H Steel, 4 decks, strengthened for use as an auxiliary cruiser. 4 hatches; fcsle 73 ft (22.25 m), promenade deck 217 ft (66.14 m), poop 42 ft (12.80 m).
Pass 215 1st, 36 2nd, 350 3rd.

1893 Mar 21: Launched by Miss Curtiss, a Director's daughter. Oct 19: Maiden voyage Southampton–Brazil–Buenos Aires. The single fares were 1st £35, 2nd £18.
1900 Jan 11: First of two voyages as Boer war transport *No 82.* Apr: Returned to Royal Mail service with white hull and buff funnels.

1901 Refrigerated machinery installed for frozen meat.
1902 Black hull.
1907 Collided at Santos with steamer *Lynfield*.
1911 Oct 6: Final voyage for Royal Mail. Nov: Sold to Nile SS Co, owned by the Southern Pacific Co, Hong Kong and operated by Pacific Mail SS Co between San Francisco–Hong Kong. Main mast removed.
1915 Sold to China Pacific SS Co, the China Mail; same route.
1917 Became a US navy transport Mediterranean and India trooping.
1918 Returned to Pacific service.
1922 Laid up.
1925 Broken up at San Francisco.

95 **DANUBE** (II)

Details as *Nile* (94) except:
T: 5,946 g, 3,425 n.

1893 May 16: Launched.
1894 Jan: Maiden voyage Southampton–Brazil–Buenos Aires.
1897 Host ship for House of Lords at the Jubilee Naval Review at Spithead.
1917 Jan 10: Last, and 107th, voyage to South America. Placed on Royal Mail's New York–Jamaica service. Sept 15: Arrived Liverpool for conversion to a troopship.
1918 Dec 6: Took the Serbian Government archives and gold from Salonika to Fiume (and thence by rail to Belgrade).
1920 Returned to Royal Mail but sold by them to Claude Langton & Co for scrap. Renamed *Mediterranean Star* for cruising.
1922 Broken up.

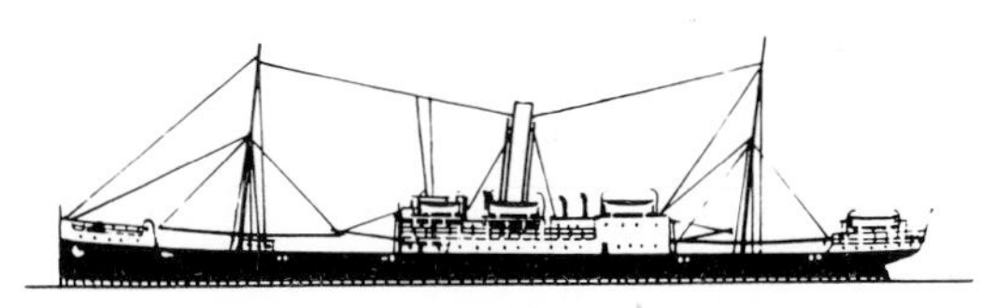

LA PLATA (III), MINHO (II) and EBRO (II)

96 **LA PLATA** (III)

Bt 1896 Robert Napier & Sons, Glasgow; *T:* 3,445 g, 2,166 n.
Dim 345 ft 8 in (105.36 m) × 44 ft 1 in (13.44 m) × 24 ft 7 in (7.49 m).
Eng sgl scr, tpl exp; 3 cyls; 440 HP; Stm P: 180 lb; 3 sgl ended boilers, 9 furnaces; 14 kts; By builder.
H Steel, 2 decks; fcsle 42 ft (12.8 m), bridge 96 ft (29.26 m), poop 30 ft (9.14 m).
Pass 135 1st, 370 Spanish or Portuguese in dormitories.

1896 Aug: Built for Southampton–Spain–South America service.
1900 Sold to Booth Line, Liverpool; renamed *Clement*.
1914 Acquired by Lawrence Smith & Co, Montreal; renamed *Freshfield*.
1918 Aug 5: Torpedoed and sunk in Mediterranean off Cape Colonne, toe of Italy.

97 **MINHO** (II)

Details as *La Plata* (96).

1896 Oct: Built for Southampton–South America service.
1899 Boer war transport.
1901 Reverted to Royal Mail.
1903 Sold to Swan, Peterson & Co, Newcastle; renamed *Halifax*.
1905 Became *Montreal,* Cie General Transatlantique, Le Havre–Bordeaux–Haiti service.
1917 Mar 24: Torpedoed by U-boat in Bay of Biscay.

98 **EBRO** (II)

Details as *La Plata* (96).

1896 Dec: Joined her sister vessels on the South America route.
1900 Boer war transport.
1901 Reverted to Royal Mail.
1903 Sold to Swan, Peterson & Co, Newcastle; renamed *Quebec.*
1905 Acquired by Cie General Transatlantique; same name. Le Havre–Bordeaux–Haiti service.
1917 Jan 24: Struck a mine and sank in Bay of Biscay off Bordeaux.

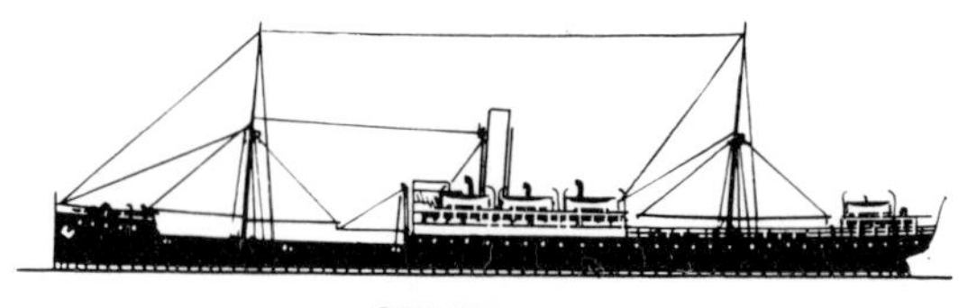

SEVERN (II)

99 **SEVERN** (II)

Bt 1898 Sir Raylton Dixon & Co, Middlesbrough; *T:* 3,760 g, 2,125 n.
Dim 350 ft (106.68 m) × 45 ft 5 in (13.84 m) × 25 ft 4 in (7.72 m).
Eng Sgl scr, tpl exp; 3 cyls; 542 NHP; Stm P: 180 lb; 4 sgl ended boilers, 12 furnaces; 14 kts; By T. Richardson.
H Steel, 2 decks; fcsle 46 ft (14.02 m), poop 214 ft (65.23 m).
Pass 130 1st, 400 steerage.

1898 Built for the Southampton–West Indies route but with the option for use on other Royal Mail services as relief ship.
1913 Sold to Cia Transatlantica Espanola, Cadiz; renamed *Fernando Poo* Captain Ferrandiz. West African services.
1918 Not in Lloyds Register.

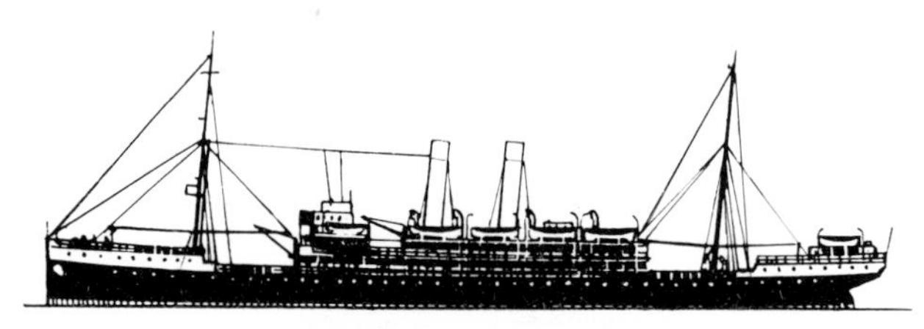

TAGUS (II) and TRENT (III)

100 **TAGUS** (II)

Bt 1899 Robert Napier Sons & Co, Glasgow; *T:* 5,545 g, 3,056 n.
Dim 410 ft (124.97 m) × 30 ft (9.14 m) × 23 ft (7.01 m).
Eng Sgl scr, tpl exp; 3 cyls; 1,050 NHP; Stm P: 180 lb; 6 sgl ended boilers and 18 furnaces; 15 kts; By builder.
H Steel, 3 decks and spar deck; fcscle 74 ft (22.56 m), poop 40 ft (12.19 m).
Pass 200 1st, 30 2nd, 250 3rd.

1899 June 27: Launched. Nov 15: Maiden voyage Southampton–West Indies.
1900 Boer war transport *No 101.*
1914–18 Hospital ship.
1920 Not reconditioned; became *Principe de Viana,* Hijos de Jose Taya, Barcelona.
1926 Broken up.

101 **TRENT** (III)

Details as *Tagus* (100) except:
T: 5,573 g, 3,085 n.

1899 Sept 19: Launched.
1909 Jan 6: Went ashore on Semedine Bank near Cartagena. Eventually salved after 4 months aground.
1910 Oct 18: Rescued crew of airship *America* 410 miles south-east of Sandy Hook during first attempt to cross the Atlantic by air.
1915 July 6: As HMS *Trent,* a monitor depot ship, mounted operations against German cruiser *Konigsberg* in Rufiji delta, Tanganyika. Mother ship to HM Montors *Severn, Mersey* and *Humber.*
1922 Broken up.

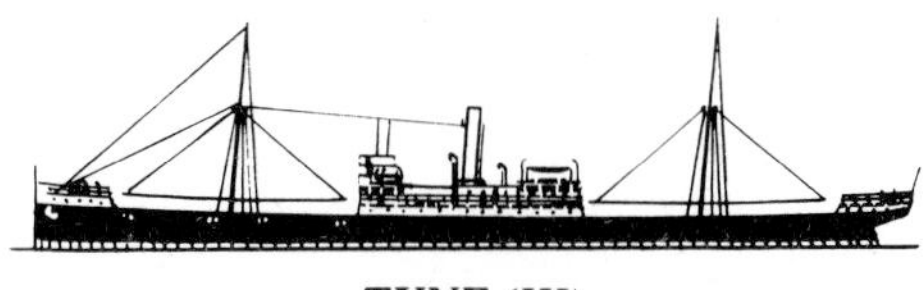

TYNE (III)

102 **TYNE** (III)

Bt 1900 Robert Napier, Sons & Co, Glasgow; *T:* 2,902 g, 1,854 n.
Dim 320 ft (97.54 m) × 44 ft 9 in (13.64 m) × 15 ft 7 in (4.75 m).
Eng Sgl scr, tpl exp; 3 cyls; 244 NHP; Stm P: 160 lb; 2 sgl ended boilers, 6 furnaces; 14 kts; By builder.
H Steel, 1 deck and awning deck; fcsle 35 ft (10.67 m), bridge 92 ft (28.04 m), poop 24 ft (7.31 m).
1900 Served on West Indies inter-island services.
1917 June 17: Torpedoed and sunk 18 miles SW of the Lizard.

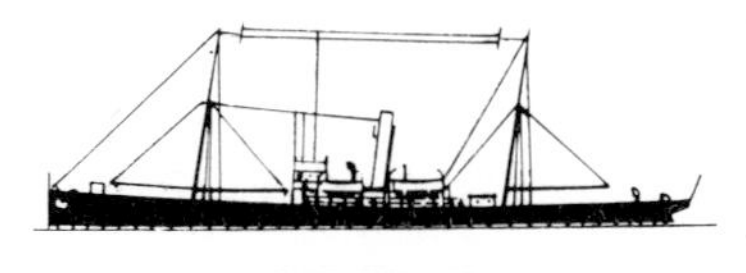

EIDER (II)

103 **EIDER** (II)

Bt 1900 Campbeltown Shipbuilding Co, Campbeltown; *T:* 1,236 g, 799 n.
Dim 230 ft 6 in (70.26 m) × 32 ft 8 in (9.96 m) × 17 ft 4 in (5.28 m).
Eng Sgl scr, tpl exp; 3 cyls; 120 NHP; Stm P: 160 lb; 10 kts; By Hutson & Sons, Glasgow.
H Steel, 1 deck; quarter deck 77 ft (23.47 m). The fore deck locker is port side only.

1900 Built as Southampton–Bremen–Hamburg feeder ship.
1914 Aug 4: *Eider* was a Bremen when war was declared. Merchant ships have 24 hours grace to leave port in the event of war. Despite attempts to delay the ship Captain W. J. Short cleared the port in the time allowed. *Eider* became the last British ship to leave Germany.
1927 Sold to Union-Castle Line for the same feeder service; same name.
1936 Sold to J. A. Billmeir; renamed *Stanhill.*
1939 Dec 25: Sold for breaking up.

ARNO (II)

104 **ARNO** (II)

Bt 1894 S. McKnight, Ayr; *T:* 607 g, 253 n.
Dim 190 ft (57.91 m) × 27 ft 1 in (8.25 m) × 13 ft 2 in (4.01 m).
Eng Sgl scr, tpl exp; 3 cyls; 99 RHP; Stm P: 160 lb; 1 sgl ended boiler, 3 furnaces; 10 kts; By Muir & Houston, Glasgow.
H Steel, 1 deck; fcsle 26 ft (7.92 m), poop 141 ft (42.98 m).

1894 Built as *Juno* for J & P Hutchison, Glasgow.
1901 Purchased to act as consort to *Spey* (93) on the inter-island services.
1917 Sold for breaking up.

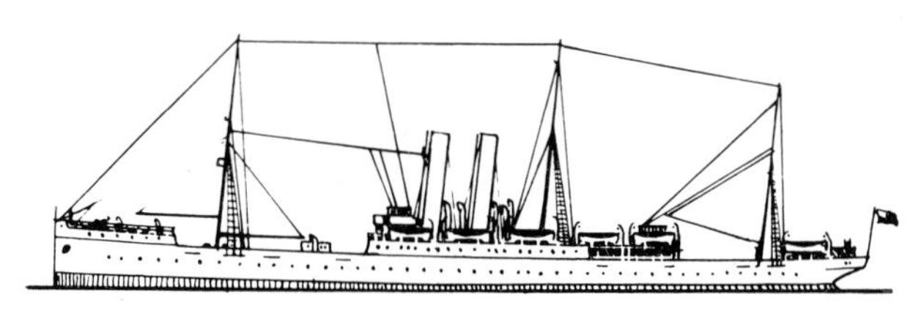

LA PLATA (IV)

105 **LA PLATA** (IV)

Bt 1882 J & G Thomson, Glasgow; *T:* 4,464 g , 2,229 n.
Dim 420 ft 7 in (128.19 m) × 45 ft 9 in (13.94 m) × 29 ft 4 in (8.94 m).
Eng Sgl scr, tpl exp; 3 cyls; 810 NHP.
H Steel, 2 decks.
Pass 120 1st, 90 2nd, 50 3rd.

1882 Built as *Moor* for Union Line.
1894 Lengthened by 44 ft (13.41 m). Profile as illustrated with second funnel.
1900 Mar: Merged into the Union-Castle fleet.
1901 Acquired by Royal Mail; renamed *La Plata.* Painted white for cruising.
1908 Jan: Sold to the Polytechnic Touring Association; renamed *The Viking,* used for Norwegian Fjord cruises.
1913 Broken up.

106 **KENNET**

Bt 1895 James Laing & Co, Sunderland; *T:* 827 g, 413 n.
Dim 210 ft (64 m) × 28 ft 2 in (8.58 m) × 13 ft 8 in (4.17 m).
Eng Sgl scr, tpl exp; 3 cyls; 150 NHP; 10 kts; By G. Clark, Sunderland.
H Steel, 2 decks; fcsle 30 ft (9.14 m), poop 138 ft (42.06 m), 3 masts.

1895 Built as *General Havelock,* R. M. Hudson, Sunderland.
1901 Purchased, renamed *Kennet* and based at Trinidad.
1914 Broken up.

107 **YARE**

Bt 1887 S. McKnight & Co, Ayr; *T:* 299 g, 149 n.
Dim 145 ft (44.19 m) × 22 ft 6 in (6.86 m) × 11 ft (3.35 m).
Eng Sgl scr, compound; 2 cyls; 70 RHP; 10 kts; By W. Kemp, Glasgow.

H Iron, 1 deck; fcsle 30 ft (9.14 m), bridge 14 ft (4.27 m), quarterdeck 33 ft (10.06 m), poop 33 ft (10.06 m).

1887 Built as *Norfolk* for H. Reeve, Yarmouth.
1901 Purchased by Royal Mail; renamed *Yare*. Stationed at Dominica.
1915 Sold and broken up.

108 **DEE** (III)

Bt 1902 Craig Taylor & Co, Stockton-on-Tees; *T:* 1,871 g, 1,182 n.
Dim 282 ft (85.95 m) × 38 ft 7 in (11.76 m) × 12 ft 6 in (3.81 m).
Eng Sgl scr, tpl exp; 3 cyls; 258 NHP; Stm P: 160 lb; 2 sgl ended boilers and 6 furnaces; 12 kts; By North East Marine.
H Steel, 1 deck and spar deck; fcsle 34 ft (10.36 m), bridge 74 ft (22.56 m).

1902 Built for West Indian local services.
1914 Taken over for use as a transport.
1918 Did not return to Royal Mail service.

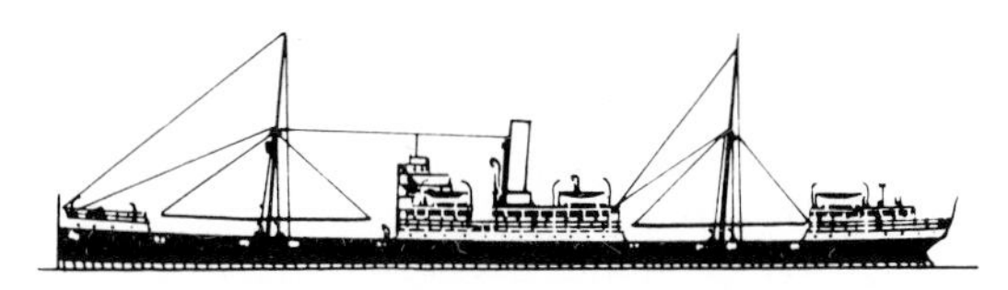

TAMAR (III) and TEVIOT (II)

109 **TAMAR** (III)

Bt 1902 Craig Taylor & Co, Stockton-on-Tees; *T:* 3,207 g, 2,065 n.
Dim 356 ft (108.51 m) oa, 331 ft 6 in (101.04 m) × 46 ft 2 in (14.07 m) × 23 ft 11 in (7.29 m).
Eng Sgl scr, tpl exp; 3 cyls; 360 NHP; Stm P: 180 lb; 3 sgl ended boilers, 9 furnaces; 14 kts; By North East Marine.
H Steel, 1 deck and spar deck; fcsle 36 ft (10.97 m), bridge 92 ft (28.04 m), poop 69 ft (21.03 m); cargo: 5,390 tons.

1902 Built for Royal Mail cargo services.
1915 Mar 24: Captured by the German raider *Kronprinz Wilhelm* whilst en route Santos–Le Havre with a cargo of coffee. Captain F. S. Hannan. Crew taken prisoner and then *Tamar* was sunk by gunfire.

110 **TEVIOT** (II)

Details as *Tamar* (109) except:
T: 3,271 g, 2,108 n.

1902 Entered service, general cargo duties.
1914 Oct 15: Evacuated refugees from Ostend as the Germans entered the outskirts of the town.
1914–18 Supply ship.
1919 Resumed Royal Mail service.
1923 Replaced the wrecked *Caraquet* (157) on the Canada–West Indies route.
1928 Broken up at Danzig.

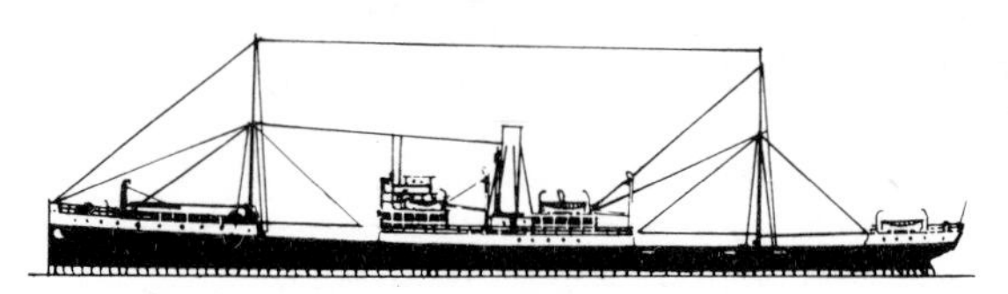

PARANA (II), PARDO (I) and POTARO (I)

111 **PARANA** (II)

Bt 1904 Workman Clark, Belfast; *T:* 4,515 g, 2,689 n.
Dim 375 ft 4 in (114.4 m) × 48 ft 4 in (14.73 m) × 24 ft 2 in (7.37 m).
Eng Sgl scr, tpl exp; 3 cyls; 430 NHP; Stm P: 205 lb; 3 sgl ended boilers, 6 furnaces; 12 kts; By builders.
H Steel, 2 decks; fcsle 99 ft (30.18 m), bridge 110 ft (33.53 m), poop 45 ft (13.72 m); refrigerated holds for meat.

1904 Built for the South American meat trade. Apr 28: Launched.
1917 Sept 10: Fought a German submarine for ninety minutes firing over 70 shells in reply to more than 100 from the U-boat. The arrival of a warship caused the U-boat to break off the engagement and dive.
1933 Broken up.

112 **PARDO** (I)

Details as *Parana* (111) except:
Bt 1904 Harland & Wolff, Belfast; *T:* 4,538 g, 2,791 n.

1904 Feb: Entered service.
1934 Broken up.

113 **POTARO** (I)

Details as *Parana* (111) except:
Bt 1904 Harland & Wolff, Belfast; *T:* 4,378 g, 2,793 n.

1904 Sept 10: Launched.
1915 Jan 10: Captured by the German commerce raider *Kronprinz Wilhelm;* used as a scouting ship.
1915 Mar 6: Scuttled by her captors.

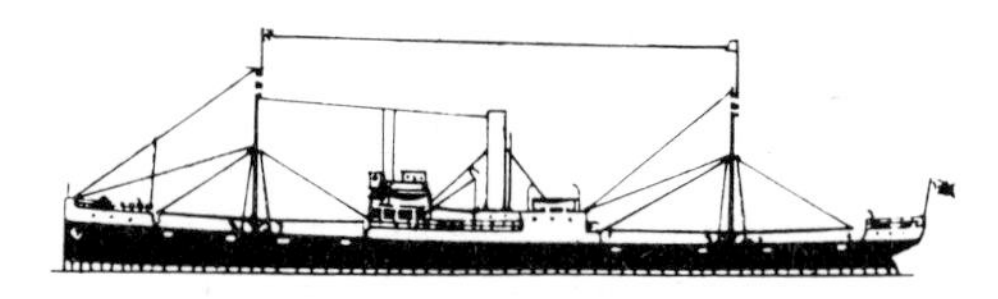

CARONI, CONWAY (II) and CATALINA

114 **CARONI**

Bt 1904 Armstrong Whitworth, Newcastle; *T:* 2,628 g, 1,671 n.
Dim 318 ft (96.93 m) × 43 ft 8 in (13.31 m) × 23 ft 4 in (7.11 m).
Eng Sgl scr, tpl exp; 3 cyls; 360 NHP; 1,900 IHP; Stm P: 180 lb; 3 sgl ended boilers, 9 furnaces; 10½ kts; By Wallsend Slipway Co, Wallsend.
H Steel, 2 decks; fcsle 33 ft (10.06 m), bridge 87 ft (26.52 m), poop 21 ft (6.40 m); Cargo: 3,300 tons; fuel: 302 tons coal; 5 holds, 9 derricks, 8 winches.

1904 June 15: Launched. Aug: Delivered.
1915 Sept 7: Captured by shell fire from a U-boat 15 miles west of Chassiron, then torpedoed.

115 **CONWAY** (II)

Details as *Caroni* (114) except:
T: 2,627 g, 1,669 n.

1904 Apr 29: Launched. June: Entered service Liverpool–Caribbean.
1930 Broken up.

116 **CATALINA**

Details as *Caroni* (114) except:
T: 2,626 g, 1,667 n.

1904 July 28: Launched.
1915 Dec 19: Damaged by explosion; sabotage suspected.
1922 Sold to Matsuoka Kisen KK; renamed *Nisshin Maru No 3,* later spelling *Nissin Maru No 3.*
1943 War loss.

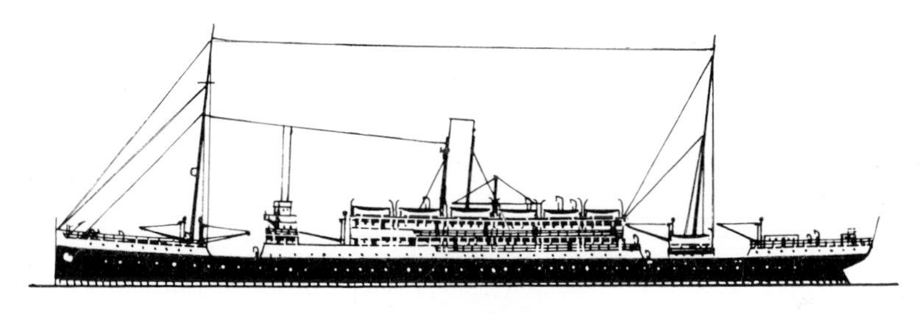

ARAGON (I)

117 **ARAGON** (I)

Bt Harland and Wolff, Belfast; *T:* 9,588 g, 6,038 n.
Dim 513 ft 4 in (156.46 m) × 60 ft 5 in (18.41 m) × 30 ft 9 in (9.37 m).
Eng Tw scr, quad exp; 4 cyls; 875 NHP; 3 sgl and 3 dbl ended cylindrical boilers; 16 kts; By builder.
H Steel, 3 decks; fcsle 54 ft (16.46 m), bridge 249 ft (75.89 m), poop 53 ft (16.15 m); 10 hydraulic cranes; fuel: 4,780 tons coal.
Pass 306 1st, 66 2nd, 632 3rd.

This class of vessels were not identical sisters; each ship differed progressively.

1905 Feb 23: Launched by Countess Fitzwilliam. The company's first built twin screw liner. July 14: Maid voyage Southampton–Brazilian ports–River Plate.
1910 Refitted, as illustrated, well abaft boat deck decked in. Poop deck house and boats added.
1915 Apr 13: Carried the troops to the Dardanelles who boarded the steamer *River Clyde* for the assault and landing.
1917 Dec 30: Torpedoed and sunk outside Alexandria harbour. The rescuing destroyer HMS *Attack* was also sunk. 610 lost, out of 2,700 abroad. *Aragon* had entered harbour but found no berth and was ordered out into the roadstead where she was promptly sunk.

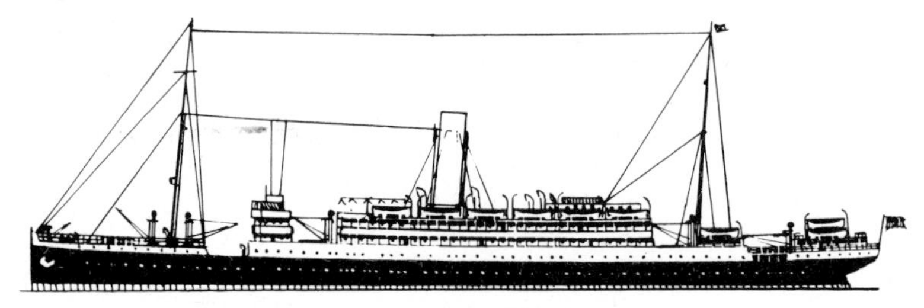

AMAZON (II) and ARAGUAYA

118 **AMAZON** (II)

Details as *Aragon* except:
Bt 1906; *T:* 10,037 g, 6,301 n.

1906 Feb 24: Launched by Mrs Owen Philipps, wife of the Chairman. June 15: Maiden voyage Southampton–South America.
1917 Jan 13: Sank U-boat. Feb 19: Chased by U-boat off SW Ireland.
1918 Mar 15: Sunk in 30 minutes by torpedo off the north coast of Ireland when outward bound from Liverpool. All saved. HMS *Moresby* depth charged *U-52* to the surface and destroyed her. 9 of the submarine's crew were saved.

119 **ARAGUAYA**

Details as *Aragon* (117) except:
T: 11,537 g, 6,637 n.

Identification note: The foremast was in the centre of the well deck between split hatch covers.

1906 June 5: Launched by the Countess of Aberdeen. Oct 12: Maiden voyage Southampton–South America.
1912 Chartered by the Thames Yacht Club to attend the Kiel Royal Regatta.
1914 Remained in commercial service.
1917 Hospital ship. Most of the time in Canadian Govt, use. 19 voyages.
1920 Oct 9: Returned to commercial service Southampton–Buenos Aires.
1926 Rebuilt as a cruise ship. *T:* 10,195 g; Pass: 365 1st.
1930 Nov 11: Sold to Jugoslavenska Lloyd, Rijeka; renamed *Kraljica Marija* (Queen Maria). Funnel shortened by 20 ft (6.1 m).
1940 Sold to the French Government; renamed *Savoie;* operated by Cie Generale Transatlantique to replace their lost *Bretagne*.
1942 Nov 8: Sunk off Casablanca during the North African landings.

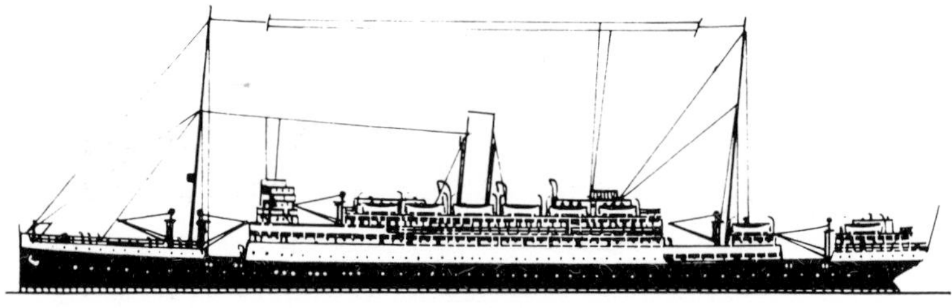

AVON (III)

120 **AVON** (III)/**AVOCA**/**AVON**

Details as *Aragon* (117) except:
Bt 1907; *T:* 11,073 g, 6,883 n.

Identification: Promenade deck extends to bridge front.

1907 Mar 2: Launched by Lady Pirrie. The only "A" with an English name. June 28: Maiden voyage Southampton–Corunna–Vigo–Oporto–Lisbon–Madeira–St Vincent–Recife–Bahia (Salvador)–Rio de Janeiro–Santos–Montevideo–Buenos Aires.
1910 Undertook summer Norwegian cruises.
1914 Aug: Trooping duties with the British Expeditionary Force Southampton–France.
1915 Feb: Taken over by the Admiralty for conversion into an Armed Merchant Cruiser. Renamed *Avoca,* there was already a destroyer *Avon.* 8×6 in (15.24 cm) guns and 2×6 pounder anti-aircraft guns. *Avoca* was attached to the 15th Cruiser Squadron at Esquimalt, Vancouver Island, for Pacific service.
1917 Took part in the hunt for the German sail raider *Seeadler* (Count von Luckner).
1919 Reverted to Royal Mail. Nov: Resumed commercial service.
1927 Operated New York–Bermuda service. White hull.
1929 Sept: Laid up at Southampton.
1930 Sold for £31,000 and broken up at Briton Ferry by Thos W. Ward & Co.

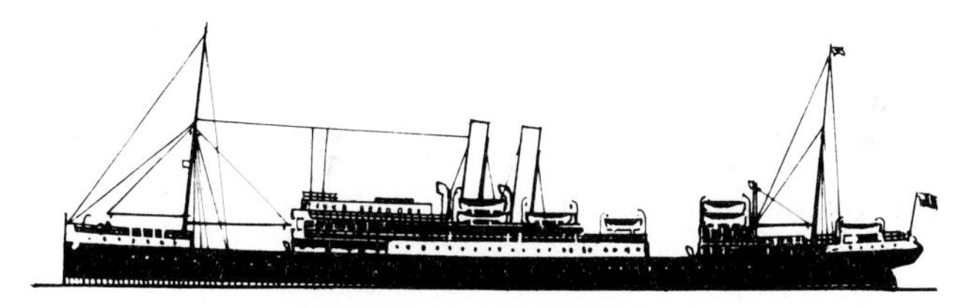

ORUBA (I) and OROTAVA

121 **ORUBA** (I)

Bt 1889 Naval Construction & Armament Co, Barrow; *T:* 5,852 g, 3,351 n.
Dim 430 ft (131.06 m) × 49 ft 4 in (15.04 m) × 34 ft 2 in (10.41 m).
Eng Sgl scr, tpl exp; 3 cyls; 764 NHP; 16½ kts; By builder.
H Steel, 2 decks; fcsle 66 ft (20.12 m), poop 48 ft (14.63 m).
Pass 126 1st, 120 2nd, 400 3rd.

1889 Built as *Oruba* for PSNC. Liverpool–Valparaiso route.
1890 Transferred to Orient Line service. July 4: First voyage to Australia.
1906 Feb: Transferred to Royal Mail Line ownership, given yellow funnels; remained on Australian route.
1908 Oct 16: Final sailing to Australia; placed on Royal Mail's South American service to Buenos Aires.
1914 Purchased by the British Admiralty and rebuilt to represent the battleship HMS *Orion.*
1915 Scuttled at Mudros Harbour, Aegean Sea, as a breakwater.

122 **OROTAVA**

Bt 1889 Barrow Shipbuilding Co, Barrow; *T:* 5,857 g, 3,096 n.
Dim 430 ft (131.06 m) × 49 ft 3 in (15.03 m) × 34 ft 2 in (10.42 m).
Eng Sgl scr, tpl exp; 3 cyl; 1,030 HP, 7,000 IHP; Stm P: 60 lb; 14½ kts; By Naval Construction & Armament Co, Barrow.
H Steel, 2 decks; fcsle 66 ft (20.1 m), poop 48 ft (14.63 m).
Pass 126 1st, 120 2nd, 400 3rd.

1889 Built for PSNC's Liverpool–Valparaiso service, made two voyages before being transferred to Orient Line management and the Australian service via Suez.
1890 June 6: First voyage London–Suez–Melbourne–Sydney.
1896 Capsized whilst coaling at Tilbury; 4 lost. Raised and renovated.

1897 Resumed service to Australia.
1899–1903 Boer War transport.
1903 Mar 13: Returned to Australian route.
1906 Feb: Ownership passed to Royal Mail Line. Yellow funnels. Remained on Australian berth.
1909 Mar 5: Last voyage to Australia; transferred to West Indies services. Pass: 250.
1914 Joined "B" Line of 10th Cruiser Squadron.
1919 Sold and broken up.

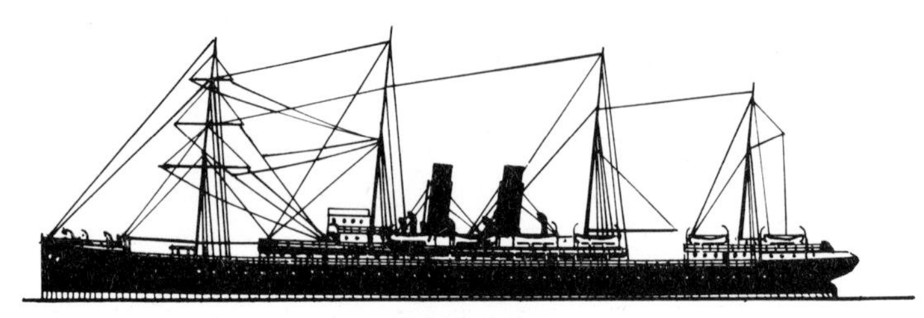

OROYA (II)

123 **OROYA** (II)

Bt 1886 Barrow Shipbuilding Co, Barrow; *T:* 6,057 g, 3,359 n.
Dim 474 ft (144.47 m) oa, 460 ft (140.21 m) × 49 ft 4 in (15.03 m) × 35 ft 4 in (10.77 m).
Eng Sgl scr, tpl exp; 3 cyl; 1,200 HP, 7,000 IHP; 12½ kts; By Naval Construction & Armament Co, Barrow.
H Steel, 4 decks and dbl bottom; fcsle 47 ft (14.32 m), poop 35 ft (10.66 m).
Pass 126 1st, 154 2nd, 412 3rd (in two tiered bunks).

1886 Aug 31: Launched as PSNC's first straight stemmed ocean liner and the largest vessel yet built for the company.

1887 Designed for the Australian service. Feb 17: Maiden voyage London–Suez Canal–Melbourne–Sydney.
1895 Mar 4: Went aground and was severely damaged in the Bay of Naples.
1905 Funnels lengthened.
1906 Feb: Sold to Royal Mail Line. Became Orient–Royal Mail Line.
1909 Sold for breaking up in Italy; renamed *Oro* for delivery voyage.

ARCADIAN (I)

124 **ORTONA/ARCADIAN** (I)

Bt 1899 Vickers, Sons and Maxim, Barrow; *T:* 7,945 g, 4,115 n.
Dim 515 ft (156.97 m) oa, 500 ft (152.4 m) × 55 ft 4 in (16.88 m) × 33 ft 7 in (10.27 m).
Eng Tw scr, tpl exp; 2 × 3 cyl; 560 HP; Stm P: 190 lb; 4 dbl ended boilers, 16 furnaces; 14 kts; By Naval Construction & Armament Co, Barrow (i.e. Builder).
H Steel, 2 decks; fcsle 66 ft (20.1 m).

Pass 130 1st, 162 2nd, 300 3rd (steerage class).

1899 Nov 24: Maiden voyage to Australia under the joint Orient–PSNC service. No sisters; not even near relatives were built.
1902 June: Trooping duties to South Africa as Transport No 112.
1903 Oct 9: Returned to the Australian route.
1906 Feb: Acquired by Royal Mail together with remainder of PSNC Australian fleet.
1909 Apr 30: Last Australian voyage.
1910 Renamed *Arcadian* and converted into a cruise ship. Pass: 320, one class (drawing).
1915 Troopship. Gallipoli Headquarters ship to Sir Ian Hamilton.
1917 Apr 15: Torpedoed in Eastern Mediterranean en-route Salonika–Alexandria. 279 lives lost out of 1,335 aboard.

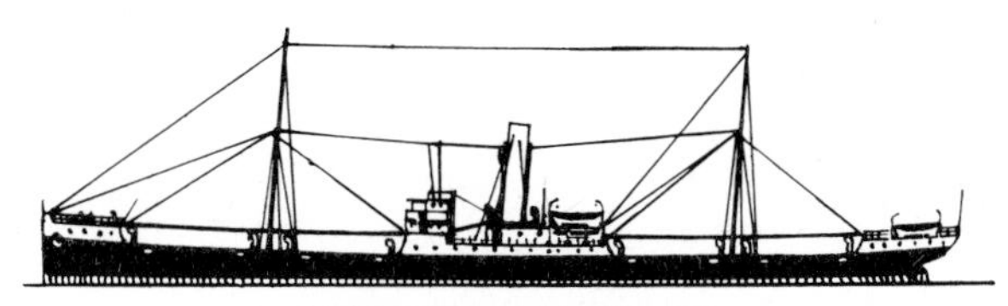

MARIMA and MANAU

125 **MARIMA**

Bt 1892 Sir W. Raylton Dixon & Co, Middlesbrough; *T:* 2,742 g, 1,760 n.
Dim 323 ft (98.45 m) oa, 309 ft 8 in (94.39 m) × 40 ft 7 in (12.37 m) × 17 ft 6 in (5.33 m).
Eng Sgl scr, tpl exp; 3 cyls; 283 NHP; Stm P: 160 lb; 2 sgl ended boilers, 6 furnaces; 12 kts; By T. Richardson & Sons, Hartlepool.
H Steel, 1 deck and spar deck; fcsle 36 ft (10.97 m), bridge 34 ft (10.36 m), poop 31 ft (9.45 m).

1892 Built as *Zulu* for Bucknall's British & Colonial Steam Nav Co.
1906 Purchased by Royal Mail; renamed *Marima.*
1911 Sold to G. Coulouras, Andros, Greece; became *Marika.*
1916 Sold to Hannevig Bros, Oslo. Apr 4: Foundered in the South Atlantic.

126 **MANAU**

Details as *Marima* (125) except:
T: 2,745 g, 1,756 n.

1892 Built as *Transvaal* for Bucknall's British & Colonial Steam Nav Co.
1906 Acquired with *Zulu* (124) and renamed *Manau.* Mar: Whilst in dry dock in Antwerp the dock flooded and *Manau* was temporarily submerged. May 22: Wrecked 7 miles north of Bahia en route Southampton–Bahia. Broke in two and became a total loss.

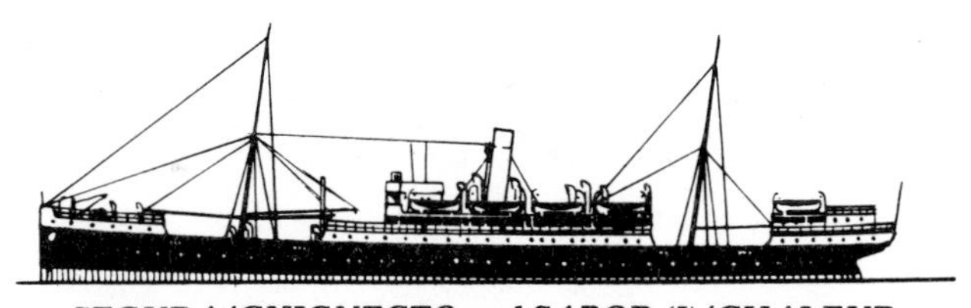

SEGURA/CHIGNECTO and SABOR (I)/CHALEUR

127 **SEGURA/CHIGNECTO**

Bt 1893 Harland & Wolff, Belfast; *T:* 4,747 g, 3,036 n.
Dim 416 ft (126.8 m) oa, 400 ft 6 in (122.07 m) × 47 ft 2 in (14.38 m) × 26 ft 10 in (8.18 m).

Eng Tw scr, tpl exp; 3 cyls; 2,200 IHP; 3 dbl ended boilers, 4 furnaces; Stm P: 180 lb; 12 kts; By builder.
H Steel, 3 decks; fcsle 55 ft (16.76 m), bridge 142 ft (43.28 m), poop 47 ft (14.33 m), 5 hatches; cargo: 5,000 tons.
Pass 52 1st, 66 2nd, 500 3rd.

1893 May: Maiden voyage as *Greek* for Union Line's Intermediate service.
1900 Mar: Transferred to Union-Castle Mail SS Co by the merger.
1906 Acquired by Royal Mail for their Southampton–Cuba–Mexico service. Renamed *Segura*.
1908 Transferred to Jenkin's Shire Line; became *Pembrokeshire* with red funnel and black top.
1913 Reverted to Royal Mail; renamed *Chignecto* and placed on Canada–West Indies run.
1927 Broken up in Holland.

128 **SABOR** (I)/**CHALEUR**

Details as *Segura* (127) except:
T: 4,745 g, 3,047 n.

1893 May: Maiden voyage as *Gaul* for Union Line's Intermediate service.
1900 Mar: Merged into Union-Castle Mail SS Co fleet.
1906 Sold to Royal Mail and renamed *Sabor* for the Southampton–Cuba–Mexico service.
1908 Transferred to Jenkin's Shire Line; became *Carmarthenshire* with red funnel and black top.
1913 Reverted to Royal Mail; renamed *Chaleur* for the Canada–West Indies service.
1927 Broken up in Holland.

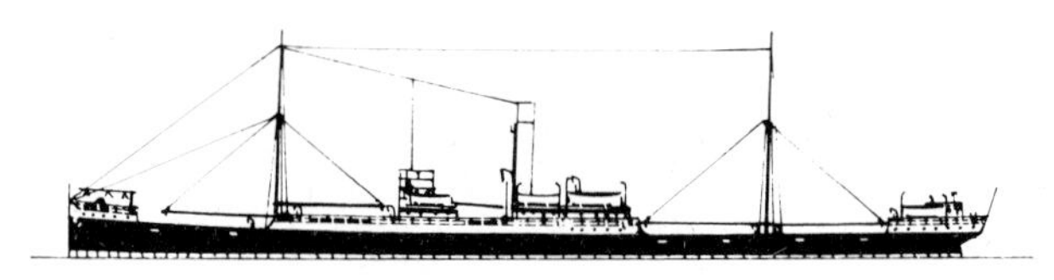

MONMOUTHSHIRE/TYNE (IV)

129 **MONMOUTHSHIRE/TYNE** (IV)

Bt 1902 Sunderland SB Co, Sunderland; *T:* 5,091 g, 3,306 n.
Dim 400 ft (121.92 m) × 52 ft (15.85 m) × 20 ft 1 in (6.12 m).
Eng Sgl scr, tpl exp; 3 cyls; 10 kts. By North East Marine Co, Sunderland.
H Steel, 1 deck and spar deck; fcsle 27 ft (8.23 m), bridge 160 ft (48.77 m), poop 41 ft (12.50 m).

1902 Built as *Monmouthshire* for Jenkin's Shire Line.
1907 Acquired by Royal Mail; same name. A new company was formed by Royal Mail called Shire Line.
1919 Became *Tyne*.
1922 Sold to Tokai Kisen KK; renamed *Toku Maru*.
1936 Broken up.

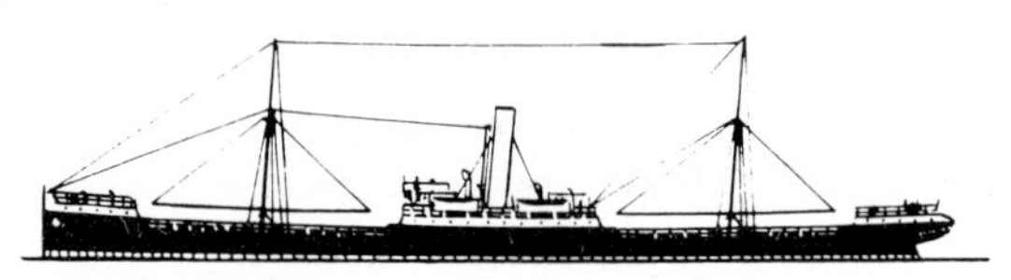

DENBIGHSHIRE TAMAR (IV) and FLINTSHIRE

130 **DENBIGHSHIRE/TAMAR** (IV)

Bt 1899 Sunderland SB Co, Sunderland; *T:* 3,844 g, 2,489 n.

Dim 356 ft (108.51 m) × 45 ft 2 in (13.77 m) × 18 ft 8 in (5.69 m).
Eng Sgl scr, tpl exp; 3 cyls; 2 sgl ended boilers, 6 furnaces; Stm P: 170 lb; 10 kts; By North East Marine Co, Sunderland.
H Steel, 1 deck and spar deck; fcsle 42 ft (12.8 m), bridge 80 ft (24.38 m), poop 38 ft (11.58 m).

1899 Built for Jenkin's Shire Line.
1907 Acquired by Royal Mail; same name and colours.
1913 Lost propeller 48 miles off Cape Race, Newfoundland. The German steamer *Elizabeth* towed her into port.
1919 Reverted to Royal Mail; renamed *Tamar*.
1922 Sold; renamed *Avgy*. Broken up.

131 **FLINTSHIRE**

Details as *Denbighshire* (130) except:
T: 3,837 g, 2,404 n.

1899 Built for Jenkin's Shire Line.
1907 Taken over by Royal Mail; same name and colours.
1913 Sold to Ellerman Lines; renamed *Algerian*.
1916 Jan: Mined 2½ miles south west of the Needles.

ASTURIAS (I)/ARCADIAN (II)

132 **ASTURIAS** (I)/**ARCADIAN** (II)

Bt 1907 Harland & Wolff, Belfast; *T:* 12,105 g, 7,509 n.
Dim 535 ft (163.07 m) oa, 520 ft 4 in (158.6 m) × 62 ft 4 in (19 m) × 31 ft 9 in (9.68 m).
Eng Tw scr, quad exp; 2 × 4 cyls; 3 dbl and 4 sgl ended boilers; Stm P: 215 lb; 16½ kts; By builder.
H Steel, 2 decks; 5 holds, 10 hydraulic cranes. The first RM vessel to be fitted with a passenger lift. Fcsle and bridge 447 ft (136.25 m), poop 52 ft (15.85 m).
Pass 300 1st, 140 2nd, 1,200 steerage.

1906 Laid down. The fifth of the "A" class but differed materially in appearance. She was half way to the new "A's" initiated by *Arlanza* (142).
1907 Sept 26: Launched.
1908 Jan 24: Maiden voyage London – Brisbane. Then Southampton – River Plate service.
1914 Aug 1: Requisitioned for use as a hospital ship.
1917 Mar 20: Torpedoed and the stern blow off. Put ashore at Bolt Head. At the time of the attack the ship was in full hospital colours. 35 lives lost. Towed to port and became an ammunition hulk at Plymouth. Owned by British Admiralty.
1919 Purchased again by Royal Mail. Laid up at Belfast.
1923 June 3: At the end of a 2 year rebuild at Harland & Wolff emerged as the cruising liner *Arcadian*.
1930 Laid up in Southampton water.
1933 Feb: Sold to Japan for scrapping.

ARZILA and AGADIR

133 **ARZILA**

Bt 1907 Sir James Laing, Sunderland; *T:* 2,722 g, 1,677 n.
Dim 285 ft (86.87 m) × 41 ft 4 in (12.6 m) × 25 ft 8 in (7.82 m).
Eng Sgl scr, tpl exp; 3 cyls; 275 NHP; 12 kts; By G. Clark, Sunderland.
H Steel, 2 decks.
Pass 72 1st, Crew: 108.

1907 Built for Mersey SS Co, Leech Forward & Harrison managers, Liverpool for Liverpool–Canary Isles–Morocco service.
1908 Acquired by Royal Mail; same name.
1918 May 23: Torpedo missed in English Channel.
1919 Chartered to PSNC.
1922 Sold to Khedivial Mail; renamed *Bilbeis.*
1934 May 5: Wrecked 2 miles south of Jaffa, Palestine.

134 **AGADIR**

Details as *Arzila* (133) except:
T: 2,722 g, 1,672 n.

1907 Built for Mersey SS Co service with *Arzila.*
1908 Taken over by Royal Mail.
1913 Mar 13: Went ashore off Mazagan, Morocco; 54 passengers and the crew of 108 taken off by Breeches buoy. May 23: Vessel finally salvaged by *Linnet.*
1914–18 Hospital ship at Scapa Flow.
1919 Chartered to PSNC.
1922 Sold to Khedivial Mail; renamed *Belkas.*
1935 Sold to Societe Orientale de Navigation; became *Damas.*
1940 Returned to Khedivial Mail but renamed *Sakara.*
1950 Broken up at Savona, Italy.

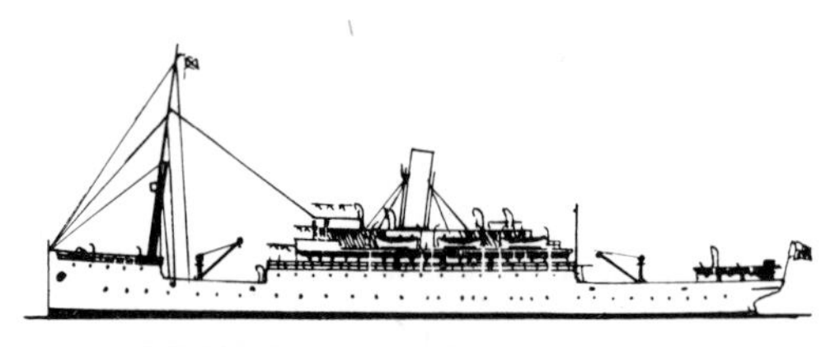

BERBICE (I) and BALANTIA (I)

135 **BERBICE** (I)

Bt 1909 Harland & Wolff, Belfast; *T:* 2,379 g, 1,387 n.
Dim 300 ft 8 in (91.64 m) × 38 ft 2 in (11.63 m) × 22 ft 10 in (6.97 m).
Eng Sgl scr, quad exp; 4 cyls; 169 NHP; 13 kts; By builder.
H Steel, 1 deck and shelter deck; fcsle 47 ft (14.33 m), bridge 144 ft (43.89 m).
Pass 100 1st, 50 2nd.

1909 May 6: Launched for West Indies inter-island and cruising services.

1914–18 Naval Hospital ship HMHS *Berbice.*
1920 Sold. Renamed *Suntemple,* Mitchell Cotts, London.
1924 Broken up.

136 **BALANTIA** (I)

Details as *Berbice* (135) except:
T: 2,467 g, 1,429 n.

1909 Oct 29: Launched for West Indies inter-island services in conjunction with *Berbice.*
1916 Fitted out as a hospital ship by public subscription. Renamed *St Margaret of Scotland,* managed by Royal Mail.
1918 Reverted to the name *Balantia.*
1922 Transferred to Khedivial Mail; renamed *Boulac.*
1929 Broken up.

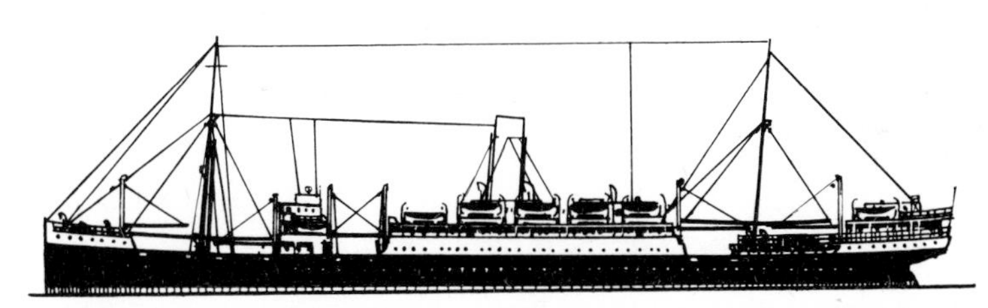

DESEADO (I), DEMERARA (II), DESNA, DARRO (I) and DRINA (I)

137 **DESEADO** (I)

Bt 1911 Harland & Wolff, Belfast; *T:* 11,475 g, 7,258 n.
Dim 500 ft 8 in (152.6 m) × 62 ft 4 in (19 m) × 40 ft 2 in (12.24 m).
Eng Tw scr, quad exp; 4 cyls; 680 NHP; 15 kts; By builder.
H Steel, 2 decks; fcsle 59 ft (17.98 m), bridge 181 ft (55.17 m), poop 50 ft (15.24 m).
Pass 98 1st, 38 Intermediate, 800 3rd (steerage).

1911 Oct 26: Launched for services from Liverpool to either West Indies or South America. Intermediate steamer.
1912 July 5: Maiden voyage Liverpool–River Plate.
1914 All of this class remained in commercial service throughout the war. Their meat carrying capacity was so important, *Drina* (141) however, became a hospital ship for four months in 1914.
1917 Jan 19: In heavy seas in the Bay of Biscay 4 U-boats surfaced and gave chase. No shot was fired because the submarines were unable to man their guns. In the gale *Deseado* escaped.
1934 Aug 7: Arrived for breaking up in Japan.

138 **DEMERARA** (II)

Details as *Deseado* (137) except:
Bt 1912; *T:* 11,484 g, 7,292 n.

1911 Dec 21: Launched.
1912 Aug 8: Delivered for Liverpool–River Plate service.
1916 Feb: Chased by the disguised German raider *Möewe* in the South Atlantic. *Demerara* identified the attacker and signalled that she would open fire. *Möewe* sheered off.
1917 July 1: Torpedoed off La Rochelle but reached port and repaired.
1933 Broken up in Japan.

139 **DESNA**

Details as *Deseado* (137) except:
Bt 1912; *T:* 11,483 g, 7,255 n.

1912 Mar 2: Launched. July: Delivered. Liverpool–River Plate service.
1912 Ran into Cie Generale Transatlantique's *La Champagne*. Neither ship badly damaged.
1914 Aug 14: Attacked by U-boat west of Ushant. 2 torpedoes missed.
1933 Broken up in Japan.

140 **DARRO** (I)

Details as *Deseado* (137) except:
Bt 1912; *T:* 11,484 g, 7,252 n.

1912 May 16: Launched for Imperial Direct Line, Elder Dempster, but now a part of the Royal Mail group and owned 100% by them.
1918 Oct 13: A U-boat torpedo missed the ship.
1933 Apr: Broken up in Japan.

141 **DRINA** (I)

Details as *Deseado* (137) except:
Bt 1912; *T:* 11,483 g, 7,255 n.

1912 June 29: Launched.
1913 Jan: Completed for Liverpool–River Plate service.
1914 Aug 1: Requisitioned for use as a hospital ship; she was in fact the first merchant ship to be taken over for this service in World War I. Not converted.
1915 Reverted to commercial service.
1917 Mar 1: Torpedoed and sunk outside Milford Haven, off Skokholm Island by *UC 65*. 15 lives lost.

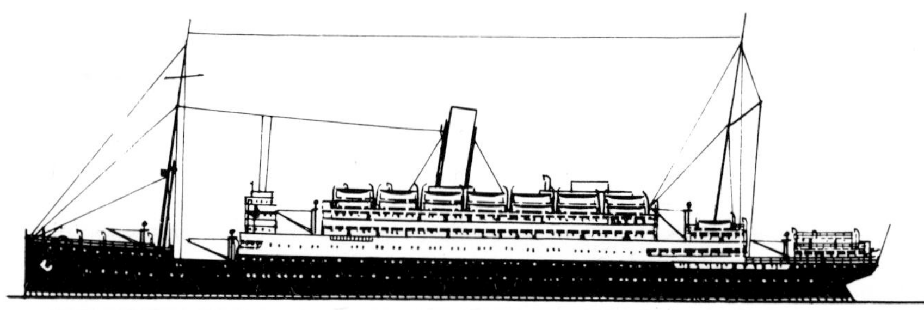

ARLANZA, ANDES (I)/ATLANTIS, ALCANTARA (I) and ALMANZORA

142 **ARLANZA**

Bt 1911 Harland & Wolff, Belfast; *T:* 15,044 g, 9,122 n.
Dim 590 ft (179.83 m) oa, 570 ft (173.74 m) × 65 ft 4 in (19.91 m) × 33 ft 4 in (10.16 m).
Eng Tpl scr, tpl exp to wing shafts exhausting into a low pressure turbine driving the centre screw. 2 × 4 cyls; 4 cylindrical boilers, 16 furnaces; 17 kts; By builder.
H Steel, 3 decks, fcsle 100 ft (30.48 m), bridge 348 ft (106.07 m), poop 53 ft (16.15 m), upper bridge 287 ft (87.48 m), promenade deck 242 ft (73.76 m), 5 hatches served by hydraulic cranes, 9 watertight compartments. Refrigerated cargo space for South American meat. Fuel: 3,880 tons coal.
Pass 400 1st, 230 2nd, 760 3rd.

1911 Nov 23: Launched for Southampton–River Plate service.

1912 Sept: Maiden voyage Southampton–River Plate.
1914 Aug 16: Captured off the coast of Brazil by the German raider *Kaiser Wilhelm der Grosse* but released after it was established that she had 335 women and 97 children aboard.
1915 Apr: Became an Armed Merchant Cruiser with 10th Cruiser Squadron. Oct 22: Mined in the White Sea; made port safely.
1920 July 27: First post war voyage Southampton–River Plate.
1929 Converted to oil fuel.
1938 Aug: 1,700 guests attended a farewell party at Montevideo. Sept 6: Paid off at Southampton. Broken up by Hughes, Bolckow & Co, Blyth.

143 **ANDES** (I)/**ATLANTIS**

Details as *Arlanza* (142) except:
Bt 1913; *T:* 15,620 g, 9,481 n.
Pass 380 1st, 250 2nd, 700 3rd.

Completed with 2×4.7 in (11.94 cm) guns right aft.

1913 May 8: Launched. Intended for PSNC but transferred to Royal Mail on the stocks. Sept 26: Maiden voyage for PSNC Liverpool–Valparaiso, then Southampton–River Plate service for Royal Mail.
1915 Apr: Converted to Armed Merchant Cruiser. 8×6 in (15.24 cm) guns; 2×6 pounders, plus depth charges.
1916 Feb 29: With her sister ship *Alcantara* (144) engaged the German raider *Greif* (masquerading as the Norwegian *Rena).* Although *Greif* was sunk *Alcantara* was herself sunk and *Andes* picked up the survivors including 115 Germans.
1917 Atlantic convoy work. Then repatriated British submarine crews trapped by the Soviet Revolution at Murmansk.
1919 Jan: Reconditioned at Belfast, resumed the River Plate Run in Oct.
1929 Converted at Gladstone Dock, Liverpool, to cruising liner, painted white; renamed *Atlantis.* Pass: 450 1st. Converted to oil fuel. A swimming pool was installed behind the bridge.
1935 Attended Silver Jubilee Naval Review at Spithead.
1939 Aug: At Danzig on a cruise when recalled. Aug 25: Reached Southampton. Converted into hospital ship *No 33* with 400 beds. 130 Medical staff joined. Initially based at Alexandria.
1940 Apr: Returned to Norwegian waters for the Norwegian evacuation campaign. Bombed twice. Sept: Indian Ocean work for two years.
1942 Took part in Madagascar operation; based at Diego Suarez.
1943 Used for the repatriation of prisoners of war. Took Italians to Lisbon and Germans to Gothenburg.
1944–46 Hospital and repatriation duties. Steamed 280,000 miles and carried 35,000 wounded.
1948 Chartered for 4 years to carry emigrants from Southampton to Australia and New Zealand. Pass: 900 3rd.
1952 Laid up in the Clyde then sold for scrapping at Faslane.

144 **ALCANTARA** (I)

Details as *Arlanza* (142) except:
Bt 1914 Harland & Wolff, Glasgow; *T:* 16,034 g, 10,323 n.
H Bridge 353 ft (107.59 m), upper bridge 348 ft (106.07 m).

Identification note: Bridge deck glassed in up to centre of second lifeboat.

1913 Oct 30: Launched at Govan. Towed to Belfast for the installation of her engines.
1914 June 19: Maiden voyage to Buenos Aires. Captain W. J. Dagnall.
1915 Converted to Armed Merchant Cruiser 8×6 in (15.24 cm) guns and 2×6 pounder

anti-aircraft guns plus depth charges.
1916 Feb 29: In command of Captain T. E. Wardle *Alcantara* was due to leave her patrol position in the Skagerrak for Liverpool. She was signalled to intercept a disguised merchant ship steaming northwards. At 08.45 a ship identified as the Norwegian *Rena* was sighted. *Andes* (143) her consort, advised that this was the ship to be intercepted. *Alcantara* closed to within 800 yards (731 m) and sent a boarding party. Then the German ship disclosed herself as the German raider *Greif* and opened fire causing great damage to *Alcantara* who began to list to port. *Greif,* too, was soon on fire but attempted to torpedo both *Alcantara* and *Andes* but missed both. It was now 09.15 and orders were given to abandon *Alcantara* and many of her crew were able to walk down her port side. The cruiser *Comus* and destroyer *Munster* came to the scene to pick up survivors. At 11.08 *Alcantara* sank. *Greif* was afloat but blazing fiercely and at 1 p.m., from the combined attack of *Comus* and *Andes,* she sank. *Alcantara* lost 72 men and *Greif* 280.

145 **ALMANZORA**

Details as *Arlanza* (142) except:
Bt 1915; *T:* 16,034 g, 10,323 n.
H Bridge 353 ft (107.59 m), upper bridge 348 ft (106.07 m).

Identification: Fore part of bridge deck glassed in from her completion.

1914 Nov 19: Launched.
1915 Sept: Completed as an Armed Merchant Cruiser 10th Cruiser Squadron.
1919 Jan 14: Reconditioned at Belfast; *T:* 15,551 g.
1920 Jan 9: Maiden commercial voyage Southampton – River Plate.
1939 Used for trooping duties.
1945 Became a Government emigration ship.
1947 Laid up off Cowes, Isle of Wight.
1948 Broken up at Blyth by British Iron & Steel Corp.

146 **JAMAICA**

Bt 1908 W. Harkess & Son, Middlesborough *T:* 1,138 g, 602 n.
Dim 220 ft (67.06 m) × 34 ft (10.36 m) × 14 ft 11 in (4.52m)
Eng Sgl scr, tpl exp; 3 cyl; 171 NHP; Stm P: 180 lb; 2 sgl ended boilers, 4 furnaces; 11 kts; By McColl & Pollock, Sunderland.
H Steel, 2 decks; fcsle 28 ft (8.53 m), bridge 79 ft (24.08 m), poop 24 ft (7.31 m).

1908 Built for Imperial Direct West India Service, Elder Dempster & Co.
1914 Acquired for Central American services; same name.
1915 Requisitioned for Government service.
1918 Shown as owned by Royal Mail Line but did not enter their service. Reverted to PSNC service.
1929 Sold, renamed *Coyhaique* Soc Industrial del Aysen, Valparaiso.
1943 Broken up.

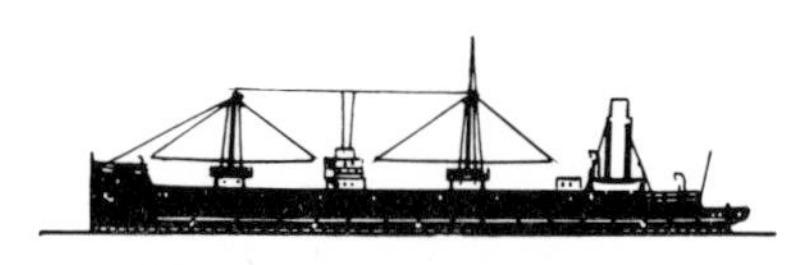

DART (II), DOON and DEVON

147 **DART** (II)

Bt 1912 Cammell Laird, Birkenhead *T:* 1,104 g, 697 n.
Dim 180 ft (54.86 m) × 42 ft 2in (12.85 m) × 9 ft 9 in (3.01m)
Eng Tw scr, compound; 2 × 2 cyls: Stm P: 140 lb; 2 sgl ended boilers, 4 furnaces; By builder.

H Steel, 1 deck, refrigerated machinery; fcsle and bridge 136 ft (41.45 m).

1912 Registered at Buenos Aires; flew Argentine flag. River Plate meat lighter.
1959 Broken up at Buenos Aires.

148 **DOON**

Details as *Dart* (147) except:
Bt 1913; *T:* 1,353 g, 751 n.
Dim 220 ft (67.06 m)
H Fcsle and bridge 166 ft (50.6 m).

1913 Mar: River Plate meat lighter, Argentine flag.
1919 Used on the London–Continent feeder service in conjunction with *Elder* (103).
1919 Sold to Blue Star Line, London; renamed *Britanica*.
1939–45 Government service in the Far East.
1946 Sold to Belgian shipbreakers.

149 **DEVON**

Details as *Dart* (147) except:
Bt 1914; *T:* 1,368 g, 737 n.
Eng Tpl exp; 3 cyls; Stm P: 180 lb.
H Fcsle and bridge 157 ft (47.85 m).

1914 July: River Plate meat lighter. Argentine flag.
1959 Broken up at Buenos Aires.

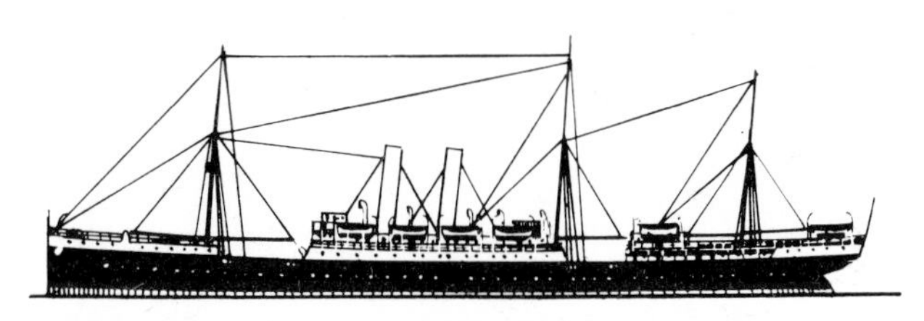

CARIBBEAN

150 **CARIBBEAN**

Bt 1889 Fairfield SB & E Co, Govan; *T:* 5,625 g, 3,139 n.
Dim 433 ft (131.98 m) oa, 420 ft (128.02 m) × 49 ft (14.93m) × 33 ft (10.06 m).
Eng Sgl scr, tpl exp; 3 cyls; Stm P: 160 lb; 4 dbl ended boilers, 16 furnaces; 15 kts; By builder.
H Steel, 3 decks; fcsle 85 ft (25.91 m), bridge 155 ft (47.24 m), poop 165 ft (50.29 m).
Pass 160 1st, 90 2nd, 100 3rd.

1890 May 22: Launched as *Dunottar Castle*, Union Castle. Oct: Maiden voyage Dartmouth–Cape Town in 17 days 19 hours 50 mins.
1894 Grounded at Eddystone Lighthouse.
1897 Funnels heightened by 6 ft (1.83 m); fcsle extended to foremast.
1904 Laid up.
1907 Chartered to Panama Railroad Co.
1909 Chartered for cruising to Sir Henry Lunn Ltd, Travel agents.
1913 Sold to Royal Mail; renamed *Caribbean*.
1914 Became an Armed Merchant Cruiser but not used, later used as a depot ship for workmen at Scapa Flow.
1915 Sept 27: Foundered off Cape Wrath; 15 lives lost.

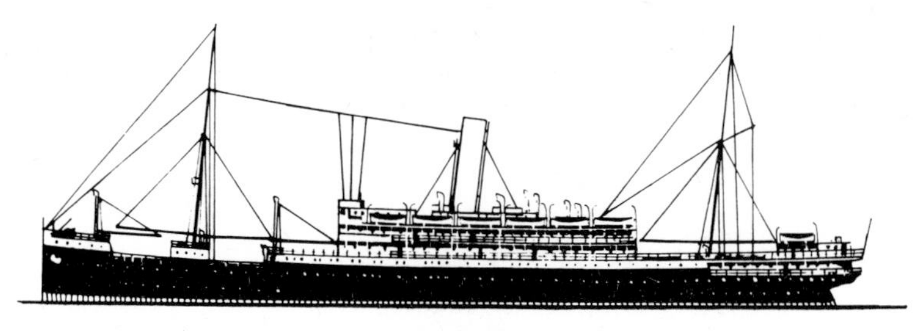

ALCALA

151 **ALCALA**

Bt 1912 Workman Clark, Belfast; *T:* 10.660 g, 6,699 n.
Dim 495 ft 6 in (151.03 m) × 60 ft 9 in (18.52 m) × 28 ft 8 in (8.74m)
Eng Tw scr, quad exp; 2 × 4 cyls; 622 NHP; 15 kts; By builder.
H Steel, 4 decks; fcsle 54 ft (16.46 m) bridge 264 ft (80.47 m).
Pass 280 1st, 130 2nd, 200 3rd; Crew: 250.

1912 Jan 20: Launched.
1913 Completed as *Vauban,* Lamport & Holt for New York–River Plate service. Taken over by Royal Mail and renamed *Alcala* pending the delivery of *Almanzora* (145) Southampton–River Plate.
1914 Jan: Returned to Lamport & Holt; reverted to *Vauban* owned by Liverpool. Brazil & River Plate SN Co.
1919 May 27: Chartered to Cunard; first voyage Liverpool–New York.
1922 Royal Mail charter, then back to Lamport & Holt's New York–River Plate service.
1930 Laid up.
1932 Jan: Sold for breaking up to Thos W. Ward, Inverkeithing.

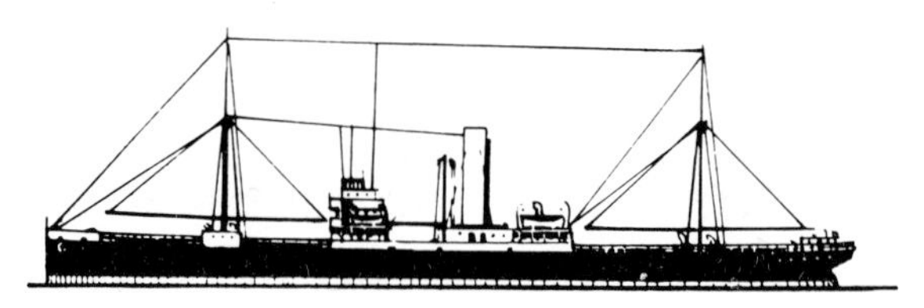

RADNORSHIRE (I) and MERIONETHSHIRE

152 **RADNORSHIRE** (I)

Bt 1913 Bartam & Sons, Sunderland; *T:* 4,310 g, 2,873 n.
Dim 385 ft (117.35 m) × 52 ft (15.85 m) × 25 ft 1in (7.65m)
Eng Sgl scr, tpl exp; 3 cyls; Stm P: 180 lb; 12 kts; By J. Dickinson & Sons, Sunderland.
H Steel, 1 deck and shade deck.

1913 Launched as *Salopian* for John Mathias, Aberystwyth, Wales. Purchased by Royal Mail to replace one of the five Brocklebank ships withdrawn in 1911. July 2: Maiden voyage, Captain Bollard, as *Radnorshire.*
1917 Jan 7: Captured and sunk by the German raider *Moewe* 110 miles north east of Pernambuco.

153 **MERIONETHSHIRE**

Details as *Radnorshire* (152) except:
T: 4,308 g, 2,869 n.

1913 Launched as *Reptonian* (II) for John Mathias, Aberystwyth, Wales. Acquired by

Royal Mail and renamed *Merionethshire*. Nov 1: Maiden voyage, Captain Lainson.
1918 May 27: Torpedoed 120 miles north of the Azores after leaving her 25 ship convoy. The survivors were picked up the following day by the Spanish schooner *Luna* and landed in the Azores.

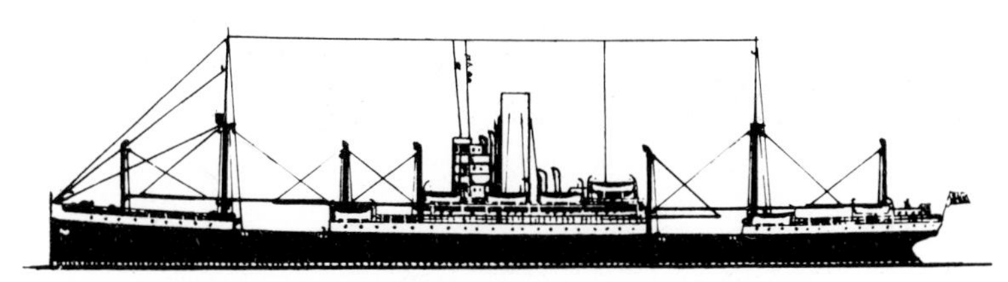

CARDIGANSHIRE and CARNARVONSHIRE

154 **CARDIGANSHIRE**

Bt 1913 Workman Clark, Belfast; *T:* 9.426 g, 5,993 n.
Dim 520 ft (158.5 m) oa, 500 ft (152.4 m) × 62 ft 5in (19.02m) × 29 ft 9 in (9.07 m).
Eng Tw scr, tpl exp; 2 × 3 cyls; Stm P: 200 lbs; 2 dbl and 2 sgl ended boilers, 18 furnaces; 13 kts; By builder.
H Steel, 2 decks; fcsle 88 ft (26.82 m), bridge 180 ft (54.86 m), poop 107 ft (32.61 m); Cargo: 13,450 tons.

Pass 12 1st, 1,000 steerage.
1913 Sept 30: Launched. Nov 25: Maiden voyage Belfast – Far East.
1929 Sold and broken up.

155 **CARNARVONSHIRE**

Details as *Cardiganshire* (154) except:
Bt 1914. *T:* 9,406 g, 5,955 n.

1913 Dec 16: Launched.
1914 Mar: 7: Maiden voyage London – Far East.
1933 Sold for breaking up.

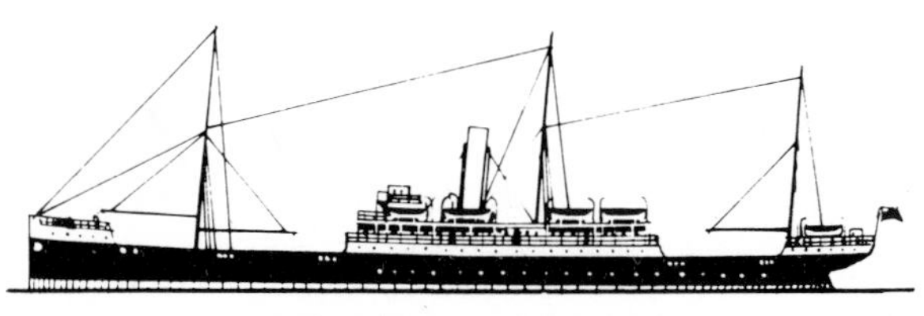

COBEQUID and CARAQUET

156 **COBEQUID**

Bt 1893 Harland & Wolff, Belfast; *T:* 4,738 g, 3,035 n.
Dim 400 ft 6in (122.07 m) × 47 ft 4in (14.43 m) × 26 ft 11in (8.21m)
Eng Tw scr, tpl exp; 2 × 3 cyls; 2,200 IHP; Stm P: 180 lb; 2 dbl ended boilers; 12¼ kts; By builder.
H Steel, 3 decks; fcsle 55 ft (16.76 m), bridge 142 ft (43.28 m), poop 47 ft (14.33 m).
Pass 56 1st, 97 2nd, 200 3rd.

1893 Built as *Goth* for Union Line, Southampton. South African Intermediate service.
1900 Transferred with the merger to Union-Castle Mail SS Co.

1913 Dec: Purchased by Royal Mail; renamed *Cobequid.*
1914 Nov 23: Placed on Canada–West Indies service with *Caraquet* (157), *Chignecto* (127) and *Chaleur* (128).
1914 Nov 23: First voyage on the Canadian service. Captain J. Howson.
1915 Jan 13: Wrecked on Trinity Ledge, Bay of Fundy, on inward leg of her first voyage. Replaced by the purchase of *Mandingo* from Elder Dempster which became *Chaudiere* (165).

157 **CARAQUET**

Details as *Cobequid* (156) except:
Bt 1894; *T:* 4,917 g, 3,112 n.

1984 Built as *Guelph* for the Union Line's Intermediate service to South Africa.
1894 Oct 6: Maiden voyage Southampton–Tenerife–Cape Town.
1900 Transferred to Union-Castle Mail SS Co, during the merger.
1913 Purchased by Royal Mail; renamed *Caraquet.*
1914 Placed on Canada–West Indies service.
1923 June 25: Wrecked near Hamilton, Bermuda. Replaced on the Canadian run by the cargo vessel *Teviot* (110).

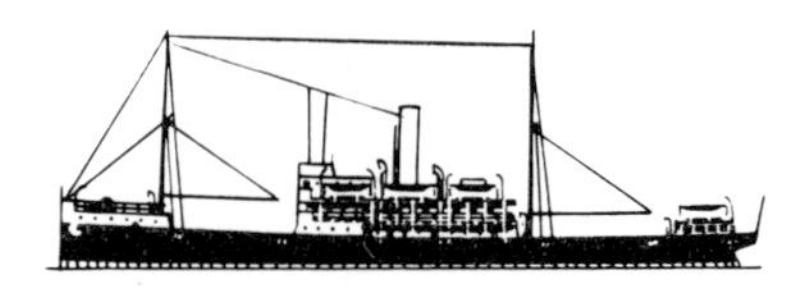

BARIMA and BELIZE (II)

158 **BARIMA**

Bt 1914 Caledon SB Co, Dundee; *T:* 1,498 g, 780 n.
Dim 220 ft 6in (62.21 m) × 37 ft 1in (11.3 m) × 12 ft 11in (3.94m)
Eng Tw scr, tpl exp; 2 × 3 cyls; 182 NHP; Stm P: 180 lb; 2 sgl ended boilers, 4 furnaces; 12 kts; By builder.
H Steel, 1 deck and shelter deck; fcsle 42 ft (12.80 m), bridge 24 ft (7.31 m); Cargo 81,000 cu ft (2,292 cu m) bale. Fuel: 250 tons.
Pass 60 1st, 350 deck.

1914 Feb 11: Launched for inter-island service between Trindad and Tobago.
1917 Sept 26: Escaped from U-boat.
1923 Sold to Straits SS Co, Singapore; renamed *Kudat.*
1941 Dec 31: Bombed and sunk by Japanese aircraft near Port Swettenham, South of Penang, Malaysia.

159 **BELIZE** (II)

Details as *Barima* (II) except:
T: 1,498 g.

1914 Mar 26: Launched for Trinidad–Tobago service.
1923 Sold to Government of Trinidad; same name.
1939 Acquired by Government of Mexico; renamed *Campeche.*
1942 Out of Lloyds Register.

TOWY, TAFF and TEIGN

160 **TOWY**

Bt 1914 Day, Summers & Co, Southampton; *T:* 204 g, 83 n.
Dim 110 ft 4in (33.63 m) × 21 ft 1in (6.43 m) × 10 ft 1in (3.07m)
Eng Sgl scr, compound; 2 cyls; 8 kts; By builder. Machinery aft.
H Steel, 1 deck; fcsle 25 ft (7.62 m).

1914 Lighter service at Southampton.
1920 Sold to Spillers Ltd, Cardiff; same name. Later Spillers Milling & Industrial Ltd.
1937 Broken up.

161 **TAFF**

Details as *Towy* (160).

1914 Entered service.
1920 Sold to J. Little & Co, Southampton; same name.
1921 Apr: Went aground, Southampton Water.
1922 May: Wrecked.

162 **TEIGN**

Details as *Towy* (160).

1914 Entered service.
1920 Sold to Spillers Ltd, Cardiff; same name. Later Spillers Milling & Industrial Ltd.
1937 Broken up.

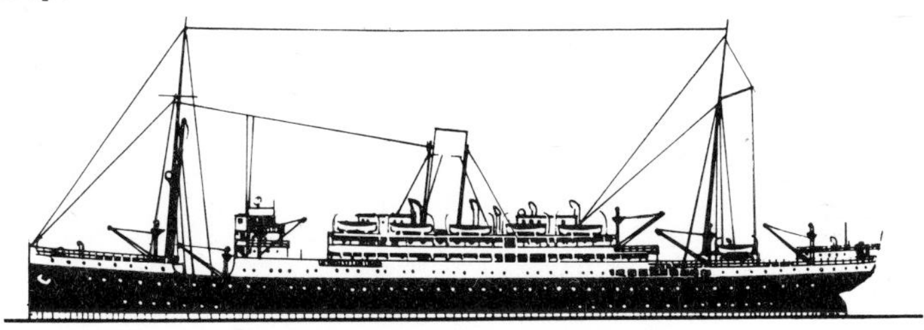

ESSEQUIBO (II) and EBRO (II)

163 **ESSEQUIBO** (II)

Bt 1915 Workman Clark & Co, Belfast; *T:* 8,489 g, 5,174 n.
Dim 450 ft 4in (137.26 m) × 57 ft 9in (17.6 m) × 30 ft 7in (9.32m)
Eng Tw scr, quad exp; 2 × 4 cyls; 1,055 NHP; Stm P: 215 lb; 2 dbl and sgl ended boilers, 24 furnaces.
H Steel, 2 decks; fcsle 71 ft (21.64 m), bridge 218 ft (66.45 m), poop 78 ft (23.77 m).
Pass 250 1st, 250 3rd. Crew: 320.

1914 July 6: Launched for Royal Mail Line. Nov 18: maiden voyage to South America, Captain J. C. Chevet.
1915 Taken over for use as a hospital ship.
1917 Stopped by U-64. Inspected, given "God speed you" and sent on her way.
1922 Acquired by PSNC; same name. Placed on New York–Panama Canal–Callao–Valparaiso service.
1930 Laid up.
1935 Mar: Sold to Arcos Ltd for £21,000, transferred to USSR and renamed *Neva.*
1957 Taken out of Lloyds Register at the owner's request.

164 **EBRO** (II)

Details as *Essequibo* (163).

1914 Sept 8: Launched for Royal Mail LIne.
1915 Apr 28: Maiden voyage to South America, then joined 10th Cruiser Squadron.
1922 Acquired by PSNC, same name; placed on New York–Panama Canal–Callao–Valparaiso service.
1930 Dec: Laid up in the River Dart.
1935 Feb: Sold to Jugoslavenska Lloyd; renamed *Princess Olga*. The price was £21,000. Dubrovnik–Haifa–Alexandria service.
1940 Sold to Cia Colonial, Lisbon; renamed *Serpa Pinto*. Lisbon–New York and Central America service.
1955 Broken up at Antwerp. Her price, by now, being £115,000.

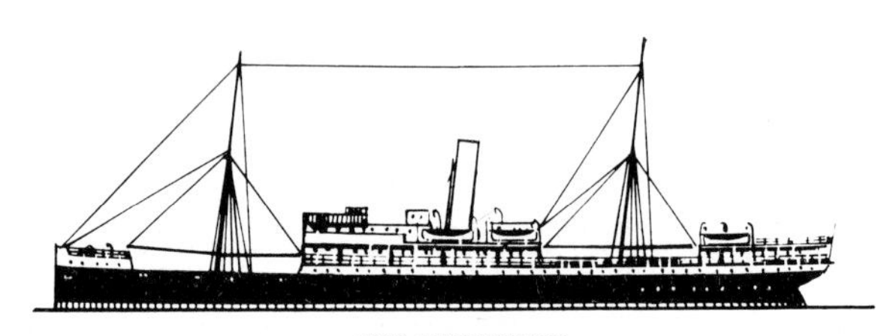

CHAUDIERE

165 **CHAUDIERE**

Bt 1899 Sir Raylton Dixon & Co, Middlesborough; *T:* 3,986 g, 2,500 n.
Dim 370 ft 1in (112.8 m) × 46 ft 2in (14.07 m) × 22 ft 6in (6.86m)
Eng Tw scr, tpl exp; 2 × 3 cyls; 584 NHP; 12 kts; By Wallsend Slipway Co, Newcastle.
H Steel, 2 decks; fcsle 42 ft (12.8 m), bridge and poop 261 ft (79.55 m).
Pass 108 1st, 52 2nd.

1899 Built as *Phillipyille* for Compagnie Maritime Belge du Congo. Purchased by Elder Dempster and renamed *Mandingo*. The sister of this ship was *Anversille* which became Elder Dempster's *Dakar*.
1914 Acquired by Royal Mail to replace the wrecked *Cobequid* (156); renamed *Chaudiere*. Placed on Canada–West Indies route.
1972 Broken up at Ardrossan, Scotland.

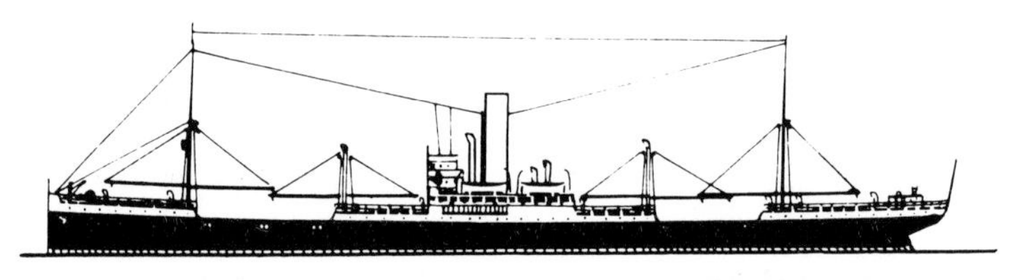

CARMARTHENSHIRE (II) and PEMBROKESHIRE

166 **CARMARTHENSHIRE** (II)

Bt 1915 Workman Clark, Belfast; *T:* 7,823 g, 4,969 n.
Dim 470 ft (143.26 m) × 58 ft 4in (17.78 m) × 27 ft 11in (8.51m)
Eng Sgl scr, quad exp; 4 cyls; 735 NHP; Stm P: 215 lb; 4 dbl ended boilers, 16 furnaces; 12 kts; By builder.
H Steel, 2 decks; fcsle 79 ft (24.08 m), bridge 171 ft (52.12 m), poop 99 ft (30.18 m).
Pass 12

1914 Nov 5: Launched.
1915 Feb 26: Maiden voyage Newport, Monmouthshire–River Plate, Captain J. Matthews.
1917 Apr 8: 200 miles south west of Lands End when attacked for two hours by U-boat gunfire. Replied shot for shot until, in heavy seas, the U-boat gave up the chase.
1929 Broken up.

167 **PEMBROKESHIRE**

Details as *Carmarthenshire* (166) except:
T: 7,821 g, 4,968 n.

1914 Dec 17: Launched.
1915 Apr 22: Maiden voyage Newport, Mon–River Plate. Captain Willats. Nov 16: Went ashore on Grand Canary; refloated.
1933 Sold and broken up.

LARNE (III)

168 **LARNE** (III)

Bt 1894 Robert Napier & Sons, Glasgow; *T:* 3,808 g, 2,410 n.
Dim 365 ft (111.25 m) × 45 ft 1in (13.74 m) × 20 ft 5in (6.22m)
Eng Sgl scr, tpl exp; 3 cyls; By builder.
H Steel, 2 decks and spar deck; fcsle 42 ft (12.8 m), bridge 80 ft (24.38 m).

1894 Oct 31: Maiden voyage as *Ninevah,* George Thomson's Aberdeen Line. London–Cape Town–Australia.
1907 Sold to Eastern & Australian SS Co; renamed *Aldenham*.
1916 Acquired by RMSP Meat Transports Ltd; became *Larne*.
1918 Sold to Zurbaran SS Co (MacAndrews & Co, managers) to become MacAndrew's first owned vessel.
1923 Broken up at Wilhelmshaven, Germany.

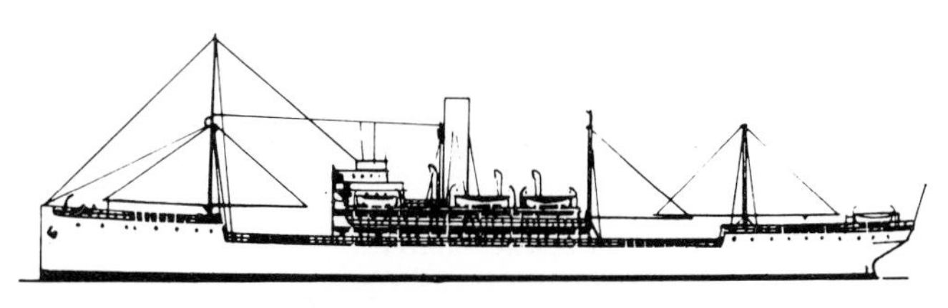

BRECKNOCKSHIRE

169 **BRECKNOCKSHIRE**

Bt 1917 Harland & Wolff, Belfast; *T:* 8,422 g, 5,201 n.
Dim 480 ft (146.3 m) × 59 ft 4in (18.08 m) × 27 ft 11in (8.51m)
Eng Sgl scr, tpl exp; 3 cyls; 12 kts; By builder.
H Steel, 2 decks. Note: illustration is taken from a blurred photograph of the sinking.

1914 Feb 9: Laid down; work suspended later in the year.
1916 Completion proceeded with.
1917 Jan 11: Maiden voyage to South America; Captain G. A. Mackenzie. Feb 15: Captured by the German raider *Moewe,* Count von Donha, and sunk.

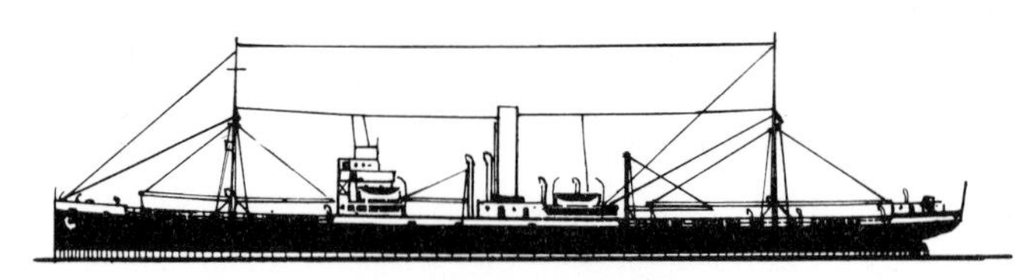

GLAMORGANSHIRE

170 **GLAMORGANSHIRE**

Bt 1918 Asano SB Co, Tsurumi, Japan; *T:* 8,192 g, 5,045 n.
Dim 445 ft (135.64 m) × 58 ft (17.68 m) × 28 ft 7in (8.71m)
Eng Tw scr, tpl exp; 2 × 3 cyls; 3,100 IHP; Stm P: 200 lb; 4 sgl ended boilers, 8 furnaces; 11 kts; By Kobe Steel Works, Kobe.
H Steel, 2 decks and shelter deck; 5 hatches; Cargo: 11,570 tons; Coal: 2,000 tons at 57 tons per day.
Pass 6.

1918 Built as *War Armour* for the Shipping Controller.
1919 Acquired by Royal Mail; renamed *Glamorganshire.*
1933 May: Broken up at Hendrik-ido-Ambracht, Holland.

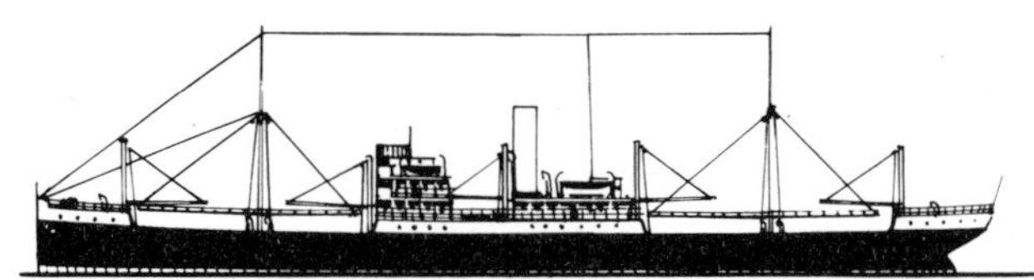

SAMBRE, SEGURA (II), SOMME, SEVERN (IV), SILARUS, SIRIS, SARTHE and SABOR (II)

171 **SAMBRE**

Bt 1919 Short Bros, Sunderland; *T:* 5,260 g, 3,226 n.
Dim 400 ft (121.92 m) × 52 ft 5in (15.98 m) × 28 ft 6in (8.69m)
Eng Sgl scr, tpl exp; 3 cyls; 517 NHP; Stm P: 180 lb; 3 sgl ended boilers, 6 furnaces; 10 kts; By G. Clark, Sunderland.
H Steel, 2 decks; fcsle 40 ft (12.19 m), bridge 110 ft (33.53 m), poop 49 ft (14.93 m); lattice work derricks.

1919 Laid down as the Standard "B" ship *War Swift* (II) Aug 29: Launched. Nov: Completed.
1920 Acquired by Royal Mail; renamed *Sambre.*
1940 July 27: Sunk by torpedo in mid-Atlantic en route Manchester–Philadelphia.

172 **SEGURA** (II)

Details as *Sambre* (171) except:
Bt 1919 Richardson, Duck & Co, Stockton-on-Tees; *T:* 5,295 g, 3,239 n.
Eng By Blair & Co, Stockton.

1919 Feb: completed as *War Pansy* (II).
1920 Renamed *Segura* by Royal Mail.

1921 Damaged by grounding.
1935 Became *Langton Grange*, Houlder Bros.
1937 Sold to Embericos Bros; renamed *Nicolaos Embericos.*
1939 Nov 4: Mined and sunk off East Goodwin Sands.

173 **SOMME**

Details as *Sambre* (171) except:
T: 5,265 g, 3,230 n.
Eng By North East Marine, Sunderland.

1919 June 17: Launched as *War Toucan.*
1920 Renamed *Somme* by Royal Mail.
1942 Feb 16: Torpedoed en route London–Bermuda.

174 **SEVERN** (IV)

Details as *Sambre* (171) except:
T: 5,246 g, 3,253 n.
Eng By North East Marine, Sunderland.

1919 Apr 2: Launched as *War Pelican.*
1932 Sold: renamed *Leonidas* (II).
1934 Ran aground at Ranzow, near Arkona, Baltic Sea, refloated and towed to Kiel. Aug: Broken up at Haulbowline, Cork.

175 **SILARUS**

Details as *Sambre* (171) except:
Bt Charles Connell & Co, Glasgow; *T:* 5,101 g, 3,237 n.
Eng By Dunsmuir & Jackson, Glasgow.

1919 Aug: Launched as *Silarus* for Royal Mail.
1931 Sold to G. N. Stathos, Piraeus; renamed *Nemea.*
1941 Jan 16: Torpedoed off Africa en route Barry Docks–Cape Town.

176 **SIRIS**

Details as *Sambre* (171) except:
Bt and **Eng** Harland & Wolff, Greenock; *T:* 5,242 g, 3,266 n. Harland & Wolff, Greenock was formerly Caird & Co.

1919 June 26: Launched. Oct: Completed as *Siris.*
1942 July 12: Sunk by torpedo and gunfire in the mid Atlantic en route Hull–Rio de Janeiro.

177 **SARTHE**

Details as *Sambre* (171) except:
Bt 1919 Wm Gray & Co; *T:* 5,271 g, 3,243 n.
Eng By Central Marine Engine Works, West Hartlepool.

1919 Nov 22: Launched as *Sarthe* for sale to Royal Mail.
1920 Purchased by Royal Mail.
1942 Oct 8: Sunk 34.50 S 18.40 E en route Aden–Rio de Janeiro.

178 **SABOR** (II)

Details as *Sambre* (171) except:
Bt and **Eng** 1920 Earle's Co, Hull; *T:* 5,212 g, 3,227 n.

1920 Jan 24: Launched as *War Whale II.* Apr 19: Completed.
1943 Torpedoed in the Indian Ocean en route Mombasa–Rio de Janeiro.

NAVASOTA, NAGARA, NARIVA and NATIA

179 **NAVASOTA**

Bt 1918 Swan Hunter & Wigham Richardson, Newcastle; *T:* 8,803 g, 5,523 n.
Dim 430 ft (131.06 m) × 61 ft 4in (18.69 m) × 39 ft (11.89 m); Dft 30 ft 4 in (9.25 m)
Eng Tw scr, quad exp; 2 × 4 cyls; 1,094 NHP; Stm P: 215 lb; 5 sgl ended boilers, 20 furnaces oil fired. Fuel: 1,982 tons oil.
H Steel, 2 decks and awning deck; fcsle 44 ft (13.41), bridge 211 ft (64.31 m).

1917 June 19. Launched. Dec: Completed.
1918 Mar 17: Entered service; owned by RMSP Meat Transports Ltd. Dazzle painted; maiden voyage North Shields–River Plate. Captain J. E. P. Williams.
1939 Dec 5: Sunk by torpedo 150 miles west of Bishops Rock en route Liverpool–Buenos Aires. 37 lost.

180 **NAGARA**

Details as *Navasota* (179) except:
T: 8,803 g, 5,455 n.

1918 June: Entered UK–River Plate service.
1927 Sept 28: Collided with Houlder's *Crofton Hall* in the River Plate and sank in shallow water. Salved.
1943 Mar 29: Torpedoed and sunk, 400 miles off Land's End.

181 **NARIVA**

Details as *Navasota* (179) except:
Bt 1920 Alex Stephen & Sons, Glasgow; *T:* 8,723 g, 5,427 n.

1920 May: Completed.
1943 Mar 17: Sunk, mid Atlantic.

182 **NATIA**

Details as *Navasota* (179) except:
Bt 1920 Alex Stephen & Sons, Glasgow; *T:* 8,723 g, 5,427 n.

1920 Dec: Completed.
1940 Oct 8: Sunk in Atlantic.

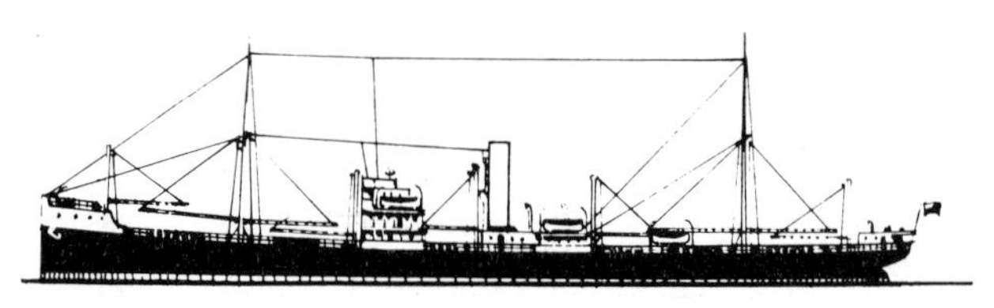

RADNORSHIRE (II)

183 **RADNORSHIRE** (II)

Bt 1919 J. L. Thompson & Sons, Sunderland; *T:* 6,723 g, 4,133 n, 10,795 dwt.
Dim 411 ft 7 in (125.45m) × 55ft 7 in (16.94 m) × 29 ft (8.84m)

Eng Sgl scr, tpl exp; 3 cyls; 3,650 IHP; Stm P: 180 lb; 3 sgl ended boilers; 12 kts; By J. Dickinson & Sons, Sunderland.
H Steel, 2 decks; fcsle 36 ft (10.97 m). Cargo: 530,000 cu ft (15,000 cu m); Crew: 60.

1919 June 12: Launched as *War Diamond.* Oct 6: Trials.
1920 Acquired by Royal Mail; renamed *Radnorshire.*
1930 Sold to Thomson S. S. Co, London; renamed *Sithonia.*
1942 July 13: Torpedoed en route Barry Dock, South Wales– Montevideo at position 29N 25W.

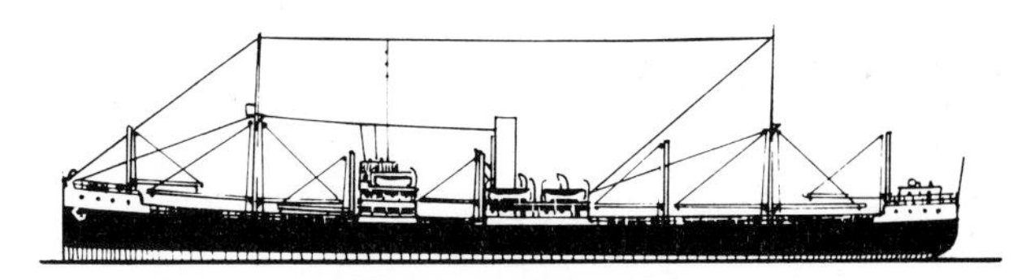

MONTGOMERYSHIRE

184 **MONTGOMERYSHIRE**

Bt 1921 Armstrong Whitworth, Newcastle; *T:* 6,650 g, 4,097 n, 14,193 disp.
Dim 412 ft 6 in (125.73 m) × 55 ft 9 in (16.99 m) × 28 ft 2 in (8.58 m).
Eng Tw scr, 2 geared turbines; 2,450 SHP; 3 water tube boilers; 10½ kts; By North East Marine Engine Co, Newcastle; turbines by Parsons Marine Turbine Co.
H Steel, 1 deck and shelter deck; fcsle 45 ft (13.72 m), poop 42 ft (12.8 m), 22 winches, 21 derricks; Cargo: 8,340 tons.

1921 Apr: Entered service.
1931 Sold to Societa Commerciale di Nav, Genoa; renamed *Riv.*
1941 Apr 6: Sunk in Mediterranean.

ARNO (III)

185 **ARNO** (III)

Bt 1916 Gebruder Bodewes, Martenshoek, Holland; *T:* 345 g, 277 n.
Dim 142 ft 4 in (43.38 m) × 25 ft 3 in (7.7 m) × 11 ft 4 in (3.45 m).
Eng Sgl scr, paraffin; 2 cyls; 46 RHP; 9 kts; By J. & C. G. Bolinders, Stockholm, Sweden.
H Steel, 1 deck.

1916 Built as the auxiliary engined Schooner *Nösted III.*
1920 Acquired by Royal Mail; renamed *Arno.*
1933 Oct: Went aground and damaged. Sold.

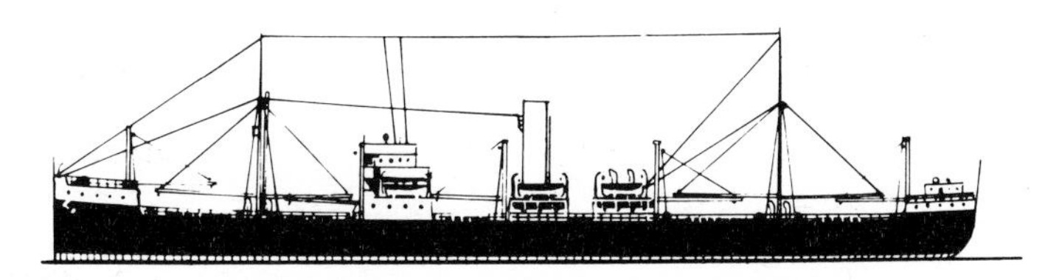

NARENTA, NICTHEROY and NEBRASKA

186 **NARENTA**

Bt 1919 Workman Clark, Belfast; *T:* 8,266 g, 5,170 n.

Dim 450 ft (137.16 m) × 58 ft (17.68 m) × 29 ft 4 in (8.94 m); Dft 40 ft (12.19 m).
Eng Sgl scr, 2 sgl reduction geared turbines; 12 kts; By builder.
H Steel, 3 decks; fcsle 44 ft (13.41 m), poop 35 ft (10.67 m); Cargo: 400,000 cu ft (11,320 cu m) refrigerated.

This class were laid down as Standard 'G' but modified during construction.

1919 Laid down as *Neganti.* Aug 27: Launched as *Narenta.* Frozen meat carrier.
1939 Sold; became *Kosei Maru,* Nippon Suisan KK, Japan.
1943 Apr 7: Sunk by submarine USS *Tunny* off Caroline Islands.

187 **NICTHEROY**

Details as *Narenta* (186) except:
T: 8,265 g, 5,159 n.

1920 May 20: Launched. Dec 22: Delivered.
1937 Sold to Achille Lauro, Naples; renamed *Cuma.*
1940 Became *Ipanemaloide,* Lloyd Brasileiro, Rio de Janeiro. Oct 18: Sunk by submarine off Licata, Sicily.

188 **NEBRASKA**

Details as *Narenta* (186) except:
T: 8,261 g, 5,163 n.

1919 Dec 9: Launched.
1920 Aug 4: Delivered.
1944 Apr 8: Torpedoed off Ascension Island en route Gibraltar–Buenos Aires.

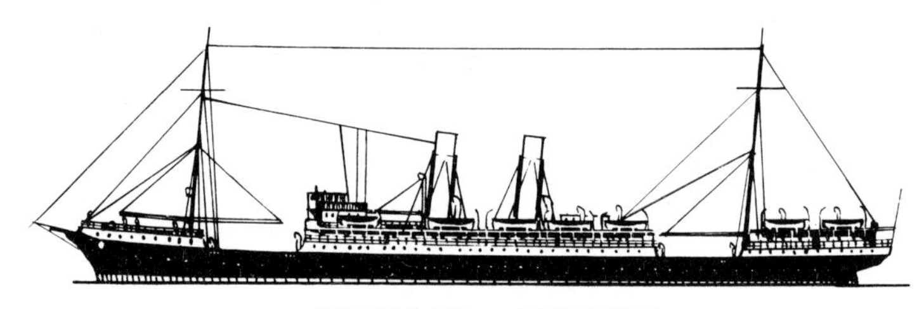

ORUBA (II) and ORCANA

189 **ORCANA**

Bt 1903 Alex Stephen & Sons, Glasgow; *T:* 6,793 g, 3,691 n.
Dim 454 ft 10 in (138.63 m) × 55 ft (16.76 m) × 30 ft (9.14 m).
Eng Tw scr, tpl exp; 2 × 3 cyls; 1,218 NHP; Stm P: 200 lb; 2 dbl ended and 1 sgl ended boiler, 21 furnaces; 15 kts; By builder.
H Steel, 3 decks; fcsle 74 ft (22.56 m), bridge 167 ft (50.9 m), poop 92 ft (28.04 m).
Pass 150 1st, 170 3rd.

1903 Built as *Miltiades* for Aberdeen Line. Nov 3: Maiden voyage London–Cape Town–Melbourne–Sydney.
1913 Lengthened to 504 ft 4 in (153.72 m); *T:* 7,814 g, 4,892 n. Bridge 217 ft (66.14 m). Second funnel, a dummy, added. Pass: 89 1st, 158 3rd.
1915 Troopship.
1920 June 4: Resumed commercial service to Australia. Nov 20: Last departure from Australia. Then acquired by Royal Mail and renamed *Orcana.*
1922 Transferred to PSNC; same name.
1924 Broken up at Hendrik-ido-Ambracht, Holland.

190 **ORUBA** (II)

Details as *Orcana* (189) except:
Bt 1904; *T:* 6,795 g, 3,695 n.

1904 Built for Aberdeen Line as *Marathon*. Jan 27: Maiden voyage London–Cape Town–Melbourne–Sydney.
1912 Lengthened and modified as *Orcana*. *T:* 7,848 g.
1915 Trooping duties.
1920 Oct 21: Reverted to Aberdeen service to Australia, made only one voyage. Sold to Royal Mail Line; renamed *Oruba*.
1922 Transferred to PSNC. Placed on South American service.
1924 Broken up in Germany.

ORCA

191 **ORCA**

Bt 1918 Harland & Wolff, Belfast; *T:* 15,120 g, 9,614 n, 11,380 dwt.
Dim 574 ft (174.96 m) oa, 550 ft 4 in (167.74 m) × 67 ft 4 in (20.52 m) × 43 ft (13.11 m).
Eng Tpl scr, tpl exp exhausting to a direct geared forward drive only turbine connected to the centre shaft. 4 cyl; 1,362 HP; Stm P: 215 lb; 6 dbl ended boilers with 36 furnaces; 15 kts; By builder. Note: Engine a duplicate of that in *Orduna* (196).
H Steel, 3 decks with a 4th deck fore and aft of the machinery space. Boat deck 230 ft (70.1 m); 10 bulkheads, 6 holds.
Pass 1918: Nil. 1922: 190 1st, 220 2nd, 480 3rd.

1918 Jan 15: Launched. Completed as a cargo carrier for PSNC.
1921 Feb 18: Arrived at builder's for completion as designed.
1922 Dec 18: After completion as a passenger liner made her first sailing Southampton–Hamburg–New York.
1923 Transferred to Royal Mail Line ownership.
1927 Jan: Sold to White Star Line service; renamed *Calgaric*. *T:* 16,063 g, 9,614 n. Pass: 290 1st, 550 tourist, 330 3rd. May 4: First voyage Liverpool–Quebec–Montreal. Pass: 100 cabin, 500 3rd.
1931 Laid up at Milford Haven, made one cruise to the Baltic with Boy Scouts.
1933 June 9: Commenced a summer season of voyages Liverpool–Montreal. Sept 9: Laid up at Milford Haven again.
1934 Sold for £31,000 and scrapped at Rosyth during 1935. The ship was only 16 years old.

CULEBRA

192 **CULEBRA**

Bt 1919 Irvine's SB Dry Dock Co, West Hartlepool; *T:* 3,044 g, 1,834 n.

Dim 331 ft (100.89 m) × 46 ft 8 in (14.22 m) × 23 ft 1 in (7.04 m).
Eng Sgl scr, tpl exp; 3 cyls; 310 NHP; 10 kts; By Richardsons, Westgarth & Co, Hartlepool.
H Steel, 2 decks.

1919 Aug 28: Built as *War Mirage,* 'C' type standard ship. Became *Riposto* for J. Glynn & Sons, Liverpool.
1922 Acquired by Royal Mail and renamed *Culebra.*
1941 Sept 26: Went aground Strait of Belle Isle, Labrador.
1942 Jan 5: Left Loch Ewe in convoy for Bermuda. A storm scattered the convoy and *Culebra* failed to regain contact. Jan 17: Sunk in North Atlantic by U-boat gunfire. All aboard, 39 crew and 6 gunners lost.

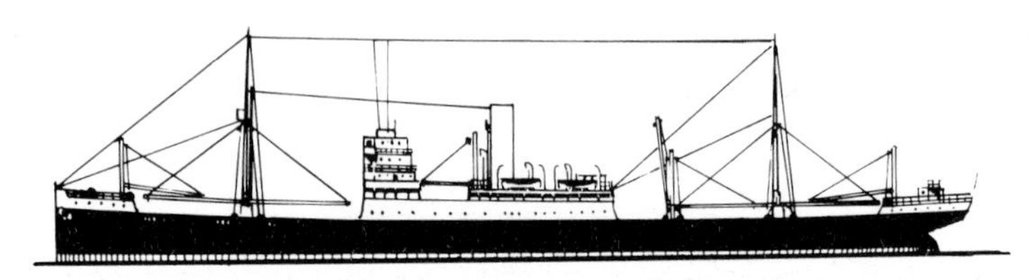

LOCHKATRINE, LOCHGOIL and LOCHMONAR

193 **LOCHKATRINE**

Bt 1921 John Brown & Co, Glasgow; *T:* 9,409 g, 5,812 n.
Dim 485 ft 6 in (147.98 m) × 62 ft 3 in (18.97 m) × 29 ft 6 in (8.99 m).
Eng Tw scr, oil 4 stroke, sgl acting; 2 × 16 cyls; 6,400 BHP; 12 kts; fuel: 1,300 tons oil at 19½ tons per day.
H Steel, 2 decks and awning deck; fcsle 59 ft (17.98 m), bridge 153 ft (46.63 m), poop 40 ft (12.19 m); Cargo: 11,000 tons, 6 hatches, 14 winches.
Pass 12.

1921 Built for UK–Panama Canal–Los Angeles–San Francisco–Vancouver service.
1942 Aug 3: Torpedoed by U-boat 300 miles east of Newfoundland. 8 crew and 1 passenger lost.

194 **LOCHGOIL**

Details as *Lochkatrine* (193) except:
Bt 1922 Harland & Wolff, Glasgow; *T:* 9,462 g, 5,873 n.

1922 Built for UK–Panama Canal–North Pacific coast ports.
1939 Oct 9: Mined but reached port. Taken over by the Government; renamed *Empire Rowan.*
1943 Mar 27: Sunk by air attack near to Gibraltar.

195 **LOCHMONAR**

Details as *Lochkatrine* (193) except:
Bt 1923 Harland & Wolff, Belfast; *T:* 9,412 g, 5,815 n.

1923 Built for UK–Panama Canal–North Pacific coast ports.
1927 Nov 30: The steering gear failed while coming up the River Mersey into Liverpool and the ship went aground breaking in two. A new fore part was built.
1949 Sold and broken up.

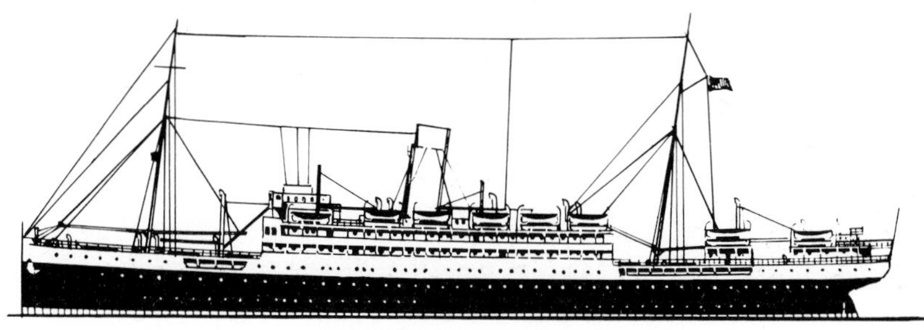

ORDUNA (I) and ORBITA (I)

196 **ORDUNA** (I)

Bt 1914 Harland & Wolff, Belfast; *T:* 15,507 g, 9,548 n, 12,370 dwt.
Dim 570 ft (173.74 m) oa, 550 ft 4 in (167.64 m) × 67 ft 4 in (20.52 m) × 43 ft (13.11 m); Dft 32 ft 6 in (9.91 m) to give 25,230 tons disp.
Eng Tpl scr, tpl exp exhausting to a direct acting turbine connected to the centre shaft; 2 × 4 cyl (2LP); 1,362 HP; Stm P: 215 lb; 6 dbl ended boilers and 36 furnaces; 15 kts; By builder. The turbine had no reverse gearing.
H Steel, 4 decks. Cargo: 9,324 tons. fuel: 2,272 tons coal.
Pass 240 1st, 180 2nd, 700 3rd.

1913 Oct 2: Launched as *Orduña* (pronounced Ordunya). Originally intended to be named *Ormeda.*
1914 Feb 19: Maiden voyage Liverpool–Straits of Megallan–West coast of South America. Oct: Chartered to Cunard for Liverpool–New York service. Recorded as being painted in Cunard colours but only the funnel was changed. Nov 1: First Cunard sailing.
1915 July 9: Attacked by submarine torpedo and gunfire 30 miles south of Queenstown. Escaped.
1918 June: Sank a German U-boat by gunfire. Dec: Collided with and sank Elder Dempster's *Konakry* off Galley Head, Ireland.
1919 End of Cunard charter; returned to PSNC.
1921 Operated by Royal Mail Line Hamburg–New York service. May 28: First sailing.
1923 Jan 1: Resumed service after a refit. Pass: 190 1st, 221 2nd, 476 3rd.
1926 Converted to oil fuel; Pass: 234 1st, 186 2nd, 458 3rd.
1927 Reverted to PSNC service to West coast of South America.
1941 Taken over as a troopship.
1950 Nov: De-commissioned as a trooper, laid up.
1951 Broken up at Dalmuir after 37 years of exemplary service.

197 **ORBITA** (I)

Details as *Orduna* (161) except:

1914 Building was slowed down because of the war.
1919 Completed as designed. A number of other liners under construction by Harland & Wolff were completed without passenger superstructure and entered service as massive cargo vessels. See *Orca* (191). *T:* 15,495 g, 10,140 n. Pass: 190 1st, 221 2nd, 476 3rd.
1914 July 7: Launched. Provision for 6 × 6 in (15.24 cm) guns was constructed into the hull.
1919 Mar: Completion work commenced. Sept: Maiden voyage Liverpool–South America via Panama Canal.
1921 Apr 30: Chartered to Royal Mail for Hamburg–New York service.
1923 Jan 1: Transferred with *Orduña* (196) to Royal Mail ownership.
1927 Fitted to burn oil fuel. Reverted to PSNC service to South America.
1941 Troopship.
1950 Broken up by Thos W. Ward at Newport, Monmouthshire.

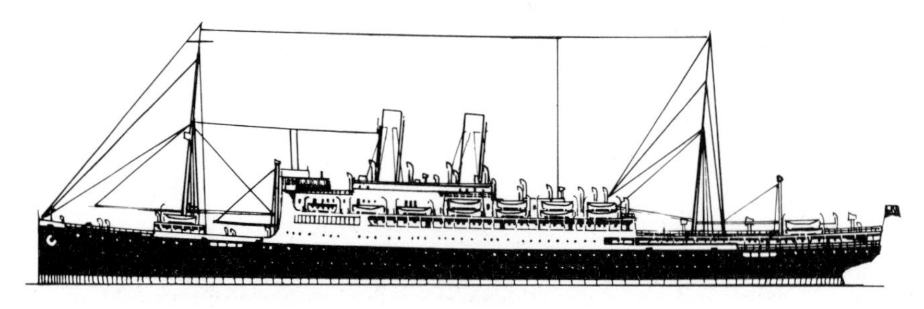

OHIO

198 **OHIO**

Bt 1919 A. G. Weser, Bremen; *T:* 18,490 g, 10,234 n.
Dim 614 ft 6 in (187.3 m) oa, 591 ft (180.14 m) × 71 ft 6 in (21.79 m) × 37 ft 1 in (11.3 m).
Eng Tw scr, quad exp; 2 × 4 cyls; 16,000 NHP; 2 boiler rooms, 6 dbl and 1 sgl ended boilers; 16,100 IHP; 17 kts; By builder.
H Steel, 3 decks, 10 watertight compartments, 6 holds.
Pass 229 1st, 523 2nd, 690 3rd.

1914 Laid down but no construction during the war.
1919 Intended as *Munchen* for Norddeutscher Lloyd's intermediate North Atlantic service.
1920 Mar 23: Launched. Surrendered as reparations to Royal Mail. Mar 27: Named *Ohio* and was the company's largest ship when she ran her trials.
1923 Apr 3: Maiden voyage Hamburg–Southampton–Cherbourg–New York in 8 days.
1925 Southampton–New York service. The German lines now served the Hamburg berth.
1927 Feb: Transferred to White Star Line; renamed *Albertic,* cost £1 million. This move followed the acquisition of the company by Royal Mail. Apr 22: First voyage Liverpool–Quebec–Montreal. Later transferred to London sailings. Pass: 270 cabin, 1,100 tst.
1928 May: Transferred to London–Southampton–Quebec–Montreal route.
1929 Replaced the lost *Celtic* on Liverpool–New York route. Pass: 218 cabin, 496 tst, 565 3rd.
1933 Mar: Laid up in the Clyde at Holy Loch.
1934 Transferred into Cunard–White Star ownership but never used by them. July: Sold to Japanese Ship breakers for £34,000. Broken up at Osaka only fourteen years old.

ARUN

199 **ARUN**

Bt 1925 Svendborg Skibsvaerf, Svendborg; *T:* 384 g, 267 n.
Dim 124 ft 4 in (37.9 m) × 24 ft 7 in (7.49 m) × 16 ft 4 in (4.98 m).
Eng Sgl scr, oil, 2 stroke direct acting; 3 cyls; 10 kts; by J. V. Svenssons Mek, Stockholm.
H Steel, 2 decks.

1925 Built as *Polonia,* A/S Svendborg Skibs, T. C. Christensen. Manager, Copenhagen.
1927 Acquired and stationed at Kingston, Jamaica.
1951(?) Sold.

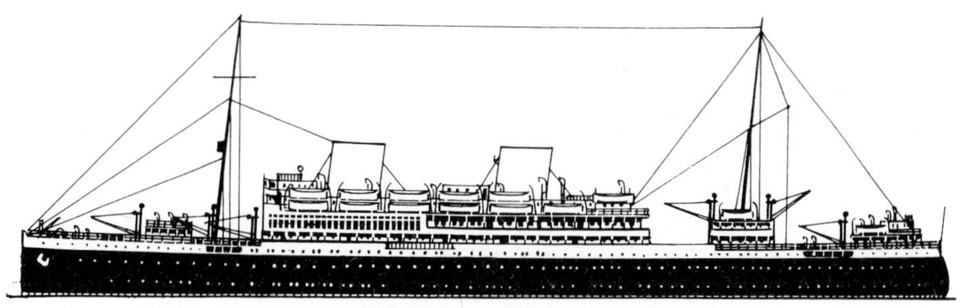

ASTURIAS (II) and ALCANTARA

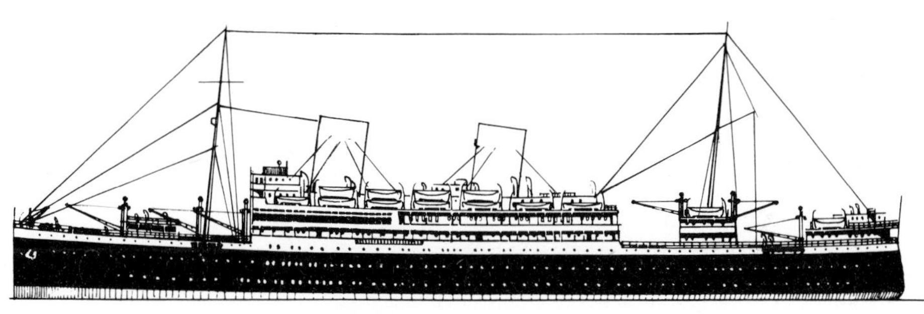

ASTURIAS (II) and ALCANTARA

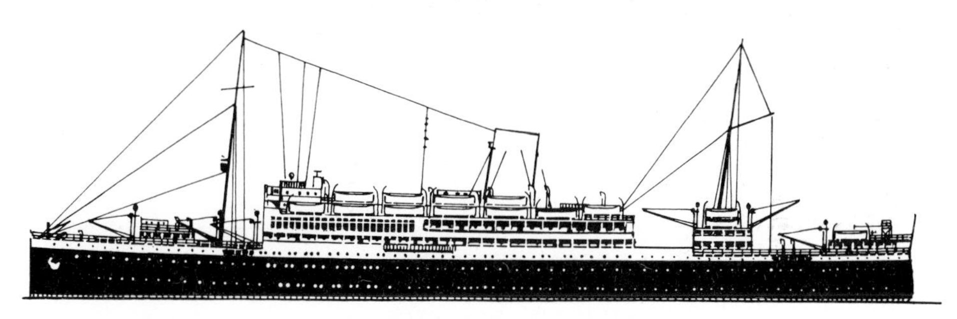

ASTURIAS (II) and ALCANTARA

200 **ASTURIAS** (II)

Bt 1925 Harland & Wolff, Belfast; *T:* 22,048 g, 13,226 n, 13,000 dwt.
Dim 655 ft 9 in (199.87 m) oa, 630 ft 6 in (192.1 m) × 78 ft 6 in (23.93 m) × 40 ft 6 in (12.34 m).
Eng Tw scr, oil; 4 stroke dbl acting with air blast injection; 8 cyls; 15,000 BHP; 10,000 IHP; 17 kts at 115 rpm and 70 tons of oil fuel per day; By builder.
H Steel, 4 decks; 6 hatches served by 1½ ton lift hydraulic cranes except No 2 hatch which had 2 × 5 ton cranes. Two CO_2 refrigeration plants electric drive.
Pass 432 1st, 223 2nd, 453 3rd; Crew: 450.

1925 July 7: Launched by the Duchess of Abercorn. The first cruiser stern passenger ship for Royal Mail. The fore funnel was a dummy. Was at that time the largest motor ship in the world. Registered as owned by RMSP Meat Transports Ltd.
1926 Feb 26: Maiden voyage Southampton–River Plate. Captained by Commodore E. W. E. Morrison. Speed poor and bad vibration.
1927 Jan and Apr: Made voyages Southampton–New York.
1934 Re-engined, the work took five months with 2 Parsons sgl reduction geared turbines

20,000 SHP. The bow was re-shaped and lengthened by 10 ft (3.05 m). New propellers fitted 17 ft 6 in (5.33 m) dia; 19 kts; Funnels heightened by 15 ft (4.57 m); 3 Johnson Boilers of 7 oil furnaces each. Pass: 331 1st, 220 2nd, 768 3rd; Crew: 425.
1935 Attended Silver Jubilee Naval Review at Spithead.
1939 Converted into an Armed Merchant Cruiser on the South Atlantic Patrol. Fore funnel and mainmast removed to improve the arc of fire of her anti-aircraft guns.
1943 July: Torpedoed in the South Atlantic, towed by *Zwarte Zee* 500 miles to Freetown. Lay for 2 years with the engine room flooded. Abandoned by Royal Mail and taken over by the Government.
1945 Towed to Gibraltar by *Zwarte Zee* and *Thames* with an escort of seven corvettes and patched up. Taken to Belfast for full repairs. Became a Government emigrant carried. One funnel. Pass: 219 1st, 185 2nd, 462 3rd.
1953 Repatriated British troops from Korea.
1954 Further refurbishing. Emerged in regular peace time troopship colours; white hull, board blue band, yellow funnel.
1957 Sold for breaking up. But just prior to commencement the ship was used at Faslane to play the part of *Titanic* in the film "A Night to Remember". The filming was done in winter and at night to create the cold atmosphere. 400 ft (121.92 m) of the white hull was painted black for the task.

201 **ALCANTARA** (II)

Details as *Asturias* (200) except:
Bt 1926; *T:* 22,181 g, 13,206 n.
Pass 410 1st, 232 2nd, 768 3rd.

1926 Sept 23: Launched as the largest motor ship in the world.
1927 Feb 8: Handed over at Belfast. May 4: Maiden voyage Southampton–Cherbourg–Lisbon–Las Palmas–Rio de Janeiro–Buenos Aires. Commodore M. S. Nicholson.
1931 Brough the Prince of Wales and Duke of Kent to Montevideo for the British Empire Exhibition.
1934 Refitted in the same way as *Asturias;* took 5 months.
1935 May 4: Under Commodore B. Shillitoe returned to service. Attended the Silver Jubilee Naval Review with *Asturias.*
1939 Sept 17: Became an Armed Merchant Cruiser at Devonport with 1 × 4 in (10.16 cm) gun. Sent to Malta for proper arming. En route, whilst zig-zagging, was run into by Cunard's *Franconia. Alcantara's* port side was badly damaged and the two ships crunched alongside each other temporarily locked together. She then proceeded to Alexandria for major repairs. Nov: Fitted with 8 × 6 in (15.24 cm) guns. Fore funnel and main mast removed. Hotchkiss anti-aircraft guns were positioned in place of the funnel. Stationed on the South Atlantic patrol.
1940 July 28: After leaving Trinidad *Alcantara* sighted a Swedish ship which turned out to be the German raider *Thor.* At 1 p.m. *Thor* opened fire. In the ensuing exchange of gunfire *Alcantara* was hit on the water line and forced to reduce speed thereby enabling *Thor* to escape *Alcantara* transferred oil to her port tanks and raised the shell hole above the waterline but *Thor* had gone.
1943 June 30: Sent for conversion into a troopship. The work took almost a year.
1944 Mar 14: First trooping voyage to the Mediterranean; Captain W. H. Wright.
1948 Oct 8: After reconditioning at Belfast returned to Commercial service. 220 1st, 185 cabin, 462 3rd; Crew: 450. Main mast re-installed but not the fore funnel.
1954 Lost her starboard propeller at Buenos Aires; came home on one screw.
1958 Apr 17: Final voyage number 172. Then sold for £240,000 to Japan for scrapping. Renamed *Kaisho Maru* for her last voyage; the first liner to go to Japan since before the war.

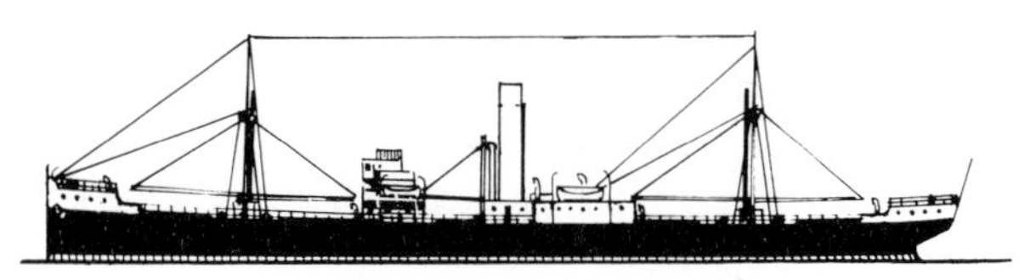

SICILY and LOMBARDY

202 **SICILY**

Bt 1913 Richardson Duck & Co, Stockton-on-Tees; *T:* 3,457 g, 2,146 n.
Dim 380 ft (115.82 m) × 48 ft 1 in (14.66 m) × 23 ft 4 in (7.11 m).
Eng Sgl scr, tpl exp; 3 cyls; 352 NHP; Stm P: 180 lb; 3 sgl ended boilers; 12 kts; By Blair & Co, Stockton.
H Steel, 1 deck and shelter deck. Cellular dbl bottom tanks carried oil fuel.

1913 Dec 13: Launched for David MacIver & Co as *Sicily*.
1914 Feb 16: Trials and handed over.
1933 Jan: Taken over by Royal Mail. July: Sold to MA Embericos, Piraeus, for £5,200 and renamed *Pagasitikos*.
1937 Nov: Sold to Societe Commerciale d'Affretments; became *Francois*.
1939 Captured by Spanish Naval forces during the Spanish Civil War. Operated by Government as *Castillo de Andrade*.
1940 Renamed *Castillo Andrade* of Cia Trasmediterranea.
1944 Caught fire and had to be scruttled at Bilbao.
1945 Raised and rebuilt as *Antartico,* Empresa Elcano, Spain.
1959 Oct 6: Stranded and lost at the entrance to Santander en route for Lobitos.

203 **LOMBARDY** (I)

Details as *Sicily* (202) except:
Bt 1920; *T:* 3,379 g, 2,067 n.

1920 Built for David MacIver as *Lombardy*.
1932 Taken over by Royal Mail.
1956 May: Sold for £72,000 to Far East Metal Industries & Shipping Co; renamed *Metal Trader*.
1957 Nov: Sold for breaking up by Hong Kong Salvage & Towage Co.
1958 Arrived Hong Kong for breaking up.

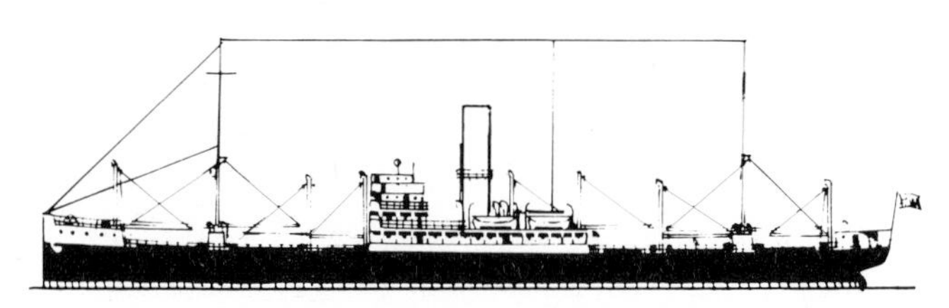

NELA, NASINA and NALON

204 **NELA**

Bt 1915 Russell & Co, Glasgow; *T:* 7,206 g, 3,400 n.
Dim 440 ft (134.11 m) × 56 ft 2 in (17.12 m) × 35 ft 7 in (10.85 m); Dft 28 ft 4 in (8.64 m).
Eng Tw scr, quad exp; 2 × 4 cyls; 885 NHP; 12 kts; By D. Rowan & Co, Glasgow.
H Steel, 3 decks and shelter deck; fcsle 48 ft (14.63 m), 6 hatches, 20 derricks.

1915 Mar: Built for Lamport & Holt as *Moliere*.
1929 Transferred to Nelson Steam Navigation Co; same name.

1932 Taken over, with Nelson fleet, by Royal Mail; renamed *Nela.*
1946 Jan: Broken up at Ghent.

205 **NASINA**

Details as *Nela* (204) except:
Bt 1915 Harland & Wolff, Belfast; *T:* 7,206 g, 4,432 n.

1915 June: Built as *Meisonnier* for Lamport & Holt.
1929 Transferred to Nelson Line; same name.
1932 Taken over by Royal Mail; renamed *Nasina.*
1935 Sold to Societa Anonima Cooperativa di Nav Garibaldi, Genoa, Italy; renamed *Asmara.*
1939 Taken over as a transport by Italian Navy.
1943 Aug 11: Sunk by the British submarine *Unshaken.*

206 **NALON**

Details as *Nela* (204) except:
Bt 1915 Harland & Wolff, Belfast; *T:* 7,206 g, 4,432 n.

1915 Sept: Built as *Murillo* for Lamport & Holt.
1929 Transferred to Nelson Line; same name.
1932 Taken over by Royal Mail; renamed *Nalon.*
1940 Nov 6: Attacked and sunk by aircraft at 53° 57′N 15° 31′W.

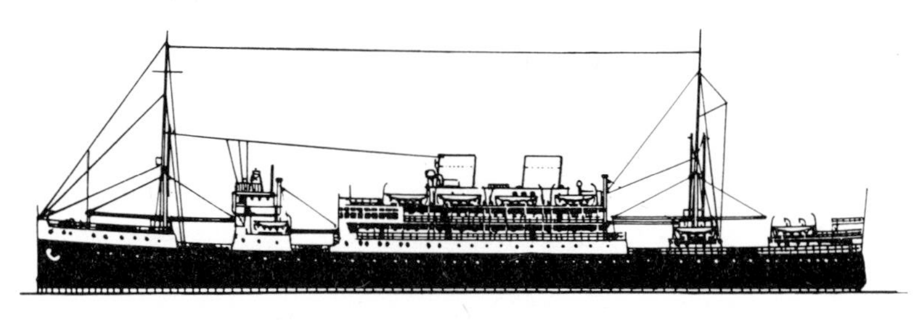

HIGHLAND MONARCH, HIGHLAND CHIEFTAIN, HIGHLAND BRIGADE, HIGHLAND PRINCESS and HIGHLAND PATRIOT

207 **HIGHLAND MONARCH**

Bt 1928 Harland & Wolff, Belfast; *T:* 14,139 g, 8,734 n.
Dim 545 ft (166.12 m) oa, 523 ft 4 in (159.41 m) × 69 ft 4 in (21.13 m) × 37 ft 1 in (11.3 m).
Eng Tw scr, oil; 4 stroke dbl acting; 2 × 8 cyls; 2,190 NHP; 15 kts; By builder to Burmeister & Wain design.
H Steel, 4 decks; fcsle 101 ft (30.78 m), bridge 97 ft (29.57 m). 520,000 cu ft (14,716 cu m) meat.
Pass 150 1st, 70 Intermediate, 500 3rd.

1928 May 3: Launched. Designed by Mr A. R. T. Wood, Director and General Manager of Nelson Line. Decorated in "Old English" style. This ship was generally the most popular of the five sisters. Oct 18: Maiden voyage London–Buenos Aires.
1932 Aug 20: Last sailing in Nelson Line colours. Transferred to Royal Mail; same name.
1939 Trooping duties.
1946 Resumed commercial service before refitting.
1948 Reverted to River Plate service; *T:* 14,216 g; Pass: 104 1st, 335 3rd.
1960 Apr 28: Broken up by W. H. Arnott Young at Dalmuir. The last surviving vessel of the Nelson Line.

208 **HIGHLAND CHIEFTAIN**

Details as *Highland Monarch* (207) except:
Bt 1929; *T:* 14,131 g, 8,730 n.

1928 June 21: Launched.
1929 Jan 26: Delivered to the Nelson Line for London – River Plate service. Feb 21: Maiden voyage London – Buenos Aires.
1932 Transferred to Royal Mail; same name.
1939 Trooping duties.
1940 Oct 11: Damaged by bombing at Liverpool.
1948 Resumed River Plate service.
1959 Jan: Sold to Calpe Shipping Co, Gibraltar; renamed *Calpean Star* for use in the whaling industry as a store, accommodation and frozen whale meat transporter.
1960 Mar: Rudder damaged off Montevideo. Left in tow for repair but went aground after a boiler room explosion and left there. Slowly disintegrated.
1965 The Wreck was cut up for scrap.

209 **HIGHLAND BRIGADE**

Details as *Highland Monarch* (207) except:
Bt 1929; *T:* 14,131 g, 8,732 n.

1928 Nov 1: Launched.
1929 Apr 27: Completed. The second ship of this name built for Nelson Line. Placed on London – River Plate run.
1932 Transferred to Royal Mail; same name.
1940 Trooping duties.
1946 Jan 18: Damaged by mine off Singapore with 2,200 Indian troops aboard; no casualties.
1947 Resumed commercial service.
1959 Sold to John Latsis, Piraeus; renamed *Henrietta*. Intended for Genoa – Australia service. Originally to have been *Hellos*.
1960 Renamed *Marianna* by Latsis to replace *Marianna* ex *Highland Princess* (210) which he sold to the Czechs. *Marianna* was rebuilt with one pepper pot design funnel and the two forward wells were filled in. Used as a Mecca Pilgrimage ship.
1965 June 29: Arrived at Kaohsiung, Taiwan, for scrapping.

210 **HIGHLAND PRINCESS**

Details as *Highland Monarch* (207) except:
Bt 1930; *T:* 14,128 g, 8,729 n.

1929 Apr 11: Launched.
1930 Feb 25: Completed for Nelson Line London – River Plate service.
1932 Transferred to Royal Mail; same name.
1939 Trooping duties.
1946 Reconditioned by Harland & Wolff, Belfast; Pass: 100 1st, 340 3rd.
1947 Jan 9: Resumed London – River Plate service.
1959 Sold to John Latsis, Piraeus; renamed *Marianna*. Intended for Genoa – Australia service. Originally to have been *Henrietta*.
1960 Sold to Czechofracht, Czechoslovakia; became *Slapy*. Sold to Peoples Republic of China; renamed *Guanghua*.
1980 Still recorded in Lloyds Register. Spelling *Guang Hua*.

211 **HIGHLAND PATRIOT**

Details as *Highland Monarch* (207) except:
Bt 1932; *T:* 14,157 g, 8,743 n.

1931 Dec 10: Launched.
1932 May 14: Completed for Nelson Line as a replacement for *Highland Hope*. See Nelson Line Entry No 30 for further details. May 28: Maiden voyage London–Buenos Aires.
1932 Transferred to Royal Mail Line; same name.
1940 Oct 1: Torpedoed by *U-38* 500 miles west of Bishops Rock inbound for the Clyde from Buenos Aires. 3 lost out of the 143 aboard.

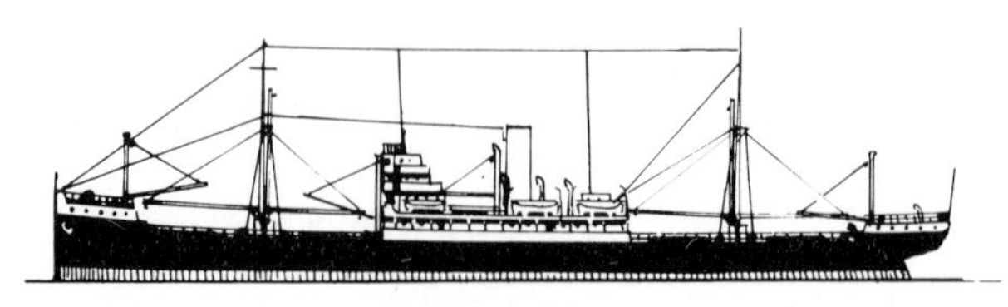

BRITTANY (I)

212 **BRITANNY** (I)

Bt 1928 Archibald McMillan & Sons, Dumbarton; *T:* 4,772 g, 2,849 n.
Dim 400 ft 4 in (122.02 m) × 55 ft 2 in (16.81 m) × 25 ft 8 in (7.82 m).
Eng Sgl scr, oil, sgl acting; 4 cyls; 646 NHP; By Harland & Wolff, Glasgow.
H Steel, 2 decks and shelter deck; fcsle 36 ft (10.97 m), poop 38 ft (11.58 m).

1928 June 29: Maiden voyage Liverpool–Rosario for David MacIver & Co.
1932 Transferred with MacIver fleet to Royal Mail.
1942 Oct 29: Sunk by torpedo en route Liverpool–Freetown.

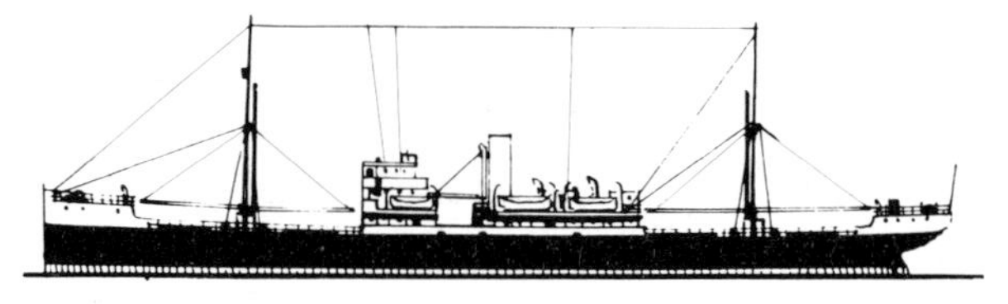

GASCONY

213 **GASCONY**

Bt 1925 Archibald McMillan, Dumbarton; *T:* 4,716 g, 2,631 n.
Dim 385 ft 4 in (117.45 m) × 53 ft 2 in (16.2 m) × 25 ft 2 in (7.67 m).
Eng Sgl scr, oil; sgl acting; 4 cyls; 1,850 BHP; By Harland & Wolff, Glasgow.
H Steel, 2 decks and shelter deck on the longitudinal system. Fcsle 33 ft (10.06 m), poop 38 ft (11.58 m).

1925 Nov 25: Maiden voyage Liverpool–S. America for David MacIver.
1932 Transferred to Royal Mail with the MacIver fleet.
1958 Sold and broken up.

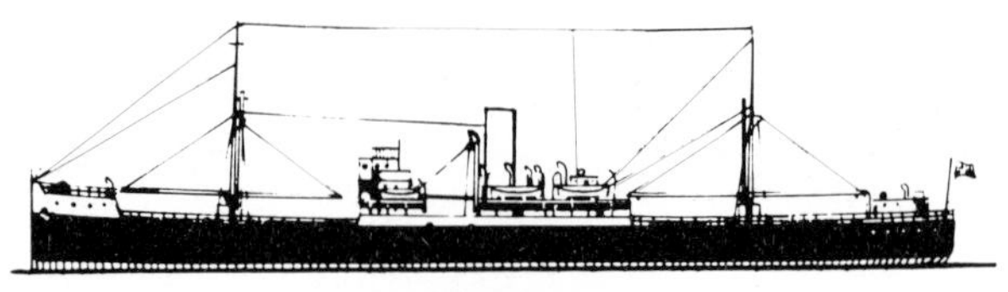

ARABY (I)

214 **ARABY** (I)

Bt 1923 Archibald McMillan, Dumbarton; *T:* 4,936 g, 2,944 n.

Dim 380 ft (115.82 m) × 53 ft 2 in (16.2 m) × 27 ft 1 in (8.25 m); Dft 26 ft 4 in (8.03 m).
Eng Sgl scr, oil, sgl acting; 4 cyls: 1,850 IHP; 12 kts; By Harland & Wolff, Glasgow. Fuel: 733 tons oil.
H Steel, 2 decks and shelter deck; fcsle 34 ft (10.36 m). Cargo: 461,000 cu ft (13,046 cu m) grain.
Pass 12. Crew: 40.

1923 Mar 24: Maiden voyage Liverpool–Buenos Aires for David MacIver.
1932 Transferred to Royal Mail.
1940 Dec 27: Sunk by U-boat in the Atlantic.

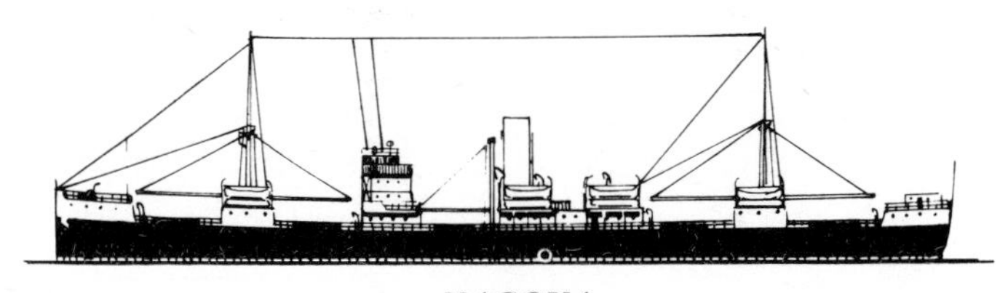

NAGOYA

215 **NAGOYA**

Bt 1920 Barclay Curle & Co, Yard No 576, Glasgow; *T:* 8,442 g, 5,337 n.
Dim 465 ft (141.73 m) oa, 450 ft 4 in (137.26 m) × 58 ft 2 in (17.73 m) × 37 ft 2 in (11.33 m).
Eng Sgl scr, dbl reduction geared turbine; 1,005 HP; 4 sgl ended boilers; 12 kts; By builder.
H Steel, 2 decks and shelter deck; fcsle 43 ft (13.11 m), poop 31 ft (9.45 m).

1920 Built as a standard 'G' class ship. Acquired by Nelson Line; named *Highland Warrior*. The bridge of this ship was one deck higher than the other standard 'G's.
1932 Taken over by Royal Mail; renamed *Nagoya*.
1936 Sold to Kaye, Son & Co; renamed *Marlene*. Tpl exp fitted by Wm Denny.
1941 Apr 4: Torpedoed south west of Freetown.

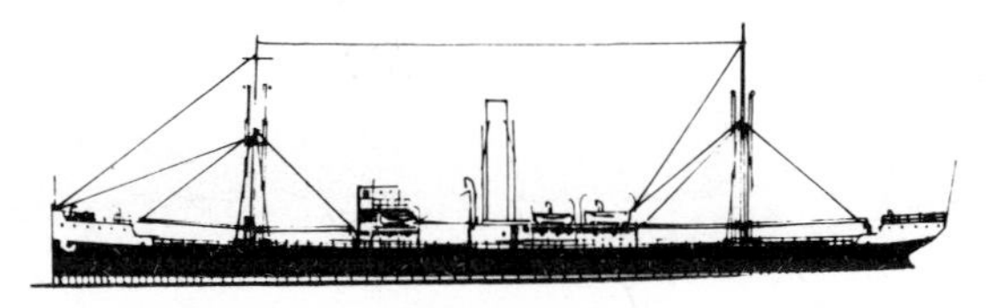

THESSALY (I)

216 **THESSALY** (I)

Bt 1909 Richardson Duck & Co, Stockton-on-Tees; *T:* 3,135 g, 1,916 n.
Dim 360 ft (109.73 m) × 48 ft (14.63 m) × 21 ft 2 in (6.45m)
Eng Sgl scr, tpl exp; 3 cyls; 321 NHP; 11 kts; By Blair & Co, Stockton.
H Steel, 2 decks and shelter deck constucted on the Isherwood longitudinal frame system; fcsle 22 ft (6.7 m), poop 38 ft (11.58 m).

1909 June 23: Launched.
1917 June 11: Attacked with gunfire by a U-boat. *Thessaly* escaped; 1 killed.
1931 July 24: Laid up at Langton Dock, Liverpool.
1932 Transferred to Royal Mail with MacIver fleet.
1933 Sold to Thos. Ward & Co, for £2,600 and broken up at Briton Ferry.

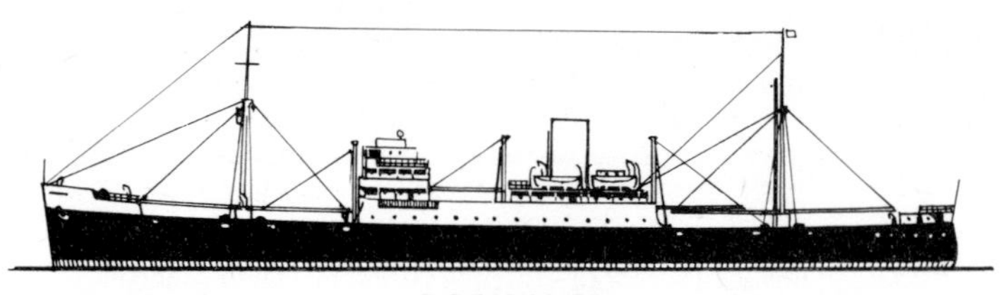

LOCHAVON

217 **LOCHAVON**

Bt 1938 Harland & Wolff, Belfast; *T:* 9,205 g, 5,700 n.
Dim 470 ft (143.26 m) × 66 ft 2 in (20.17 m) × 41 ft ((12.5 m)
Eng Tw scr, oil, dbl acting airless injection; 2 × 12 cyls; 16 kts; By builder.
H Steel, 2 decks. Cargo: 530,000 cu ft (14,999 cu m) grain.

1938 Aug 6: Maiden voyage Rotterdam – London – South America. Captain F. Cooke.
1939 Oct 14: Torpedoed 200 miles west of Bishop's Rocks en route Vancouver – Liverpool.

ANDES (II)

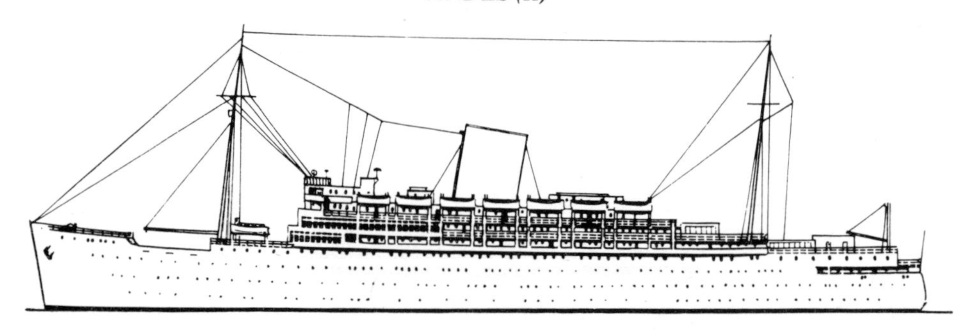

218 **ANDES** (II)

Bt 1939 Harland & Wolff, Belfast; *T:* 26,689 g, 14,787 n.
Dim 669 ft 4 in (204.01 m) oa, 643 ft 4 in (196.09 m) × 83 ft 6 in (25.45m) × 43 ft 7 in (13.28 m).
Eng Tw scr, 2 sets of 3 steam turbines sgl reduction geared; 5,599 SHP: 3 watertube boilers; Stm P: 485 lb; 21 kts; By builder.
H Steel, 5 decks; fcsle and bridge 573 ft (174.65 m), upper fcsle 73 ft (22.25 m), upper bridge 357 fr (108.81 m); Cargo: 133,000 cu ft (3,764 cu m) refrigerated.
Pass 403 1st, 204 2nd. Crew: 451.

1939 Mar 7: Launched. Sept 26: *Andes* was due to make her maiden voyage Southampton – South America on the 100th anniversary of the founding of the company. Instead the ship

proceeded to Liverpool in peacetime colours for conversion into a troopship for 4,096 men. Dec 9: First trooping voyage to Halifax, Nova Scotia.
1945 May: Carried the Norwegian Government-in-exile back to Oslo.
1946–7 Reconditioned at Belfast; *T:* 25,676 g; Pass 324 1st, 204 2nd.
1948 Jan 22: First commercial voyage to South America. Southampton–Buenos Aires, 18 days.
1959 Rebuilt for cruising by De Schelde, Flushing. Appearance altered as 218A. *T:* 25,895 g; **Pass:** 480 one class.
1960 June 10: Entered cruising.
1971 Feb: Sold for breaking up to Van Heyghen Freres, Ghent, for over £300,000. In her 31½ years service *Andes* had steamed 2,750,000 miles (4,426,000 km). May 7: Arrived Ghent.

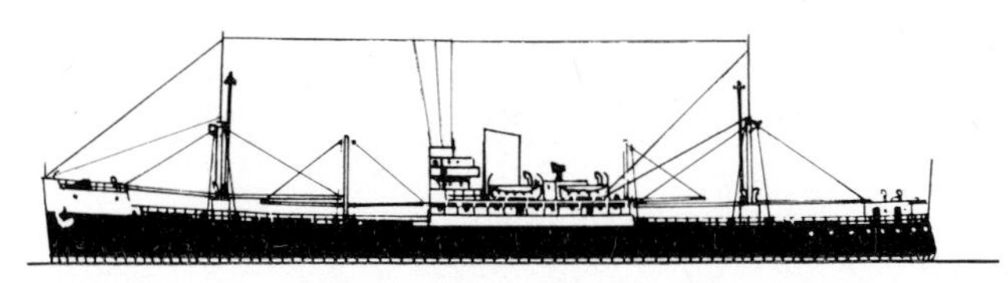

PARDO (II), PAMPAS (I), POTARO (II), PALMA, PARAMATTA (II)/PAMPAS (II) PARAGUAY (II)

219 **PARDO** (II)

Bt 1940 Harland & Wolff, Belfast; *T:* 5,405 g, 3,067 n.
Dim 450 ft 4 in (137.26 m) oa, 433 ft 4 in (132.08 m) × 61 ft 4 in (18.69m) × 22 ft 8 in (6.91 m).
Eng Sgl scr, oil, direct acting; 6 cyls; 1,236 NHP: 13 kts; By builder..
H Steel, 1 deck and shelter deck; fcsle 43 ft (13.11 m), 6 watertight divisions.

1940 Aug: Entered service. Dec: Damaged by a bomb on fcsle at Liverpool.
1964 Dec: Sold to Ioannitsa Cia Nav (Karageorgis Group), Piraeus; renamed *Aristarchos.* £440,000 was paid for the group of 4, *Pardo, Pampas* (220), *Paraguay* (224) and *Pilcomayo* (226).
1971 Broken up.

220 **PAMPAS** (I)

Details as *Pardo* (219) except:
T: 5,415 g, 3,070 n.

1940 Completed.
1942 Mar 26: Sunk during the seige of Malta; the ship arrived safely but damaged. During the unloading of her cargo she was bombed to destruction being hit 18 times.

221 **POTARO** (II)

Details as *Pardo* (219) except:
T: 5,416 g, 3,072 n.

1940 Nov: Completed.
1965 Sold to Ioannitsa Cia Nav, Piraeus; renamed *Aristipos.*
1971 Broken up.

222 **PALMA**

Details as *Pardo* (219) except:
T: 5,419 g, 3,079 n.

1941 Apr: Entered service.
1944 Feb 29: Sunk by Japanese submarine 400 miles south of Ceylon en route Liverpool–Calcutta. 7 lost.

223 **PARAMATTA** (II)/**PAMPAS**(II)

Details as *Pardo* (219) except:
T: 5,576 g, 3,144 n.

1944 Launched as *Paramatta* but completed as *Pampas* to commemorate *Pampas* (I) lost at Malta. Converted into a Headquarters Infantry landing ship for 650 men. Carried 18 landing craft on 2 tiers of davits. Took part in the Normandy landings.
1944 Oct: Designated for Far East service; renamed HMS *Persimmon* after King Edward VII's famous Derby winner.
1945 Apr: Under the command of Commander W. E. Gelling took part in the landings on the Irrawraddy delta and the capture of Rangoon. Thereafter ferried troops India–Burma.
1946 Apr: Made a trooping voyage Clyde–India then refitted for commercial service by builder.
1964 Dec: Handed over on the Tyne to Ioannitsa Cia Nav, Panama; renamed *Aristodimos*. In the same year *Paramatta* (but spelled Parramatta) was also acquired from the Swedish Company Transatlantic and renamed *Aristoteles*. In some records these two ships are transposed.
1970 Broken up.

224 **PARAGUAY**

Details as *Pardo* (219) except:
T: 5,564 g, 3,126 n.

1944 Completed.
1964 Dec: Sold to Ioannitsa Cie Nav. Piraeus.
1965 Resold to M.A. Karageorgis, Mountpleasant Cia, Nav, Piraeus; renamed *Elire*.
1969 Broken up.

225 **PARIMA**

Details as *Pardo* (219) except:
T: 5,596 g, 3,094 n.

1944 Entered service.
1962 Sold to Mary Shipping Co S.A., Panama; renamed *Michalios X*.
1969 Broken up.

226 **PILCOMAYO**

Details as *Pardo* (219) except:
T: 5,574 g, 3,130 n.

1945 Completed.
1964 Dec: Sold to Ioannitsa Cia Nav., Piraeus; renamed *Aristagelos,* Then Varkiza Cia. Nav., M.A. Karageorgis group, Panama.
1970 Broken up.

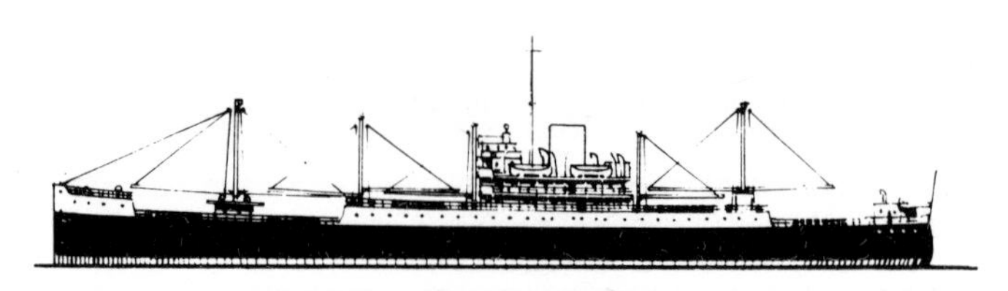

DESEADO (II) and DARRO (II)

227 **DESEADO** (II)

Bt 1942 Harland & Wolff, Belfast; *T:* 9,641 g, 5,773 n.

Dim 469 ft 10 n (143.21 m) oa, 453 ft 4 in (138.18 m) × 65 ft 3 in (19.89 m) × 35 ft 3 in (10.74 m).
Eng Tw scr, oil, 2 stroke dbl acting; 2 × 6 cyls; 1,803 HP; 14 kts; By builder.
H Steel, 4 decks; fcsle 41 ft (12.5 m), bridge 219 ft (66.75 m).

1942 Built for dual purpose work on South American or North Pacific ports.
1967 July: Laid up at Belfast.
1968 Sold for scrap to Eisen und Metall, Hamburg.

228 **DARRO** (II)

Details as *Deseado* (227) except:
Bt 1943; *T:* 9.733 g, 5,725 n.

1943 Completed for South American or North Pacific coast service.
1967 Sold to Embajada Cia Nav; renamed *Surrey* Nov 22: left Hong Kong in tow for breaking up at Kaohsiung, Taiwan.

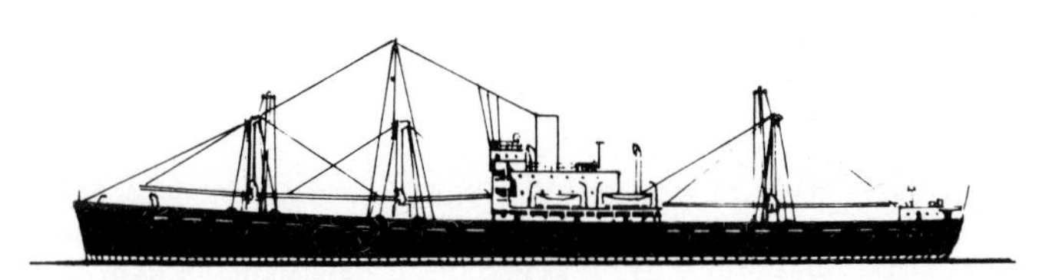

BARRANCA, BERESINA, BERBICE (II) and BALANTIA (II)

229 **BARRANCA**

Bt 1943 Oregon S.B. Corp; Portland Oregon; *T:* 7,252 g, 4,380 n.
Dim 441 ft 8 in (134.62 m) oa, 423 ft 10 in (129.18 m) × 57 ft (17.37 m) × 34 ft 8 in (10.57 m).
Eng Sgl scr, tpl exp; 3 cyls: 12 kts; By Iron Fireman Manufacturing Co.
H Steel, 2 decks; part electric welded.

1943 Launched as *Charles A. Broadwater* but completed as *Samthar* for Ministry of War Transport. Managed by Royal Mail.
1947 Acquired by Royal Mail; renamed *Barranca.*
1957 Sold; renamed *Cesco Corrado*, Soc Anon. di Nav. Corrado, Genoa.
1967 July: Broken up at Spezia.

230 **BERESINA**

Details as *Barranca* (229) except:
Bt 1943 New England S.B. Corp, Portland, Maine; *T:* 7,298 g, 4,380 n.
Eng By General Machinery Corp, Hamilton, Ontario,

1943 Launched as *Charles A. Young* but completed as *Samspring;* managed by Royal Mail.
1947 Acquired by Royal Mail and renamed *Beresina.*
1956 Sold; renamed *African Monarch,* General Navigation Ltd of Monrovia, Monrovia.
1969 Nov: Broken up at Split. Yugoslavia.

231 **BERBICE** (II)

Details as *Barranca* (229) except:
Bt: 1943 New England S. B. Corp, Portland, Maine; *T:* 7,219 g, 4,380 n.
Eng By Springfield Machine and Foundry Co, Springfield, Mass.

1943 Launched as *Barrett Wendell;* completed as *Samphill* and managed by Royal Mail.
1947 Purchased by Royal Mail and renamed *Berbice.*
1958 Sold; renamed *Nikolas S,* Cia Nav. Aisnicolas S.A., Beirut, Lebanon.
1967 Mar: Broken up at Kaohsiung, Taiwan.

232 **BALANTIA** (II)

Details as *Barranca* (229) except:
Bt: 1944 Bethlehem Fairfield Shipyard Inc, Baltimore; *T:* 7,210 g, 4,389 n.
Eng By General Machinery Corp, Hamilton, Ontario.

1944 Built for Ministry of War Transport as *Samfaithful.*
1947 Purchased by Royal Mail; renamed *Balantia.*
1958 Sold; renamed *Betamar,* Cia Nav. Betacruz S.A., LIberia.
1965 Became *Acme,* Acme Shipping, Famagusta, Cyprus.
1969 Apr: Broken up at Shanghai.

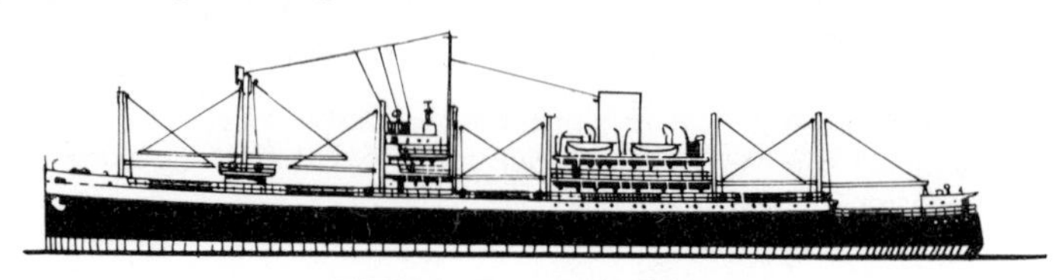

DRINA (II) and DURANGO

233 **DRINA** (II)

Bt 1944 Harland & Wolff, Belfast; *T:* 9,785 g, 5,823 n.
Dim 468 ft 9 in (142.87 m) oa, 453 ft 1 in (138.1 m) × 65 ft 4 in (19.91 m) × 33 ft 4 in (10.16 m).
Eng Tw scr, oil, 2 stroke direct acting; 6 cyls; 1,802 NHP; 15 kts; By builder.
H Steel, 4 decks; fcsle and bridge 375 ft (114.3 m). 6 watertight compartments.
Pass 12.

1944 Built for North Pacific route.
1965 Transferred to Shaw Savill & Albion; renamed *Romanic.*
1967 Laid up at Belfast.
1968 June 22: left Lyttleton for scrapping at Kaohsiung.

234 **DURANGO**

Details as *Drina* (233) except:
T: 9,806 g, 5,786 n.

1944 Built for North Pacific ports route.
1966 Transferred to Shaw Savill & Albion; became *Ruthenic.*
1967 Sold to Embajada Cia de Nav. Renamed *Sussex.*
1968 Dec 26: arrived Kaohsiung for breaking up.

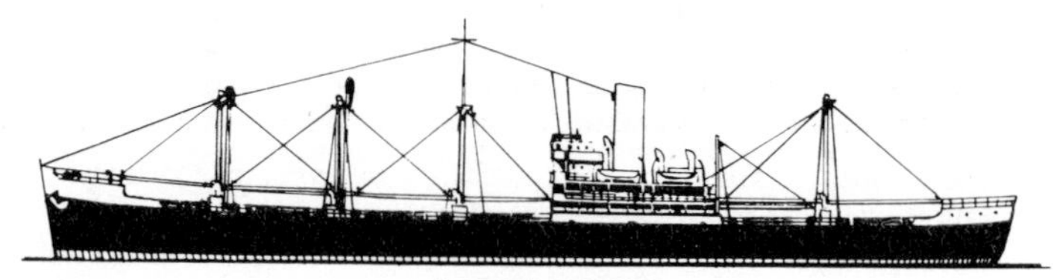

LOCH RYAN

235 **LOCH RYAN**

Bt 1943 Furness S.B. Co, Haverton Hill-on-Tees; *T:* 9.904 g, 7,165 n.
Dim 497 ft 6 in (151.64 m) oa, 475 ft 5 in (144.91 m) × 64 ft 4 in (19.61 m) × 40 ft (12.19 m).
Eng Sgl scr, 2 steam turbines dbl reduction geared; 1,210 IHP; 15 kts; By Richardsons, Westgarth, Hartlepool.
H Steel, 2 decks; fcsle 40 ft (12.19 m), poop 33 ft (10.06 m).

1943 Built as *Empire Chieftain* for Ministry of War Transport.
1946 Purchased by Royal Mail; renamed *Loch Ryan.*
1967 Sold; renamed *Pacific Envoy* and transferred to Furness Withy but still registered as

owned by Royal Mail.
1971 Sold; renamed *Aegis Strength,* Ammon Shipping Co, Famagusta.
1973 Broken up.

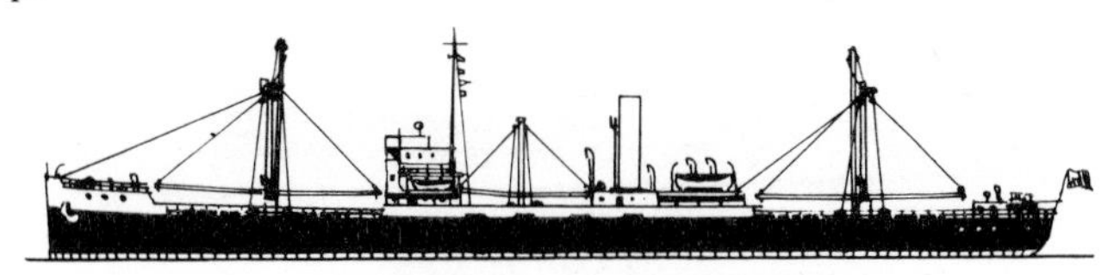

TEVIOT (III) and TWEED (II)

236 **TEVIOT** (III)

Bt 1944 Shipbuliding Corp, Tyne branch, Newcastle; *T:* 7,085 g, 4,140 n.
Dim 446 ft 4 in (136.04 m) oa, 430 ft 10 in (131.32 m) × 56 ft 2 in (17.12 m) × 35 ft 2 in (10.72 m)
Eng Sgl scr, tpl exp; 3 cyls; Stm P: 220 lb; 2 sgl ended boilers; 12 kts; By North East Marine.
H Steel, 2 decks; fcsle 40 ft (12.19 m).

1944 Built as *Empire Abbey* for Ministry of War Transport.
1946 Purchased by Royal Mail; renamed *Teviot.*
1960 Broken up.

237 **TWEED** (II)

Details as *Teviot* (236) except:
T: 7.046 g, 4,747 n.

1944 Built as *Empire Lady* for Ministry of War Transport.
1946 Bought by Royal Mail; renamed *Tweed.*
1959 Broken up.

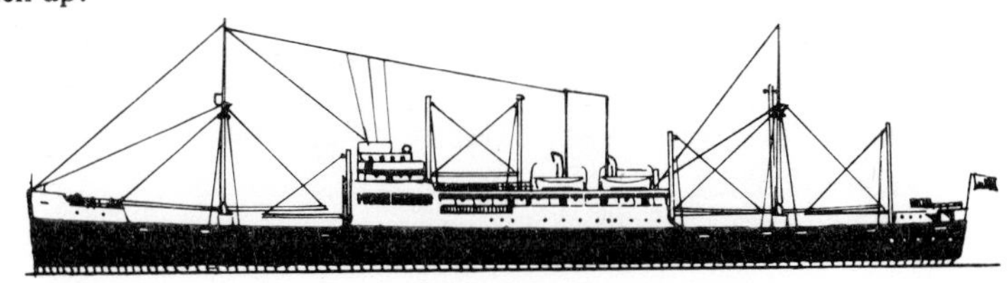

LOCH AVON and LOCH GARTH

238 **LOCH AVON**

Bt 1947 Harland & Wolff, Belfast; *T:* 8,617 g, 5,132 n.
Dim 498 ft 4 in (151.89 m) oa, 477 ft 10 in (145.64 m) × 66 ft 4 in (20.22 m) × 30 ft (9.14 m)
Eng Sgl scr, 3 steam turbines, dbl reduction geared to one shaft; Stm P: 585 lb; 2 water tube boilers; 16 kts; By builder.
H Steel, 2 decks and shelter deck; fcsle 49 ft (14.93 m), bridge 173 ft (52.73 m); Refrigerating machinery.
Pass 12.

1947 Built for North Pacific service.
1967 Sold to Singapore Malaysia Overseas Line; renamed *Hongkong Observer.*
1971 Broken up, Taiwan.

239 **LOCH GARTH**

Details as *Loch Avon* (238) except:
T: 8,617 g, 5,132 n.

1947 Entered service on the North Pacific service.
1968 Sold for scrap.

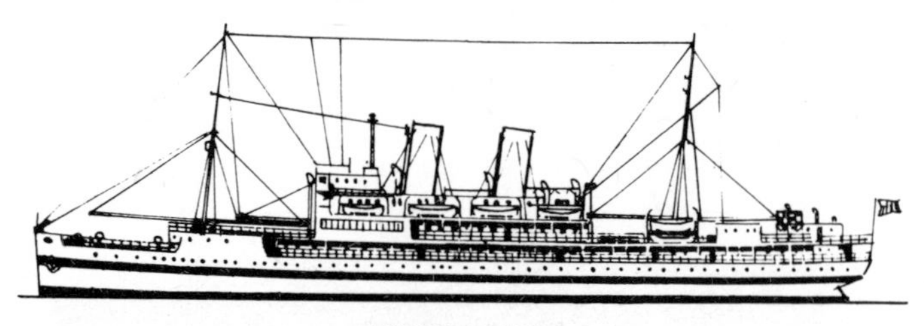

EMPIRE KEN

240 **EMPIRE KEN**

Bt 1928 Blohm & Voss, Hamburg; *T:* 9,523 g, 5,573 n.
Dim 464 ft (141.43 m) oa, 445 ft 6 in (135.79 m) × 60 ft 4 in (18.39 m) × 29 ft 8 in (9.04 m)
Eng Sgl scr, 4 steam turbines sgl reduction geared; 14½ kts; By builder.
H Steel, 3 decks.
Pass 124 1st, 78 2nd, 132 3rd. Crew: 165.

1928 Mar 31: Launched as *Ubena* for Deutsche–Ost Afrika Linie. July 31: Maiden voyage on Round Africa service.
1934 Lengthened by 22 ft 9 in (7 m) by builder. Speed increased by 1 kt.
1939 Aug 30: Arrived Hamburg. Nov 24: Taken over by German Navy. Became mother ship to 7th U-boat Flotilla at Kiel.
1942 Aug 17: Mother ship to 21st Flotilla at Pillau.
1945 Feb: Made 7 evacuation voyages from East Germany. Brought 27,170 persons to the West. July 17: Surrendered to Great Britain; renamed *Empire Ken*. Operated by Royal Mail Line.
1957 Sept 20: Broken up by W. H. Arnott Young at Dalmuir.

ARABY (II) and BRITTANY (II)

241 **ARABY** (II)

Bt 1947 Lithgows, Port Glasgow; *T:* 5,040 g, 2,796 n, 8,258 dwt.
Dim 425 ft 1 in (129.57 m) oa, 407 ft 6 in (124.21 m) × 56 ft 2 in (17.12 m) × 25 ft 7 in (7.8 m)
Eng Sgl scr, oil, 4 stroke sgl acting, supercharged; 6 cyls; 3,340 BHP; 12 kts; By J. G. Kincaid, Gourock.
H Steel, 2 decks; fcsle 35 ft (10.67 m).

1947 Jan: Completed.
1961 Sold to Shamrock Shipping Co, Larne; renamed *Glynn*. Chartered for 15 months to Orient Mid East Line.
1964 Broken up.

242 **BRITTANY** (II)

Details as *Araby* (241) except:
Bt: 1946 Wm Pickersgill & Sons, Sunderland; *T:* 5,089 g, 2,823 n.
Dim 422 ft (128.63 m) oa, 407 ft 10 in (124.31 m).

1946 Entered service.
1962 Broken up.

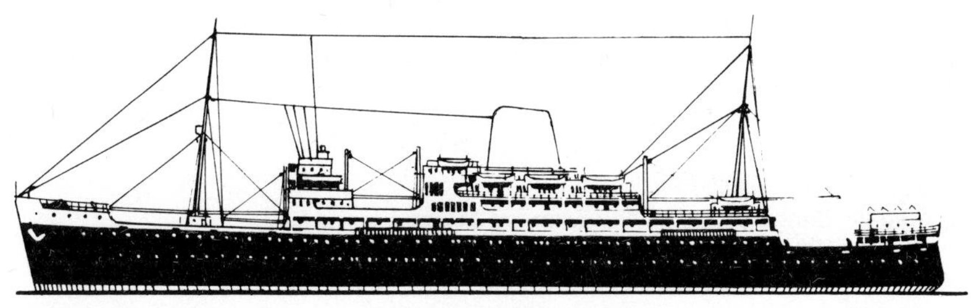

MAGDALENA (III)

243 **MAGDALENA** (III)

Bt 1949 Harland & Wolff, (Yard No. 1,354), Belfast; *T:* 17,547 g.
Dim 570 ft (143.26 m) × 73 ft 2 in (22.3 m) × 28 ft 6in (8.69 m)
Eng Tw scr, 4 geared turbines; 19,800 SHP; 18 kts; By builder.
H Steel, 7 decks, 9 watertight compartments, swimming pool.
Pass 133 1st, 346 3rd. Crew: 224.

1948 May 11: Launched as a replacement for *Highland Patriot* (211) the only war loss of this class.
1949 Mar 9: Maiden voyage London–Buenos Aires. Apr 25: Lost on inward leg of her maiden voyage en route Rio de Janeiro–London. *Magdalena* grounded on Tijucas Reef between Cagarras and Palmas islands. Apr 26: She was refloated but off Fort Sao Joao broke in two between the bridge and the boat deck. The fore part sank and the remainder of the hull went ashore in Imbui Bay where it was sold for breaking up.

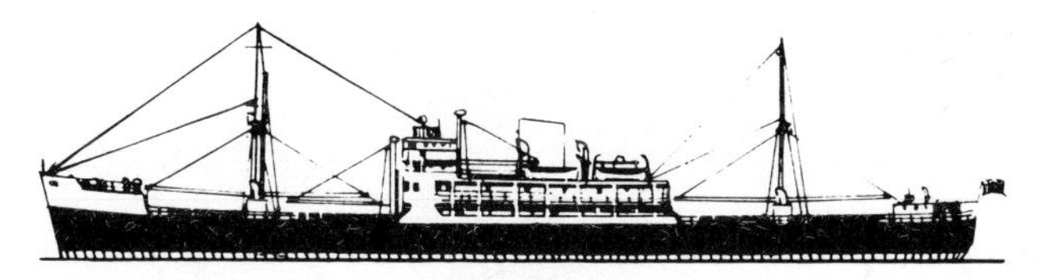

EBRO (IV)

244 **EBRO** (IV)

Bt 1952 Harland & Wolff, Govan; *T:* 7,784 g, 3,621 n, 12,290 disp.
Dim 444 ft 6 in (135.48 m) oa, 427 ft 6 in (130.3 m) × 56 ft 8in (17.27 m) × 24 ft (7.31 m)
Eng Sgl scr, oil; 2 stroke sgl acting; 6 cyls; 14 kts; By builder.
H Steel, 1 deck and shelter deck; fcsle 44 ft (13.41 m). Cargo 478,370 cu ft (13,538 cu m) bale.
Pass 12.

1952 June: Delivered.
1969 Sold; renamed *Fortune Victory*, Fortune Maritime, Hong Kong.
1970 Sold to Union of Burma Five Star Line Rangoon; renamed *Kalemyo*.
1978 Dec: Broken up at Tsingtao.

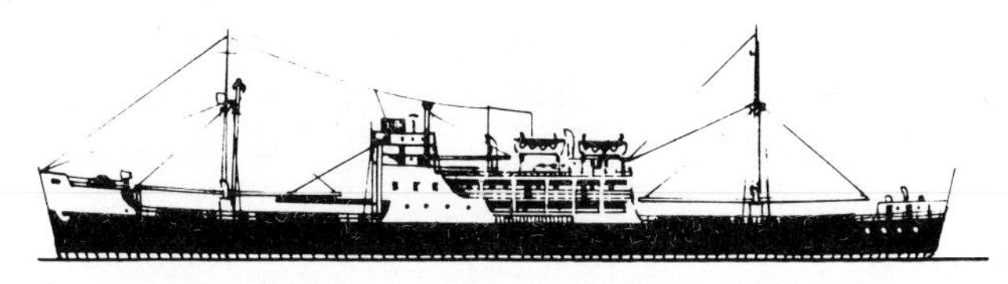

ESSEQUIBO (III), ESCALANTE and EDEN (II)

245 **ESSEQUIBO** (III)

Bt 1952 Harland & Wolff, Govan; *T:* 7,791 g, 3,261 n.

Dim 444 ft 6 in (135.48 m) oa, 415 ft (126.5 m) × 58 ft (17.68 m) × 38 ft 4 in (11.68 m)
Eng Sgl scr, oil, 2 stroke sgl acting opposed piston, cross head type; 6 cyls; 4,500 BHP at 115 rpm; 14 kts; By builder.
H Steel, 7 sub-divisions, 1 deck and shelter deck. Cargo 478,370 cu ft (13,538 cu m) bale.
Pass 12.

1952 Sept: Completed.
1968 Sold to China Navigation Co; renamed *Ningpo.*
1970 Became *Kalewa,* Union of Burma Five Star LIne Corp, Rangoon.
1979 Broken up.

246 **ESCALANTE**

Details as *Essequibo* (245) except:
Bt: 1955; *T:* 7,791 g, 4,483 n. Identifications: 4 windows in bridge deck.
1955 Entered service.
1970 Sold to Marescencia Cia de Nav SA, Panama. Renamed *Manes P.* Feb 2: Lost on first voyage at St Johns, NB; grounded on rock breakwater.

247 **EDEN** (II)

Details as *Essquibo* (245) except:
Bt: 1956; *T:* 7,791 g, 4,464 n. Identification: No jumbo derrick at foremast.

1956 Delivered.
1969 Sold to Neptine Orient Lines, Singapore; renamed *Neptune Garnet.*
1979 Broken up.

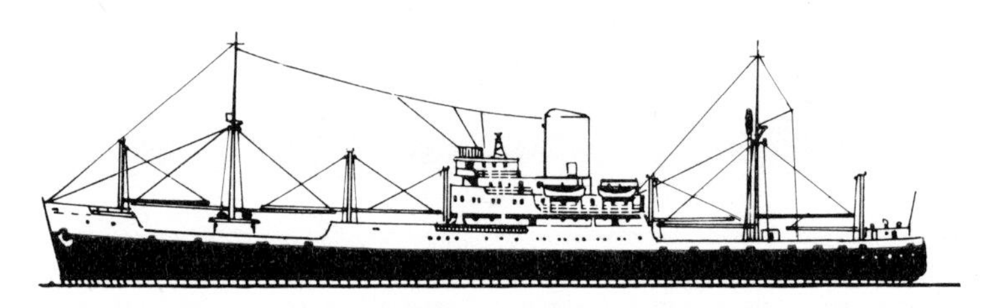

LOCH GOWAN and LOCH LOYAL

248 **LOCH GOWAN**

Bt 1954 Harland & Wolff, Belfast; *T:* 9,718 g, 5,549 n.
Dim 502 ft 10 in (153.26 m) oa, 470 ft (143.26 m) × 68 ft 4 in (20.83 m) × 28 ft 6 in (8.69 m)
Eng Sgl scr, steam turbine, dbl reduction geared; 16 kts; By builder.
H Steel, 8 watertight compartments; 2 decks; fcsle 54 ft (16.46 m) Bridge 181 ft (55.17 m); Tiled swimming pool. 30 ton derrick on mainmast. Cargo: 424,750 cu ft (12.020 cu m) grain.
Pass 12.
Identification: 2 mushroom shaped cowls immediately abaft funnel.

1954 Entered a joint service to North Pacific ports with Holland America Line.
1970 Sold and broken up at Kaohsiung.

249 **LOCH LOYAL**

Details as *Loch Gowan* (248) except:
Bt: 1957; *T:* 11,035 g, 6,447 n.

1957 Built for joint North Pacific service with Holland America Line.

1969 Oct: disabled by engine room fire.
1971 Sold to Aegis Group, Piraeus; renamed *Aegis Loyal;* operated by Aeakos Cia Nav. S.A., Piraeus.
1974 Broken up.

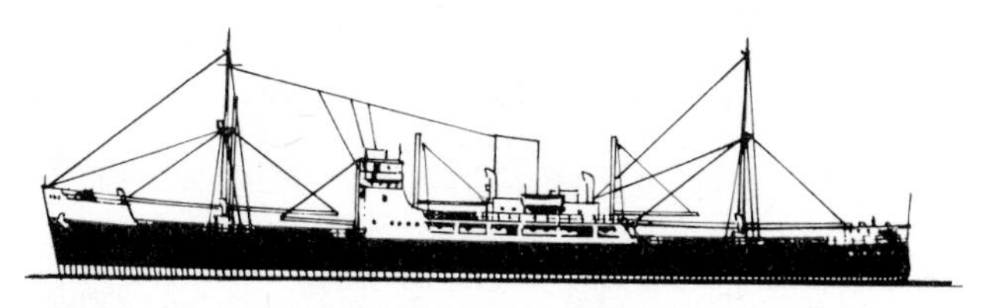

TUSCANY, THESSALY (II), PICARDY and ALBANY

250 **TUSCANY**

Bt 1956 Harland & Wolff, Govan; *T:* 7,455 g, 4,102 n.
Dim 440 ft (134.11 m) oa, 415 ft 6 in (126.64 m) × 58 ft 6 in (17.83 m) × 38 ft 4 in (11.68 m)
Eng Sgl scr, oil; sgl acting opposed piston, turbo-charged; 6 cyls; 4,500 BHP at 115 rpm; 13 kts; By builder; Turbo blower by Napier.
H Steel, 7 bulkheads, 1 deck and open shelter deck. Cargo: 8,000 tons.
1956 Delivered.
1970 Sold to Random Ltd; renamed *Federal Hudson,* managed by H & J Denholm Management.
1973 Became *Golden King,* Goldtopps Navigation S.A., Panama.
1975 Sold; renamed *Char Hsiung*, Chaffinch Shipping S.A., Panama.
1980 Aug: Broken up at Kaohsiung, Taiwan.

251 **THESSALY** (II)

Details as *Tuscany* (250) except:
Bt: 1957; *T:* 7,299 g, 4,036 n.
1957 Entered service.
1971 Sold to Union Steamship Co, Monrovia; renamed *Japan*.
1976 Became *Liho*, Lina Shipping Co, Singapore.
1979 March: Broken up by Chi I Enterprises, Kaohsiung.

252 **PICARDY**

Details as *Tuscany* (250) except:
Bt: 1957; Harland & Wolff, Belfast; *T:* 7,306 g, 4,028 n.
1957 Entered service.
1971 Sold to Union Steamship Co, Monrovia; renamed *Europe*.
1976 Sold to Lira Shipping Co, Singapore; renamed *Lira*.
1977 Caught fire and sank in the Indian Ocean.

253 **ALBANY**

Details as *Tuscany* (250) except:
Bt: 1957; *T:* 7,299 g, 4,026 n.
1957 Feb 14: Maiden voyage Middlesborough – West Indies.
1971 Sold to Union Steamship Co, Monrovia; renamed *Taiwan*.
1976 Became *Lido*, Li-Ta Shipping (Pte) Singapore.
1979 Mar 29: arrived Kaohsiung for scrapping.

YACARE and YAGUARETE

254 **YACARE**

Bt 1959 N.V. Scheepswerf Gebrudder van der Werf, Deest, Holland; *T:* 1,344 g, 652 n.
Dim 216 ft 7 in (66.01 m) oa, × 40 ft 9 in (12.42 m) × 8 ft 4 in (2.53 m).
Eng Tw scr, oil 4 stroke sgl acting; 7 cyls; 12 kts; By Masch Augsburg-Nurnberg.
H Steel, 2 decks.

1959 July: The first of two ships. *Yaguarete* (255) being the other, built abroad. They were the only ships ordered and built outside of Great Britain in 120 years. Others were purchased after building. Registered as owned by La Mala Real, Argentina, S.A. (ie, Royal Mail Argentina) and flew the Argentinian flag. Built for River Plate service limited seaward to the port of La Plata.
1972 Transferred to Comercial e Immobiliara Paraguayo Argentina S.A., Buenos Aires; same name.
1982 Still in service.

255 **YAGUARETE**

Details as *Yacare* (254)

1959 Oct: Entered River Plate feeder services.
1972 Transferred with her sister ship to C e I Paraguayo Argentina S.A., same name.
1982 Still in service.

256 **TWEED** (III)

Bt 1959 Rowhedge Iron Works Co, Rowhedge; *T:* 170 g, 108 n.
Dim 112 ft 6 in (34.29 m) × 22 ft 6 in (6.86 m) × 11 ft 6 in (3.51 m)
Eng Sgl scr, oil 2 stroke sgl acting; 6 cyls; 132 BHP; 7 kts; By Bergius & Co, Glasgow.
H Steel, 1 deck, water tanker.

1959 Completed at Rowhedge, dismantled and shipped to Port of Spain, Trinidad. Re-assembled for service as water-boat at Port of Spain. Registered as owned by Furness Withy but given a Royal Mail traditional name. Therefore included in the Royal mail fleet list.
1982 Still in service.

DERWENT (III)

257 **DERWENT** (III)

Bt 1949 Cammell Laird, Birkenhead; *T:* 13,594 g, 7,794 n, 14,447 dwt.
Dim 561 ft 2 in (171.04 m) × 72 ft 3 in (22.02 m) × 31 ft 11 in (9.73 m)
Eng Tw scr, 2 × 3 steam turbines sgl reduction geared; 2 watertube boilers; Stm P: 490 lb; 16 kts; By builder.

H Steel, 3 decks.

1949 Nov: Built as *Persic* for Shaw Saville & Albion.
1969 Transferred to Royal Mail; became *Derwent.*
1971 Operated for the Furness Withy Group. owners of Shaw Savill & Albion as well as Royal Mail, by Prince Line; same name. Became one of 23 ships of the Group. Sold for further trading or scrap. Broken up.

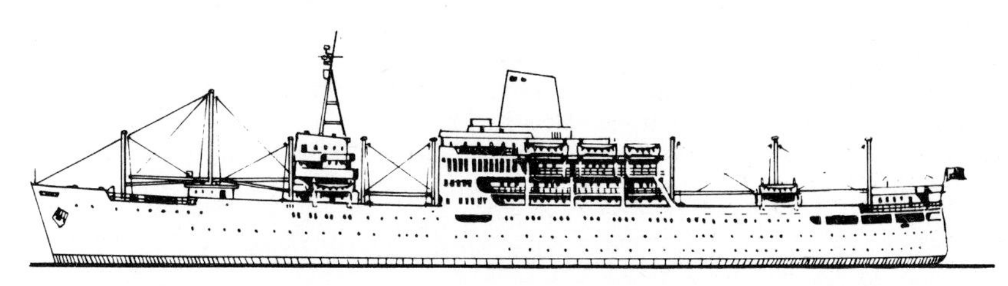

AMAZON (III), ARAGON (II) and ARLANZA (II)

258 **AMAZON** (III)

Bt 1959 Harland & Wolff, Belfast; *T:* 20,348 g, 11,100 n.
Dim 584 ft (178 m) oa, 540 ft (164.59 m) × 78 ft 3 in (23.85 m) × 28 ft 10 in (8.79 m)
Eng Tw scr, oil; 2 stroke sgl acting, opposed piston; 2 × 6 cyls: 17,000 BHP; 18 kts at 114 rpm; By builder, Burmeister & Wain type of self cleaning design. Superchargers by Napier.
H Steel, welded, 4 decks. Cargo: 435,000 cu ft (12,310 cu m) refrigerated; 45,000 cu ft (1,273 cu m) general.
Pass 107 1st, 82 cabin, 275 3rd.

1959 July 7: Launched by HRH Princess Margaret, Dec: Completed. Notable for still having substantial numbers of 3rd class.
1960 Jan 22: Maiden voyage London–South America service. Registered as owned by Welldeck Shipping Co.
1967 *T:* 18,565 g.
1968 Transferred to Shaw Savill & Albion for New Zealand service; renamed *Akaroa.* May 28: First voyage Southampton–Australia–New Zealand.
1971 Sold to A/S Uglands Rederi, Grimstad, Norway and stripped by Nymo AB for conversion into a new motor car transporter; renamed *Akarita;* all Ugland ships end in "ita".
1972 Apr: Rebuilt by Victor Lenac Yard, Rijeka, into car carrier; *T:* 10,886 g. Oct: Into service.
1977 Sold to Sagitta (Liberia) Ltd; renamed *Hual Akarita.*
1980 Renamed *Akarita,* Ace Autoline Co, Liberia.
1982 Jan: Broken up at Kaohsiung.

259 **ARAGON** (II)

Details as *Amazon* (258) except:
Bt: 1960; *T:* 20,362 g, 11,100 n.

1959 Oct 20: Launched.
1960 Apr: Completed. Apr 29: Maiden voyage London–Buenos Aires.
1967 *T:* 18,575 g.
1969 Transferred to Shaw Savill & Albion for New Zealand route; renamed *Aranda.* Mar 28: First voyage Southampton–Australia–New Zealand.
1971 Sold to Lief Hoegh for conversion to an automobile transporter. May 12: Arrived at Rijeka for conversion with *Akarita* (258) renamed *Hoegh Traveller* by Hoegh-Ugland Autoliners; *T:* 10,912 g.

1972 Entered service.
1977 Sold to Ace Navigation Co, Liberia; renamed *Hual Traveller*
1980 Renamed *Traveller*, Ace Autoline Co, Monrovia.
1981 Nov: Broken up at Kaohsiung.

260 **ARLANZA** (II)

Details as *Amazon* (258) except:
Bt 1960; *T:* 20,362 g, 11,470 n.

1960 Apr 13: Launched. Oct 7: Maiden voyage London–Buenos Aires. *T:* 18,595 g.
1969 Transferred to Shaw, Savill & Albion; New Zealand route; renamed *Arawa.* Feb 28: First voyage Southampton–Australia–New Zealand.
1971 Sold to Leif Hoegh & Co, Oslow; renamed *Hoegh Transit.* July 1: Arrived Victor Lenac Yard, Rijeka, for conversion into a car transporter.
1972 June: Renamed *Hoegh Trotter; T:* 10,895 g. Entered service.
1977 Sold to Ace Transportation Co, Liberia; renamed *Hual Trotter.*
1980 Renamed *Trotter;* Ace Autoline Co, Liberia.
1981 Dec: Broken up at Kaohsiung.

DOURO

261 **DOURO** (II)

Bt 1946 Hawthorn Leslie & Co, Newcastle; *T:* 10,783 g, 6,524 n.
Dim 279 ft 6 in (146.15 m) oa, 460 ft 10 in (140.46 m) × 65 ft 10 in (20.07 m) × 37 ft 10 in (11.53 m).
Eng Tw scr, oil; 2 cycle sgl acting Doxford type; 2 × 4 cyls: 26¼ in (67 cm); Stroke: 91¼ in (232 cm); 8,900 BHP; 14 kts; By builder; 2 auxiliary steam boilers.
H Steel, 3 decks; fcsle and bridge 401 ft (122.22 m).
Pass 12.

1946 Built as *Hornby Grange,* Houlder Line Ltd.
1969 Transferred to Royal Mail; renamed *Douro;* same service. Later registered as owned by Prince Line Ltd, London.
1972 June 6: arrived Aviles, Spain for breaking up.

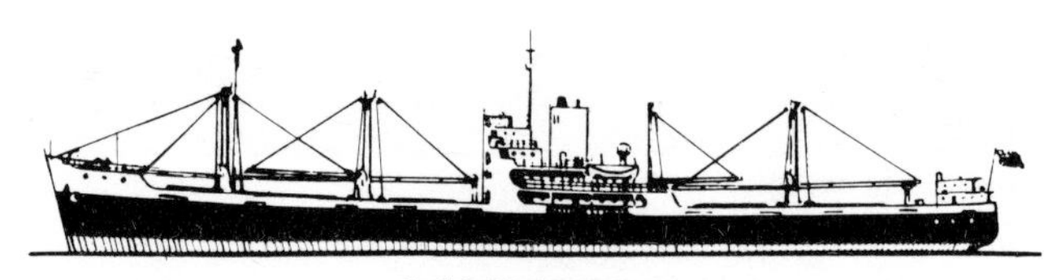

LOMBARDY (II)

262 **LOMBARDY** (II)

Bt 1958 Burntisland Shipbuilding Co, Burntisland; *T:* 8,105 g, 3,858 n.
Dim 459 ft 6 in (140.06 m) oa, 430 ft (131.06 m) × 59 ft 11 in (18.26 m) × 27 ft (8.23 m).
Eng Sgl scr, oil, Doxford 2 stroke sgl acting; 4 cyls; 4,400 BHP; 14 kts; By Hawthorn Leslie & Co, Newcastle.
H Steel, strengthened for ice, 2 decks; fcsle 39 ft (11.89 m).

1958 Built for Cairns, Noble & Co, Newcastle as *Cairnforth*.
1965 Transferred to Manchester Liners Ltd; became *Manchester Freighter*.
1969 Transferred to Royal Mail; renamed *Lombardy*.
1970 Laid up at Falmouth.
1971 Sept: Sold to Premier Shipping Co, Monrovia; renamed *Premier Pacific*. Premier S Co is owned by Maldivian Nationwide Trading Corp (Ceylon) Ltd, Singapore.
1975 Renamed *Tara Sea*.
1976 Became *Georgios,* Sergeant S Co, Piraeus.
1981 Still in service.

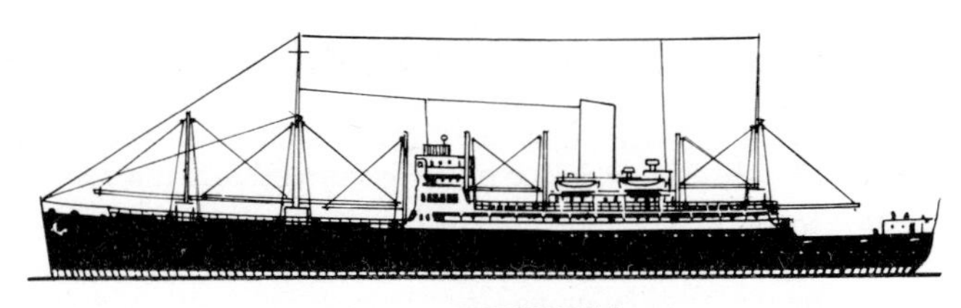

DUQUESA

263 **DUQUESA**

Bt 1949 Hawthorne Leslie & Co, Newcastle; *T:* 9,762 g, 6,564 n.
Dim 479 ft 6 in (146.15 m) × 65 ft 9 in (20.04 m) × 30 ft 11 in (9.42 m).
Eng Sgl scr, 2 steam turbines, reduction geared; 15 kts; By builder.
H Steel, 3 decks; fcsle and bridge 402 ft (122.53 m). Refrigerated cargo for carriage of meat.

1949 Mar: Built as *Duquesa* for Furness-Houlder Argentine Lines.
1968 Transferred to Royal Mail; same name.
1970 Broken up.

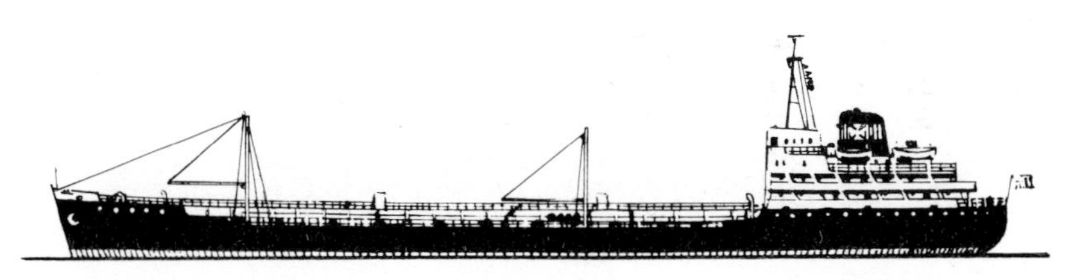

ABADESA

264 **ABADESA**

Bt 1962 Swan Hunter & Wigham Richardson, Newcastle; *T:* 13,398 g, 7,706 n, 21,150 dwt.
Dim 565 ft 2 in (172.26 m) oa, 535 ft (163.07 m) × 72 ft 2 in (22 m) × 33 ft 2 in (10.11 m).
Eng Sgl scr, oil, Doxford-Swan 2 stroke sgl acting; 6 cyls; 9,500 BHP.
H Steel, 1 deck; fcsle 67 ft (20.42 m), poop 126 ft (38.4 m); Oil tanker 901,757 cu ft (25,520 cu m) oil.

1962 Built as *Abadesa* for Furness-Houlder Argentina Line.
1968 Transferred to Royal Mail operation; same name; retained Furness-Houlder funnel.
1969 Mar: Placed on long term charter to J. Stolt Nielsen (Pacific Maritime Services, London) for the carriage of chemicals, fats and general liquid cargoes. Converted at Horten, Norway; renamed *Stolt Abadesa*.
1973 Sold to Aberdeen Shipping Inc, Monrovia; renamed *Stolt Tiger;* still on charter to Stolt-Nielsen.
1974 Became *Stolt Viking* owned by Dundee Shipping Inc, Monrovia. Still in service.

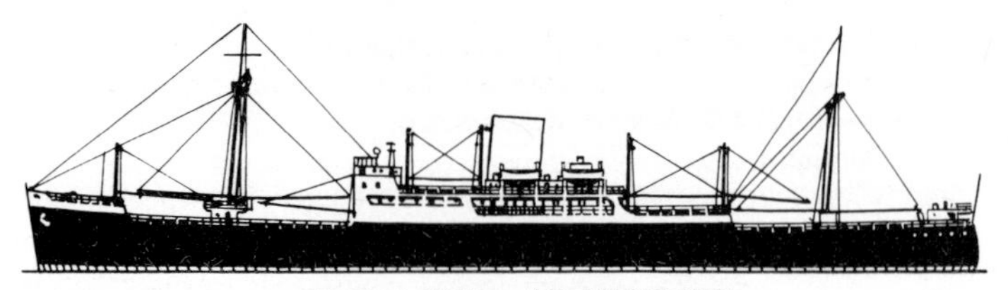

DRINA (III) and DARRO (III)

265 **DRINA** (III)

Bt 1953 Harland & Wolff, Belfast; *T:* 10,961 g, 6,319 n.
Dim 512 ft (156.06 m) oa, 481 ft 10 in (146.86 m) × 69 ft 3 in (21.11 m) × 41 ft 6 in (12.65 m).
Eng Tw scr, oil; 2 stroke sgl acting; 2 cyls; 14,300 BHP; 17 kts at 114 prm; By Burmeister & Wain at Harland & Wolff.
H Steel, 3 decks; fcsle 57 ft (17.37 m), bridge 206 ft (62.79 m); 6 holds; Cargo: 303,890 cu ft (8,600 cu m) general; 333,430 cu ft (9,460 cu m) refrigerated; 1 × 70 ton derrick.

1953 Built as *Cymric* for Shaw Savill & Albion UK-Australia service.
1972 Transferred to Royal Mail management, not ownership; renamed *Drina.*
1977 Transferred to the Blackhall Shipping Co, a Shaw Savill & Albion subsidiary; same name.
1978 Dec 23: Arrived for breaking up at Kaohsiung, Taiwan.

266 **DARRO** (III)

Details as *Drina* (265) except:
Bt 1957 Cammell Laird, Birkenhead; *T:* 11,144 g, 6,343 n.

1957 Built as *Carnatic* for Shaw Savill & Albion, London. UK–Australia service.
1973 Transferred to Royal Mail management; renamed *Darro,* shown as owned by Ardgowan Shipping Co, Southampton.
1977 Sold to Universal River Inc, Piraeus; renamed *Litsa K.*
1979 Renamed *Dimitra,* P. Perimenis, Piraeus, and sold for breaking up.

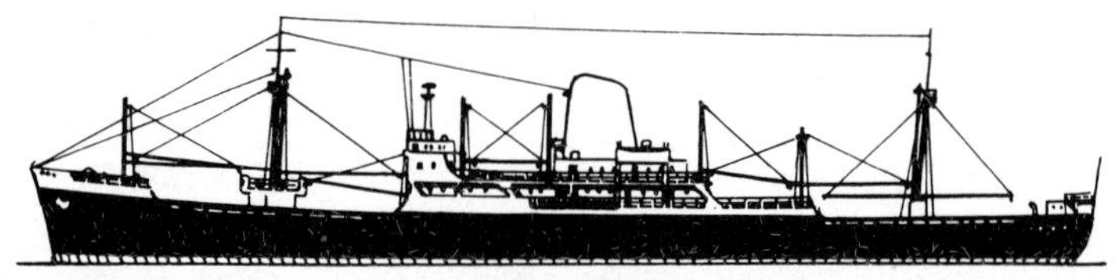

DESEADO (III)

267 **DESEADO** (III)

Bt 1961 Alex Stephen & Sons, Glasgow; *T:* 11,034 g, 6,339 n.
Dim 510 ft 5 in (156.58 m) oa, 479 ft 1 in (146.02 m) × 70 ft 5 in (21.47 m) × 41 ft 6 in (12.65 m).
Eng Sgl scr, oil; 2 stroke sgl acting; 8 cyls; 13,300 BHP; 17 kts; By Harland & Wolff, Belfast.
H Steel, 3 decks; fcsle 58 ft (17.7 m), bridge 203 ft 6 in (62.2 m); Cargo: 679,000 cu ft (19,241 cu m) grain plus 411,700 cu ft (11,665 cu m) refrigerated.

1961 Built as *Iberic* for Shaw Savill & Albion, London.
1976 Transferred to Royal Mail management and renamed *Deseado.* The ship was never owned by the company.
1980 Sold to Metcalfe Shipping Co; same name.

268 **REINA DEL MAR**

In 1969, during the period of charter to Union-Castle Mail SS Co this ship was transferred to Royal Mail ownership until sold to Union-Castle in 1973. The vessel saw no Royal Mail service and is thus mentioned here for record purposes.

Bt 1956 Harland & Wolff, Belfast; *T:* 20,750 g, 8,260 n.
Dim 600 ft 8 in (183.09 m) oa, 560 ft (170.69 m) × 78 ft 4 in (23.88 m) × 44 ft (13.41 m).
Eng Tw scr, 2 dbl reduction geared Parsons's turbines; 18,700 SHP at 112 rpm; 18 kts; By builder.
H Steel, 3 decks. Denny Brown stabilisers, 5 holds.
Pass 207 1st, 216 cabin, 343 tourist. Crew: 327.

1955 June 7: Launched.
1956 Apr: Cost £5 million. May 3: Maiden voyage Liverpool–Panama Canal–Valparaiso.
1963 Chartered to the Travel Savings Association.
1964 Mar 10: Arrived Belfast for conversion to a cruise liner. *T:* 21,501 g; Pass: 1,047 one class. June 10: Placed under Union-Castle Management; first cruise Southampton–New York. Nov: Painted in Union-Castle colours.
1967 *T:* 20,750 g.
1969 Transferred to Royal Mail Line ownership.
1973 Sept: Sold to Union-Castle SS Co.
1975 July: Arrived Kaohsiung, Taiwan. Broken up by Tung Cheng Steel Co.

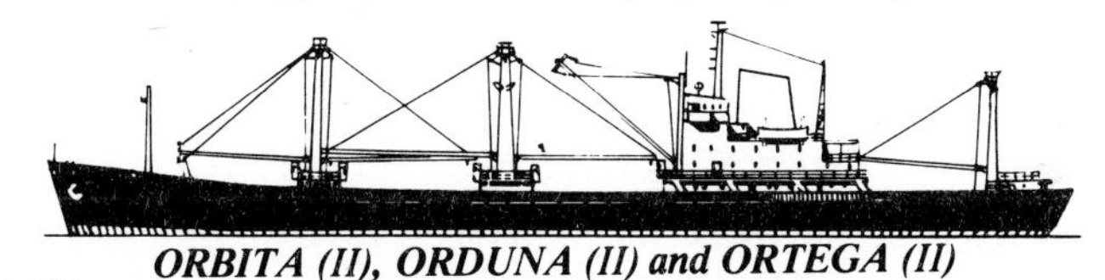

ORBITA (II), ORDUNA (II) and ORTEGA (II)

269 **ORBITA** (II)

Bt 1972 Cammell Laird & Co, Birkenhead; *T:* 8,396 g, 4,302 n.
Dim 529 ft 8 in (161.45 m) oa, 501 ft 10 in (152.97 m) × 73 ft 4 in (22.36 m) × 44 ft (13.42 m).
Eng Sgl scr, oil 2 stroke sgl acting; 8 cyls; 15,000 BHP; 18 kts; Burmeister & Wain type; By J. G. Kincaird & Co.
H Steel, 2 decks; fcsle 47 ft 3 in (14.4 m). Cargo: 858,869 cu ft (24,306 cu m) grain.

1972 Built for PSNC but part of the Royal Mail Line Division of Furness Withy.
1980 Apr: Sold to Cia Sud Americana de Vapores; renamed *Andalien.*
1981 Sold to Wallem Ship Management; renamed *Morning Sun.*

270 **ORDUNA** (II)

Details as *Orbita* (215) except:
Bt 1973.

1973 Mar: Completed for South American service.
1982 Sept: Renamed *Beacon Grange,* Furness Group

271 **ORTEGA** (II)/**ANDES** (III)

Details as *Orbita* (215) except:
Bt 1973

1973 July: Entered service.
1980 Apr: Renamed *Andes* (III); same owner.
1982 Sold; renamed *Oceanhaven,* Bluehaven Co, Hong Kong.

STEAM LAUNCHES

272 **WALTHAM**
T: 87 g.
A steam launch listed in the Annual Report and Balance Sheet of 1893. No other information.

273 **EXE**
T: 61 g.
A steam launch listed in the Annual Report and Balance Sheet of 1893. No other information.

NELSON LINE

Chronological History

1880 James Nelson, father of Hugh and William Nelson, began life as a butcher in County Meath, Ireland and from this trade expanded into cattle breeding. These he began to export across the Irish Sea to Liverpool. In that city he set up as James Nelson & Sons. The company expanded by opening retail branches to a point where the Irish exports were insufficient to meet demand.

1886 Hugh Nelson was dispatched to the Argentine to investigate and set up a supply of the finest beef. He established the Las Palmas Meat Factory at Zarate near the mouth of the Parana River, 50 miles from Buenos Aires. There the cattle were collected and then processed for shipment; the carcasses were transported to Buenos Aires.

1887 Nelson's River Plate Meat Company was founded to operate the Argentine end of the business. Steel, Young & Co's steamer *Ranmoor* shipped home the first cargo of meat.

1889 The Argentine company became Nelsons (New) River Plate Meat Company. It was decided that the Nelson organisation should enter into the refrigerated shipowning business in order to ensure a proper flow of high standard meat. The first vessel to be owned by James Nelson and Sons was *Spindrift* which was acquired from G. C. Gillchrest & Co. The first task was to convert the ship for the carriage of refrigerated meat and this conversion was onto the cold air system.

1890 *Spindrift* was renamed *Highland Scot* and registered as owned by Highland Scot Steamship Co, Liverpool, with Hugh and William Nelson as managers. Thus began the practice of using the prefix *Highland* for Nelson ships. *Highland Chief* was the first ship to be built for the group's Liverpool–River Plate service.

1891 *Highland Lassie* entered service followed by *Highland Mary* and *Highland Glen*. All were individual ship companies managed by H. & W. Nelson.

1892 The holding company James Nelson and Sons Ltd was formed to operate the Liverpool meat firm of James Nelson and Sons plus Nelsons (New) River Plate Meat Co.

1893 The Argentine subsidiary was renamed Las Palmas Produce Co Ltd and extended its activities into grain and general cargo distribution. Nelson's ships carried miscellaneous produce to the Argentine and loaded frozen meat for the northbound voyage.

1897 Mr A. R. T. Woods became General Manager.

1898 Nelson Line (Liverpool) Ltd acquired the six single ship companies and the vessels were transferred into their ownership. However Hugh and William Nelson still acted as manager and the services out of Liverpool continued.

1899 James Nelson died.

1900 The fleet comprised six ships: *Highland's Scot, Chief, Lassie, Mary, Glen* and *Laird.*

1901 The management of Nelson Line (Liverpool) Ltd changed to H. & W. Nelson Ltd. *Highland Brigade* was delivered. She heralded the company's entry into the passenger business. Lloyds Register also records the managers of this and the other single ship companies as being W. & H. Nelson then changes the title to H. & W. Nelson Ltd.

1902 A fleet renewal programme was planned with five ships for delivery over the ensuing two years.

1903 *Highland Enterprise* and *Highland Hope* were delivered.

1904 Russell's yard completed the trio *Highland Harris, Highland Heather* and *Highland Watch.* On Dec 10 *Highland Lassie* left Swansea for South America and disappeared without trace.

1905 J. B. Westray's *Duke of Portland* was bought and renamed *Highland Fling.* The fleet now comprised 15 ships of which ten were less than ten years old and *Highland Scot* was the oldest at 16 years. In only 15 years the Nelson Line had become the foremost rivals to the Royal Mail SP Co on the South American meat route. At this stage the Nelson Line commenced a period of fleet consolidation and for five years no new ships were built.

1907 Jan 7: Saw *Highland Fling* ashore at Kennock Bay, Cornwall. Her transfixed bows were cut away and the afterpart towed to Falmouth for breaking up. *Highland Lassie* became Adelaide SS Co's *Lammeroo.*

1909 The company was re-planned. The forward policy was to go for passenger ships. The older tonnage was to be disposed of and new ships introduced. As a start *Highland Scot, Highland Corrie* (I) and *Highland Glen* were all sold for scrapping.

1910 The Nelson Line entered into the passenger business in a substantial way by constructing a series of ships aboard which the revenues from passenger berths was as important as the general cargo south and frozen meat north contribution. They were, in style, similar to the equivalent ships operated by the Germans not only to South America but also to West, South and East Africa and were designed by Mr A. R. T. Woods, the Line's General Manager. Sailings of the new fleet of passenger ships was to be from London and to acquire and manage this new activity. Nelson Line (London) Ltd was formed to take its place alongside Nelson Line (Liverpool) Ltd. The holding company became Nelson Steam Navigation Co Ltd.

1910 The new ships were heralded by the delivery of *Highland Rover* in February, to be followed by both *Highland Laddie* and *Highland Pride* in April. These three ships were slightly shorter in length than the remainder and had a greater rake. Next came *Highland Corrie* (II), *Highland Glen, Highland Brae* and *Highland Scot* (II) to complete seven ships delivered in the year; by the end of which the new services out of London were fully launched on a weekly departure basis.

1911 Saw delivered *Highland Loch, Highland Piper* and the last of the ten *Highland Warrior* (I). All these ten new ships were registered as owned by Nelson Steam Navigation

Co and not by Nelson Line (London) Ltd who confined their interest to the wharfinger's role. *Highland Mary* was sold to the Vestey Group as part of the formation of Blue Star Line and became *Brodland.*

1912 *Highland Chief* and *Highland Ghillie* were sold to the Hamburg owner Michael Jebsen.

1913 The ordinary shares of Nelson Steam Navigation Co Ltd, Nelson Line (Liverpool) Ltd and Nelson Line (London) Ltd were bought by the Royal Mail Steam Packet Co. Sir William Nelson retired and the new Chairman became Sir Owen Philipps, later Lord Kylsant, Chairman of Royal Mail.

1914 Aug 4: The First World War began. Sept 14: *Highlana Hope* (I) was captured by the German raider *Karlsrühe* and later scuttled in the South Atlantic.

1915 Jan: *Highland Mary* was wrecked on the coast of South Wales and in Oct *Highland Warrior* (I) was lost on the north west coast of Spain.

1916 To replace *Highland Mary* J. P. Corry's *Star of Ireland* was acquired and renamed *Highland Star.*

1917 May: *Highland Corrie* (II) was torpedoed off Selsey Bill.

1918 In April *Highland Brigade* (I) was torpedoed to be followed in August by the loss to a German submarine of *Highland Harris.* Nov 11: The war ended with the signing of the Armistice. The fleet at this juncture numbered eleven ships: *Highland's Laird, Enterprise, Heather, Watch, Glen, Laddie, Pride, Rover, Loch, Piper* and *Star.*

1920 *Highland Warrior* (II), a wartime standard 'G' ship, without passenger accommodation, joined the fleet and remained in the refrigerated meat service until the amalgamation into Royal Mail. She was the first new built addition to the Nelson Line in nine years.

1925 Nelson Line (Liverpool) Ltd was wound up and the four ships owned were transferred to Nelson Steam Navigation Co so that all the fleet now traded under the one name.

1926 Oct: A Board meeting of the Royal Mail and Nelson Line directors, with Lord Kylsant in the chair, decided to negotiate with Harland & Wolff for five replacement passenger ships, and that the Director and General Manager Mr A. R. T. Woods would be responsible for their design and construction.

1927 Jan: The new group of five *Highland* ships was ordered to replace the 17 year old class of 1910/11. There were to be twice the size of their predecessors but were to carry on with the tradition of good cheap reliable accommodation in competition with Royal Mail SP's express mail vessels. It is worth remembering that the Nelson Line was a Royal Mail subsidiary so the policy of serving two markets must, for the group, have been an economic success. Three ships *Highland Heather, Highland Watch* and *Highland Star* were laid up at Dunston-on-Tyne.

1928 Oct: *Highland Monarch* entered service as the first of the five motor ships built as the replacements for the ten *Highland Rover* class. *Highland Laird* was sold, at 29 years of age, for further service in Canadian waters.

1929 The delivery of four of the 14,000 ton class, *Highland Brigade, Highland Chieftain,*

Highland Hope (II) and *Highland Princess* completed the new building for the company. Their arrival released five of the 1910/11 class for disposal. Unfortunately *Highland Pride* was wrecked off Vigo but four were taken by a new subsidiary of Kaye, Son & Co, the Jamaica Banana Producers Steamship Co. The name changes were: *Highland Laddie* to *Jamaica Settler; Highland Glen* to *Jamaica Producer; Highland Loch* to *Jamaica Planter; Highland Piper* to *Jamaica Merchant.*

1930 Kaye, Son & Co took *Highland Enterprise* to replace their intended purchase of *Highland Pride* but retained her in their fleet as *Northland Highland Heather, Highland Star* and *Highland Watch* were sold in a single transaction to Thos W. Ward for £27,000 and were broken up. To replace them Lamport & Holt also a Royal Mail group company transferred *Meisonnier, Moliere* and *Murillo* but without change of name.

1932 *Highland Rover* the first of the 1910 group had become the last survivor when she was sold for breaking up by Thos W. Ward Ltd at Grays, Essex. During the year the Royal Mail Group collapsed in the financial crash involving Lord Kylsant. Aug: A completely new company was formed Royal Mail Lines Ltd and into this concern was transferred the remaining nine Nelson SN ships; five, *Highland Monarch, Highland Chieftain, Highland Brigade, Highland Princess* and *Highland Patriot,* retained Nelson names. *Highland Warrior* became *Nagoya* and even the three ex Lamport & Holt ships were given Royal Mail names. All of them received Royal Mail livery and by the end of the year the famous colouring of the Nelson Line had disappeared.

Routes

1880–1932 Liverpool–Rio de Janeiro–Buenos Aires

1910–1932 London–Boulougne (mail call)–Corunna–Vigo–Rio de Janeiro–Montevideo–Buenos Aires (Passenger service). The company's cargo vessels made calls at numerous UK ports which were additional to the two base ports of Liverpool and London.

Livery

Funnels Red with white, black, white bands below the black top.

Hull 1880–1910 Black, red waterline; 1910–1932 Grey, red waterline.
Uppers 1880–1910 White; 1910–1932 Light apple green.

Masts 1880–1910 Buff; 1910–1932 Grey some white posts.

Lifeboats 1880–1910 White, light buff interiors; 1910–1932 White, apple green interiors.

Fleet index

Illustrated Fleet List

1 **SPINDRIFT/HIGHLAND SCOT** (I)

Bt 1888 Russell & Co, Greenock; *T:* 3,060 g, 2,010 n.
Dim 320 ft 7 in (97.71 m) × 40 ft 1 in (12.22 m) × 18 ft 4 in (5.59 m)
Eng Sgl scr, tpl exp; 3 cyls; 288 NHP; Stm P: 150 lb; 2 dbl ended boilers, 12 furnaces; 10 kts; By Dunsmuir & Jackson, Glasgow.
H Steel, 1 deck and spar deck; fcsle 41 ft (12.5 m), bridge 81 ft (24.69 m).

1888 Built as *Spindrift* for G.C. Gillchrist & Co.
1889 Acquired by James Nelson & Sons, and refrigerated machinery with insulated holds was installed.
1890 Transferred to Highland Scot S.S.Co, H & W Nelson, managers. Renamed *Highland Scot* (I)
1909 Sold for breaking up by Harris & Co, Falmouth.

HIGHLAND CHIEF, HIGHLAND MARY and HIGHLAND GLEN

2 **HIGHLAND CHIEF**

Bt 1890 Alex Stephen & Sons, Glasgow; *T:* 2,648 g, 1,707 n.
Dim 310 ft (94.49 m) × 41 ft (12.5 m) × 23 ft 6 in (7.16m)
Eng Sgl scr, tpl exp; 3 cyls; 284 NHP; 3 sgl ended boilers, 9 furnaces; 10 kts; By builder.
H Steel, 2 decks; fcsle 38 ft (11.58 m), bridge 68 ft (20.73 m), poop 40 ft (12.19 m).

1890 The first ship completed for James Nelson & Sons.
1912 Sold to Michael Jebsen & Co, Hamburg; renamed *Alexander.*
1913 Became *Ville de Mostaganem,* Compagnie Havraise Peninsulaire de Navigation a Vapeur, Le Havre.
1915 Sold to French Line (Cie General Transatlantique); same name.
1915 Sept 9: Torpedoed.

3 **HIGHLAND MARY**

Bt 1891 Craig Taylor & Co, Stockton-on-Tees; *T:* 2,989 g, 1,949 n.
Dim 310 ft (94.49 m) × 41 ft 2 in (12.55 m) × 17 ft 9 in (5.41m)
Eng Sgl scr, tpl exp; 3 cyls; 272 NHP; Stm P: 160 lb; 2 sgl ended boilers, 6 furnaces; 10 kts; By Westgarth English & Co, Middlesbrough.

H Steel, 1 deck and spar deck; fcsle 41 ft (12.5 m), bridge 80 ft (24.38 m), poop 37 ft (11.28 m).

1891 July: Completed. Virtually a sister of *Highland Chief* (2).
1911 Sold to Blue Star Line, renamed *Brodland.*
1915 Jan 20: Wrecked on Aberavon Beach, South Wales en route Port Talbot–Punta Arenas.

4 HIGHLAND GLEN (I)

Details as *Highland Chief* (2) except:
T: 2,974 g, 1,939 n.

1891 Oct: Entered service owned by Highland Glen S S C, H & W Nelson, managers.
1909 Aug: Sold for breaking up.

5 HIGHLAND LASSIE

Bt 1891 Mackie & Thomspon, Glasgow; *T:* 2,488 g, 1,606 n.
Dim 296 ft (90.22 m) × 40 ft 4 in (12.29 m) × 22 ft 2 in (6.76m)
Eng Sgl scr, tpl exp; 3 cyls; 207 NHP; Stm P: 160 lb; 3 sgl ended boilers, 6 furnaces; 10 kts; By Dunsmuir & Jackson, Glasgow.
H Steel, 2 decks; fcsle 33 ft (10.06 m), bridge 60 ft (18.29 m), poop 28 ft (8.53 m).

1891 Mar: Completed for W & H Nelson & Co.
1899 Transferred to Nelson Line (Liverpool) Ltd.
1904 Feb 10: Left Swansea for River Plate. Disappeared without trace to become one of the mysteries of the sea.

6 HIGHLAND LAIRD

Bt 1899 R. Duncan & Co, Port Glasgow; *T:* 4,117 g, 2,648 n.
Dim 375 ft 2 in (114.35 m) × 48 ft (14.63 m) × 26 ft 5 in (8.05 m).
Eng Sgl scr, tpl exp; 3 cyls; 330 NHP; 11 kts; By Rankin & Blackmore, Greenock.
H Steel, 2 decks; fcsle 38 ft (11.58 m), bridge 100 ft (30.48 m), poop 38 ft (11.58 m).

1899 Entered service; *T:* 4,020 g raised to 4,117 g same year.
1915 May 31: Escaped from submarine attack in St George's Channel.
1928 Sold; renamed *Blue Peter*, Job Bros & Co, St Johns, Newfoundland.
1938 Broken up.

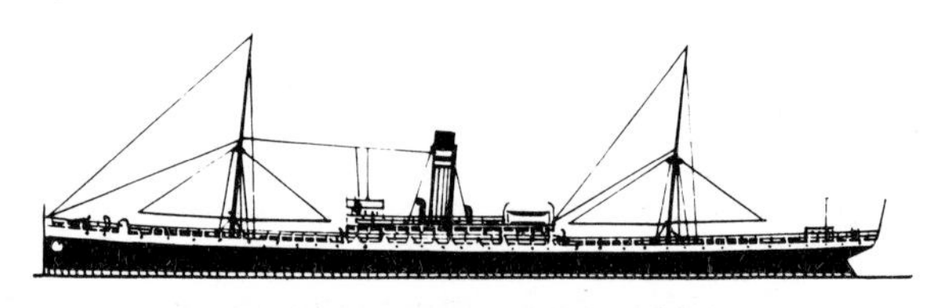

HIGHLAND BRIGADE (I)

7 HIGHLAND BRIGADE (I)

Bt 1901 W. Beardmore & Co, Glasgow; *T:* 5,662 g, 3,694 n.
Dim 384 ft 8 in (117.25 m) × 50 ft 2 in (15.29 m) × 26 ft 9 in (8.15 m)
Eng Sgl scr, tpl exp; 3 cyls; 653 NHP; Stm P: 200 lb; 4 sgl ended boilers, 12 furnaces; 11 kts; By builder.
H Steel, 2 decks.
Pass 40 1st.

1901 Completed for Nelson LIne (Liverpool) Ltd.
1918 Apr 7: Torpedoed south east of St Catherine's Point.

8 HIGHLAND CORRIE (I)

Bt 1890 Wm Gray & Co, West Hartlepool; *T:* 4,050 g, 2,646 n.
Dim 365 ft 1 in (111.28 m) × 47 ft 1 in (14.35 m) × 26 ft 9 in (8.15 m).
Eng Sgl scr, tpl exp; 3 cyls; 412 NHP; Stm P: 160 lb; 3 dbl ended boilers, 12 furnaces; 10 kts; By Central Marine Engine Works, West Hartlepool.
H Steel, 2 decks; fcsle 38 ft (11.58 m), bridge 88 ft (26.82 m), poop 31 ft (9.45 m).

1890 Built as *Tekoa* for New Zealand Shipping Co, London. With her sister these were the first two NZSC refrigerated pure cargo ships.
1902 Acquired by Nelson Line; renamed *Highland Corrie.*
1909 Apr: Sold for breaking up at Rotterdam by F. Rijsdijk.

9 HIGHLAND GHILLIE

Details as *Highland Corrrie* (8) except:
Bt: 1890 Wm Doxford & Sons, Sunderland; *T:* 3,935 g, 2,537 n.
Dim Beam 44 ft 2 in (13.46 m).
Eng 359 NHP; By builder.

1890 Apr: Built as *Sea King* for Wm Ross & Co. Acquired by J. B. Westray who installed the refrigerated machinery and insulated stowage.
1890 Late: Renamed *Otarama,* New Zealand Shipping Co, London.
1902 Acquired from New Zealand Shipping Co; renamed *Highland Ghillie.*
1912 Sold to Michael Jebsen, Hamburg; renamed *Constantin.*
1914 Aug 4: In Varna at the outbreak of war. Sold to M. Gumuchdjian, Varna, Bulgaria.
1924 Renamed *River Tyne*, same name but British registered.
1925 Renamed *Spa* and transferred to the Belgian flag, same owner but registered at Antwerp as managed by Cie Internationale de Commerce et d'Armement.
1933 Broken up by F. Rijsdijk, Rotterdam.

HIGHLAND ENTERPRISE, HIGHLAND HOPE, HIGHLAND HARRIS, HIGHLAND HEATHER and HIGHLAND WATCH

10 HIGHLAND ENTERPRISE

Bt 1903 Russell & Co, Port Glasgow; *T:* 5,155 g, 3,324 n.
Dim 385 ft (117.35 m) × 51 ft (15.54 m) × 24 ft (7.31 m).
Eng Sgl scr, tpl exp; 3 cyls; 546 NHP; Stm P: 180 lb; 3 sgl ended boilers, 9 furnaces; 10 kts; By Rankin and Blackmore, Greenock.
H Steel, 2 decks and shelter deck.

1903 Entered service for Nelson Line (Liverpool) Ltd, for the Liverpool–River Plate service.
1930 Sold; renamed *Northland*, Kaye, Son & Co, London.
1932 Sold to London Whaling Co, renamed *Thorland* and used as a frozen whale meat carrier.
1938 Sold to Christian Salvesen & Co, Leith; same name, same owner.
1946 Sold to Norwegian Government, same name. Used as a store ship at Oslo.
1951 Broken up by Metal Industries Ltd at Faslane.

11 **HIGHLAND HOPE** (I)

Details as *Highland Enterprise* (10) except:
T: 5,150 g, 3,320 n. **Dim** 384 ft 5 in (117.m).

1903 Entered service for Nelson Line (Liverpool) Ltd.
1914 Sept 14: Captured by German raider *Karlsrühe* and then scuttled 190 miles south west of St Paul's Rocks, South Atlantic.

12 **HIGHLAND HARRIS**

Bt 1904 Russell & Co, Port Glasgow; *T:* 6.023 g, 3,862 n.
Dim 390 ft (118.87 m) × 52 ft 5 in (15.98 m) × 26 ft 8 in (8.13 m).
Eng Sgl scr, tpl exp; 3 cyls; 640 NHP; Stm P: 200 lb; 3 sgl ended boilers and 1 aux. refrig. boiler, 12 furnaces; 12 kts; By Rankin & Blackmore, Greenock.

H Steel, 2 decks and shelter deck. Promenade deck and shelter deck 121 ft (36.88 m).

1904 Apr: Delivered.
1915 Aug 6: Chased by submarine north of Scilly Isles.
1918 Aug 6: Torpedoed 82 miles north west of Eagle Island, County Mayo. 24 lives lost.

13 **HIGHLAND HEATHER**

Details as *Highland Harris* (12) except:
T: 6,027 g, 3,835 n.

1904 June: Entered service.
1916 Nov 26: Damaged by torpedo attack in the Mediterranean but reached port and repaired.
1927 Laid up at Dunston-on-Tyne with her sister *Highland Watch* (14).
1930 Broken up at Hayle, Cornwall, by Thos. W. Ward Ltd.

14 **HIGHLAND WATCH**

Details as *Highland Harris* (12) except:
T: 6,022 g, 3,860 n.

1904 May: Delivered.
1918 May 2: West of Gibraltar two torpedoes missed the ship.
1927 Laid up at Dunston-on-Tyne.
1930 Broken up at Inverkeithing, Firth of Forth by Thos. W. Ward Ltd.

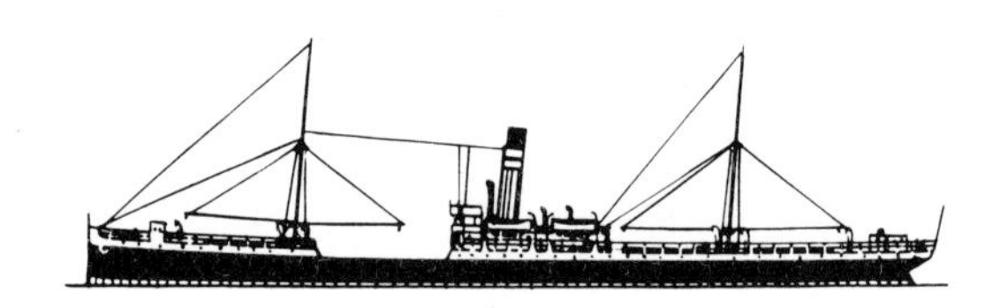

HIGHLAND FLING

15 **HIGHLAND FLING**

Bt 1890 Hawthorn, Leslie & Co, Newcastle; *T:* 3,822 g, 2,481 n.
Dim 350 ft 6 in (106.83 m) × 47 ft 8 in (14.53 m) × 24 ft 1 in (7.34m)
Eng Sgl scr, tpl exp; 3 cyls; 407 NHP; Stm P: 160 lb; 3 dbl ended boilers, 12 furnaces; 10 kts; By builder.
H Steel, 2 decks; fcsle 98 ft (29.87 m), poop 208 ft (63.4 m).

1890 Feb: Built as *Morayshire,* Turnbull Martin's Scottish Shire Line. Originally square

rigged on foremast. Became *Duke of Portland*, J. B. Westray & Co, London; employed on the Australian refrigerated meat trade.
1905 Acquired; renamed *Highland Fling*.
1907 Jan 7: Wrecked at Kennock Bay, near The Lizard, Cornwall. Jan 20: Cut in two and afterpart towed to Falmouth for breaking up by Harris & Co. Her sister was *Nairnshire* then *Duke of Norfolk,* same owners.

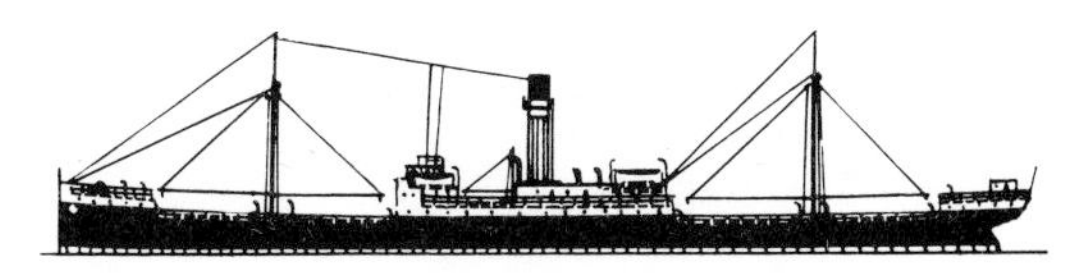

HIGHLAND LADDIE (I)

16 **HIGHLAND LADDIE** (I)

Bt 1905 W. Beardmore & Co, Glasgow; *T:* 3,750 g, 2,399 n.
Dim 360 ft (109.73 m) × 48 ft (14.63 m) × 26 ft 4 in (8.03 m)
Eng Sgl scr, tpl exp; 3 cyls; 355 NHP; Stm P: 180 lb; 3 sgl ended boilers, 9 furnaces; By builder.
H Steel, 2 decks; fcsle 43 ft (13.11 m), bridge 108 ft (32.92 m), poop 37 ft (11.28 m).

1905 Entered service.
1907 Sold to Adelaide Steamship Co, Port Adelaide; renamed *Lammeroo.*
1931 Sold to Shun Foo S.N.Co, Shanghai; renamed *Shun Foo.*
1934 Broken up.

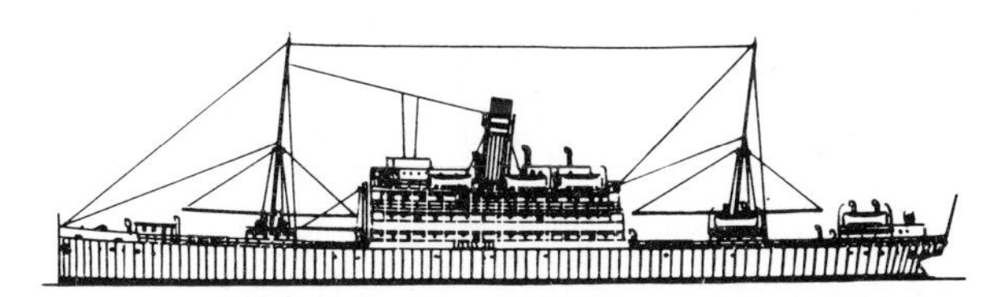

HIGHLAND ROVER and HIGHLAND PRIDE

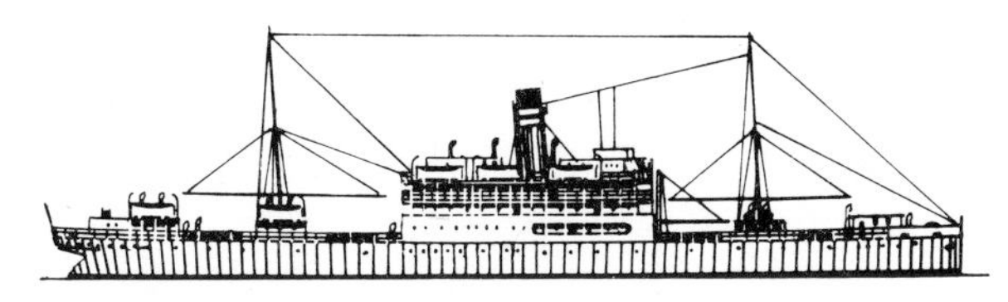

HIGHLAND ROVER and HIGHLAND PRIDE

17 **HIGHLAND ROVER**

Bt 1910 Russell & Co, Port Glasgow; *T:* 7,244 g, 4,550 n.
Dim 405 ft (123.44 m) × 56 ft 2 in (17.12 m) × 34 ft 9 in (10.59 m)
Eng Sgl scr, tpl exp; 3 cyls; 830 NHP; Stm P: 210 lb; 3 forced draft sgl ended and 1 auxiliary refrigeration boiler, 16 furnaces; 13 kts; By Rankin & Blackmore, Greenock.
H Steel, 3 decks and shelter deck. The house on the fcsle mounted a forward docking bridge. Cargo: 2,000 tons meat; 2,000 tons general, space including live cattle accommodation.
Pass 80 1st, 36 Intermediate, 400 steerage. When carrying the 'tween deck passengers canvas collapsible lifeboats were hoist at bridge deck level to give the appearance of having two parallel banks of boats.
Highland Rover and *Highland Pride* (19) had a closed in promenade deck on the starboard

side (17a). The mast deck houses had a wide walkway each side. The remainder of the class had a very narrow walkway about 2 ft (61 cm) wide. This gave the impression that their deck houses were flush with the hull breadth.
1910 Feb: The first of the new class of passenger vessels. Designed by General Manager A. R. T. Woods. Introduced grey hulls and pale apple green upperworks, said to be non-glare. This ship with *Highland Laddie* (18) and *Highland Pride* (19) had perceptibly more rake than the remaining seven ships.
1910 Mar: Inaugurated London–Vigo–Las Palmas–Rio de Janeiro–Montevideo–Buenos Aires service. The passage time was 21 days. The first class fare was £34 compared with the equivalent in Royal Mail and PSNC of £47. Royal Mail's second class was £28 single for much less spacious cabins.
1932 Broken up by Thos. W. Ward at Grays, Essex.

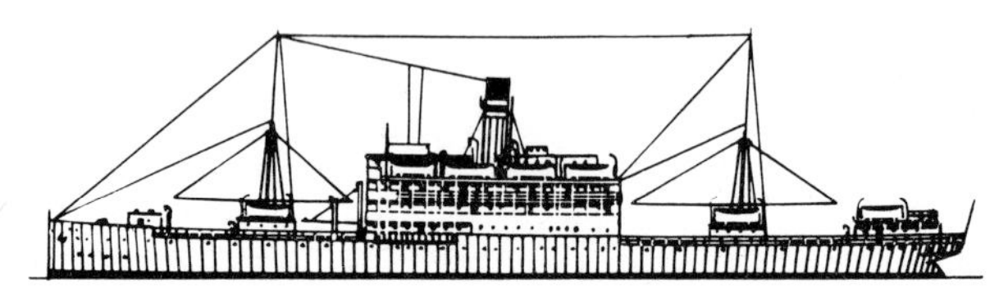

HIGHLAND LADDIE (II), HIGHLAND CORRIE (II), HIGHLAND GLEN (II), HIGHLAND SCOT (II), HIGHLAND BRAE, HIGHLAND LOCH, HIGHLAND PIPER and HIGHLAND WARRIOR (I)

18 HIGHLAND LADDIE (II)

Details as *Highland Rover* (17) except:
Bt: 1910 Cammell Laird & Co, Birkenhead; *T:* 7,117 g, 4,486 n.
Dim 405 ft 9 in (123.67 m) × 56 ft 1 in (17.09 m) × 26 ft 10 in (8.18 m).
Eng By builder.

1910 Apr: Entered London–Vigo–Las Palmas–South America service.
1929 Sold to Jamaica Banana Producers S.S.Co, renamed *Jamaica Settler;* converted for the carriage of bananas.
1935 Oct: Broken up at Dalmuir by W. H. Arnott Young.

19 HIGHLAND PRIDE

Details as *Highland Rover* (17) except:
T: 7.469 g, 4,706 n.

1910 Apr: Delivered. May: Entered London–South America service.
1929 Sept 8: Wrecked near Vigo, Spain. The ship had just left Vigo with 63 passengers and 89 crew aboard when she grounded in heavy rain on Roca Negra, Cies Islands. Captain Alford was on the bridge at the time. All the passengers were taken off in lifeboats and Spanish fishing boats. By the early hours of Sept 9 there were several feet of water in the engine room and the crew abandoned ship. All the survivors were landed at Bayona, a fishing village 22 miles from Vigo.
By daylight *Highland Pride* was lying on an even keel with her bows submerged and her stern out of the deep water beyond the ledge of rocks. During thd day by strenuous efforts all the pedigree bulls, heifers and sheep from the afterpart of the ship were rescued. Only after that was done was all the mail salvaged. It was a race against time.
Sept 10: As has been expected the afterpart broke away and sank. The forepart was eventually dismantled as it lay.

20 **HIGHLAND CORRIE** (II)

Details as *Highland Rover* (17) except:
T: 7,344 g, 4,261 n.
Dim 414 ft (126.19 m) × 56 ft 4 in (17.17 m) × 27 ft 1 in (8.25 m).

1910 July: Entered service. The first of a slightly lengthened version. London–South America service.
1915 Aug 14: Mined off Elbow Buoy, Ulster; towed into Tilbury. Repaired.
1917 May 16: Torpedoed and sunk 4 miles south of Owers Light, Selsey Bill, in the English Channel. Five lives lost.

21 **HIGHLAND GLEN** (II)

Details as *Highland Rover* (17) except:
T: 7,343 g, 4,616 n.
Dim As *Highland Corrie* (20).

1910 Oct: Placed on London–South America service.
1929 Sold to Jamaica Banana Producers S S Co, London; renamed *Jamaica Producer.* Became a banana carrier.
1933 Nov 20: Destroyed by fire at East India Dock, London. Towed to Holland and broken up by F. Rijsdijk & Co.

22 **HIGHLAND SCOT** (II)

Details as *Highland Rover* (17) except:
T: 7,343 g, 4,617 n.
Dim As *Highland Corrie* (20).
1910 Sept: Delivered for London–South America service.
1915 Mar 16: Chased by submarine in the English Channel.
1918 May 6: Wrecked on Maricas Island, Brazil, en route Buenos Aires–Rio de Janeiro.

23 **HIGHLAND BRAE**

Details as *Highland Rover* (17) except:
Bt: 1910 Cammell Laird & Co, Birkenhead; *T:* 7,365 g, 4,646 n.
Dim 413 ft 9 in (126.11 m) × 56 ft 2 in (17.12 m) × 27 ft 1 in (8.25 m).

1910 Nov: Entered London–South America service.
1915 Jan 14: Captured by German raider *Kronprins Wilhelm* 630 miles north of Pernambuco (Recife). Jan 31: Scuttled after the removal of all usable stores and frozen meat.

24 **HIGHLAND LOCH**

Details as *Highland Rover* (17) except:
Bt: 1911 Cammell Laird & Co, Birkenhead; *T:* 7,493 g, 4,730 n.
Dim As *Highland Brae* (23).

1911 Mar: Delivered for London–South American route.
1918 Jan 20: Torpedo missed in English Channel.
1929 Sold to Jamaica Banana Producers S S Co, renamed *Jamaica Planter*. Became a banana carrier.
1935 Mar: Broken up at Bo'ness, Scotland by P & W MacLellan & Co.

25 **HIGHLAND PIPER**

Details as *Highland Rover* (17) except:
Bt: 1911 Cammell Laird & Co, Birkenhead; *T:* 7.490 g, 4,728 n.
Dim As *Highland Brae* (23).

1911 Mar 18: Launched. July 11: Maiden voyage Liverpool–Vigo–Lisbon–Las Palmas–Rio de Janeiro–Montevideo–Buenos Aires arriving July 31. Thereafter London–South America service.
1929 Sold to Jamaica Banana Producers S S Co; renamed *Jamaica Merchant*. Converted to carry bananas.
Oct 29: First sailing. Liverpool–Kingston. Then from London.
1935 Sold to Standard Fruit and Steamship Company, New Orleans.
1937 Broken up at Trieste. Sold for £25,000. The last survivor of the class of ten.

26 **HIGHLAND WARRIOR** (I)

Details as *Highland Rover* (17) except:
Bt: 1911; *T:* 7,485 g, 4,717 n.
Dim As *Highland Corrie* (20).
1911 Aug: Delivered for London–South America service.
1915 Oct 2: Wrecked on Cape Prior, Santa Comba Point, north east of Spain en route London–Corruna–South America. She was carrying a general cargo. All aboard were saved.

27 **HIGHLAND STAR**

Bt 1903 Workman Clark, Belfast; *T:* 4,331 g, 2,743 n.
Dim 380 ft (115.82 m) × 48 ft 8 in (14.83 m) × 28 ft 4 in (8.64m).
Eng Sgl scr, tpl exp; 3 cyls; 452 NHP; Stm P: 200 lb; 3 sgl ended boilers, 9 furnaces; 10 kts; By builder.
H Steel, 2 decks; fcsle 107 ft (32.61 m), bridge 116 ft (35.36 m), poop 35 ft (10.67 m).
1903 Built for J. P. Corry's Star Line as *Star of Ireland*.
1916 Acquired by Nelson Steam Nav Co, renamed *Highland Star*.
1927 Laid up at Dunston-on-Tyne with *Highland Heather* (13) and *Highland Watch* (14).
1930 Broken up at Inverkeithing, Scotland, by Thos. W. Ward.

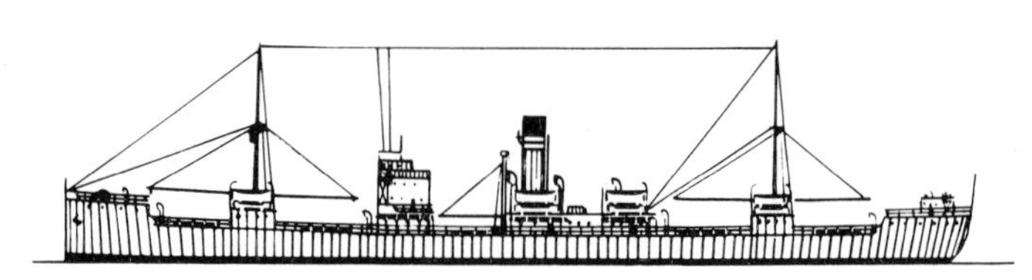

HIGHLAND WARRIOR (II)

28 **HIGHLAND WARRIOR** (II)

See Royal Mail Line Entry No. 215.

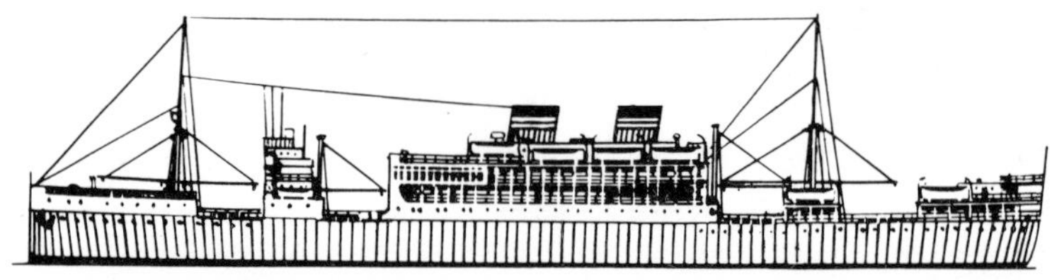

HIGHLAND MONARCH, HIGHLAND CHIEFTAIN, HIGHLAND BRIGADE, HIGHLAND HOPE, HIGHLAND PRINCESS and HIGHLAND PATRIOT

29 **HIGHLAND MONARCH**

For details of this ship see Royal Mail Entry No. 207. Nelson Line had wished to use this name in 1910 for one of their first passenger ships but were prevented from doing so because Monarch Line, Raeburn & Verel already possessed a ship with this name.

30 HIGHLAND CHIEFTAIN

See Royal Mail Line Entry No. 208.

31 HIGHLAND BRIGADE (II)

See Royal Mail Line Entry No. 209.

32 HIGHLAND HOPE (II)

Details as *Highland Monarch* (29) except:
Bt: 1929 Harland & Wolff, Belfast: *T:* 14,129 g, 8,730 n.

1930 Nov 15: Left London for Buenos Aires; Captain Thomas Jones 150 passengers and 139 crew. Embarked the mails at Boulogne and 12 passengers. Nov 18: At Vigo 217 Spanish and Portuguese emigrants were boarded. Nov 19: 4 am. The look-out reported a light in heavy mist which may have been Burling Lighthouse but it disappeared into the mist. By now the ship was enveloped in dense fog and at 4.57 am *Highland Hope* struck the north east section of Farilhoes Rock, Peniche, running over them for almost her entire length and puncturing the hull in numerous places. In the swell the liner lurched from side to side but was firmly held and not in danger of sinking.
All the passengers were safely lowered away in the lifeboats with the exception of one emigrant who jumped into a boat and was fatally injured. He died in hospital next day and was the only casualty. After the abandoning of the ship the Portuguese Government salvage ship *Patrao Lopez* stood by all night playing a searchlight on the wreck in order to prevent looting.

Most of the valuable cargo was salvaged but the ship itself was a complete loss.

33 HIGHLAND PRINCESS

See Royal Mail Line Entry No. 210.

34 HIGHLAND PATRIOT

See Royal Mail Line Entry No. 211.

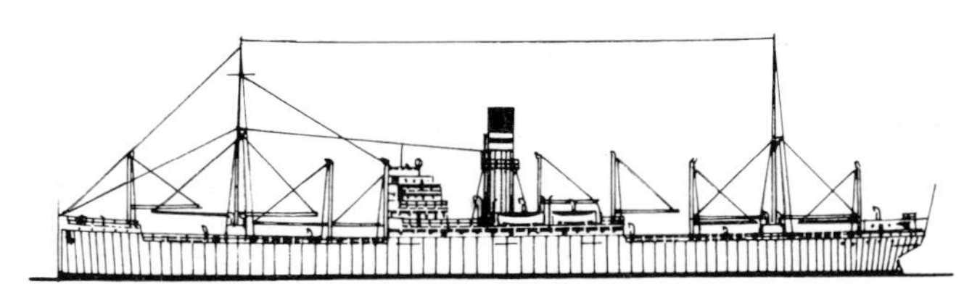

MEISONNIER, MOLIERE and MURILLO

35 MEISONNIER

See Royal Mail Line Entry No. 205.

36 MOLIERE

See Royal Mail Line Entry No. 204.

37 MURILLO

See Royal Mail Line Entry No. 206.